Why American Prisons Fail

Why American Prisons Fail

How to Fix Them without Spending More Money (Maybe Less)

Peyton Paxson
George H. Watson

CAROLINA ACADEMIC PRESS

Durham, North Carolina

Library of Congress Cataloging-in-Publication Data

Names: Paxson, Peyton, author. | Watson, George H., author.
Title: Why American prisons fail : how to fix them without spending more
money (maybe less) / Peyton Paxson and George H. Watson.
Description: Durham, North Carolina : Carolina Academic Press, [2016] |
Includes bibliographical references and index.
Identifiers: LCCN 2015037803 | ISBN 9781611635188 (alk. paper)
Subjects: LCSH: Prisons--United States. | Corrections--United States. |
Criminal justice, Administration of--United States.
Classification: LCC HV9471 .P39 2016 | DDC 365/.70973--dc23
LC record available at http://lccn.loc.gov/2015037803

CAROLINA ACADEMIC PRESS
700 Kent Street
Durham, North Carolina 27701
Telephone (919) 489-7486
Fax (919) 493-5668
www.cap-press.com

Printed in the United States of America

Contents

Acknowledgments

Peyton Paxson thanks:
Beth Hall at Carolina Academic Press, for her guidance and patience.
My program chair, Lynda J. Pintrich, for providing access to the field of corrections.
My assistant dean, Michelle Elias Bloomer, for giving me room to grow professionally.
My wife and best friend, Karen L. Muncaster, for her enduring support and encouragement.

George Watson thanks:
Peyton Paxson for recognizing the relevance of this subject matter to our society and working with me to bring it to the public's attention. I truly appreciate his time, energy, and devotion to this work.
Beth Hall for giving me the opportunity to help make the world a better place.
My wife and eternal soulmate Holly and my son Lance for their constant love and encouragement.
All my friends and family who stood by me with their unwavering support.

Introduction

Although Paxson is not a big fan of Facebook, he was using its private e-mail function a few years ago to correspond with a friend from his years spent living in Austin. She told Paxson that their mutual friend from law school, George Watson, was doing time in federal prison, and that she thought Paxson should contact him because Watson was having a tough time. As soon as Paxson heard that Watson was in trouble, he knew he had to do what he could to offer him some comfort. Despite Watson being a convicted felon, Paxson knew that he was a good man. In many ways, Watson's situation falls within the maxim "There, but for the grace of God, go I."

Watson is a bibliophile, as you'll see in Chapter 2, and Paxson's local library has great book sales. Sending books was easy on Paxson's end, and much appreciated by Watson. The two corresponded regularly. The more Watson told Paxson about prison life, the more Paxson, who teaches criminal justice courses, thought that Watson's observations on the criminal justice system in general, and the corrections system in particular, should be shared with a larger audience. The book before you is our effort to do so.

The week before our manuscript was sent to the publisher, the British magazine *The Economist* ran a cover story entitled "Jailhouse Nation; 2.3 Million Reasons to Fix America's Prison Problem." As the article states, "No country in the world imprisons as many people as America does, or for so long."[1] After having a relatively stable incarceration rate for decades, American political institutions shifted to a mass incarceration model in the last quarter of the twentieth century. In Chapter 1, we look at the reasons why the United States has about five percent of the world's population but twenty-five percent of the world's prisoners. These reasons include the post-World War II baby boom, the War on Drugs, the belief that "nothing works" in corrections, and the implementation of mandatory minimum prison sentences. We further address the incongruence of incarceration rates increasing while criminal activity decreased. Chapter 1 concludes with a brief discussion of the ultimate metric for determining if the corrections system is working—recidivism, or the rates of repeated criminal activity. Recidivism rates remain startlingly high, an indicator that the current system is broken.

Chapter 2 tells of Watson's experience of being "involuntarily embedded" in the prison system. While there, Watson, who holds bachelor's and master's degrees in psychology, observed how the prison system fails both prisoners and the taxpayers who pay for our prisons. Watson experienced things he would really prefer he hadn't, but in the process he was able to identify some things that could be changed to make American prisons more effective and more efficient.

In Chapter 3, we provide a brief overview of criminological theories about why people chose to engage in criminal activity. We also discuss how choice theory has become the dominant behavioral theory underlying the American criminal justice system. We will see that this cultural emphasis on rational choice theory—that the majority of criminals choose to be criminals—is unfounded. Chapter 3 also surveys the primary goals of the corrections system, and concludes with a brief history of American prisons and the underlying penological theories and practices that those prisons represent.

Chapter 4 compares the societal attitudes reflected in the American corrections system with those of some other Western democracies. We provide examples of how the American ways of responding to crime are at odds with the successful practices of other nations. We analyze why other nations imprison fewer people for shorter periods, and how other nations often have different perceptions about what constitutes crime and its acceptable punishment.

Chapter 5 examines how politics has contributed to mass incarceration. When deciding what behaviors to punish and how to punish them, politicians are subjected to intense lobbying by groups with conflicting interests, as well as pressure from a panicky public. This yields a criminal justice system that is similar to our income tax system: overly complex, confusing, and contradictory. It is very different from the black-and-white, good guy/bad guy system most people think of. Another complication is that criminals can be "manufactured" through vague legislation. This gives prosecutors great latitude in determining which activities to try as crimes and which suspects to prosecute.

In Chapter 6, we look at the economics of the American corrections system and the institutions and industries that benefit from the criminalization of certain behaviors. These include prison workers' unions, law enforcement agencies, private prison corporations, and industries that provide goods and services to prisons. Prison workers' unions spend millions of dollars to lobby for longer prison sentences and against alternatives to prison in an effort to provide job security for their members. A private prison company was behind

Arizona's controversial new immigration law, which created a new crime in the state in order to populate privately operated prisons. These institutions' and industries' economic models require a constantly increasing supply of prisoners whose food, clothing, housing, medical care, and supervision is paid for with American tax dollars.

We conclude with a vision of a better corrections system in Chapter 7. We look at what seems to work best in the U.S., as well as best practices in some other nations. We offer suggestions that focus on the best use of resources to prevent future criminal activity. In some areas, it is simply expanding effective rehabilitation and education programs already in use. In other areas, new legislation and approaches are required.

We appreciate that our corrections system strives to help keep us safe. We do not make excuses for criminal behavior; most of the people in prison did break the law. However, we show that there are better means available to reduce repeated criminal activity and to keep criminal behavior and criminal lifestyles from being passed on from one generation to the next. The issue is a bipartisan one. We quote Ted Cruz, the American Civil Liberties Union, one of the Koch brothers, and the National Lawyers Guild, among others. Their motivations vary, but the goal is the same: a more efficient, less expensive means of dealing with crime in America. We hope that once readers come to better understand the systemic problems within our corrections system, they will ask our government leaders to examine those problems and develop alternative policies and practices.

Notes

1. "Jailhouse Nation; 2.3 Million Reasons to Fix America's Prison Problem," *The Economist,* June 20, 2015, 23.

Why American Prisons Fail

Chapter 1

Mass Incarceration

The United States Census of 1980 estimated that there were 226,545,805 Americans that year. In 2010, the Census Bureau estimated the U.S. population to be 308,400,408, an increase of thirty-six percent over thirty years. In 1978, there were 307,276 inmates in state and federal prisons. In 2009, the U.S. prison population peaked at 1,615,487 inmates.[1] This was a 525 percent increase over thirty-one years. In this chapter, we will explain how this happened.

Causes of Mass Incarceration

Criminologists commonly measure crime statistics in rates per 100,000 people. To determine an incarceration rate, correctional statisticians typically look at the year-end population of people serving sentences in prison and jails; some statisticians include those who are detained but not yet convicted of a crime. They then compare the number of people incarcerated to the total population. By this measure, the incarceration rate in the U.S. hovered between 100 and 200 per 100,000 people from the beginning of the 1880s until the 1970s. The rate them climbed to 461 per 100,000 in 1990, 703 per 100,000 in 2000, and peaked at 756 per 100,000 in 2007.[2] That same year, one out of every 100 American adults was incarcerated.[3] The U.S. has firmly embraced what many observers refer to as mass incarceration.

As we discuss in Chapter 4, there was not a similar rise in the incarceration rates among most other nations during this period. As the National Research Council tells us, "The growth in incarceration rates in the United States over the past forty years is historically unprecedented and internationally unique."[4] The U.S.'s incarceration rate now exceeds that of all other nations. By 2008, the U.S. had five percent of the world's population but almost twenty-five percent of the world's prisoners.[5] Although many Americans complain that we are not locking up enough criminals, the U.S. reigns as the most punitive nation in the world.

The incarceration rates vary significantly among the states, with those in the South generally incarcerating people at much higher rates than states in

Figure 1.1. U.S. Incarceration Rate
(per 100,000 people)

New England and in the upper Midwest. We discuss the cultural and sociological reasons for these differences in Chapter 3. According to the Sentencing
Project, Louisiana's prison population increased from less than 10,000 in 1980
to about 40,000 in 2011; Louisiana has the highest incarceration rate among
the states, at well over 800 prisoners per 100,000 residents. During the same
period, Florida's prison population increased from 20,000 to over 100,000, and
Texas saw a rise from 30,000 prisoners to over 160,000. California, the most pop-
ulous state, saw its prison population increase from a little over 20,000 prisoners in 1980 to a peak of over 170,000 in 2006.[6]

Did crime in the U.S. dramatically increase? Although the 1980s saw a high
incidence of property crimes and an increase in violent crimes, the incidence
of crime has steadily decreased since the early 1990s. Property crime has been
generally decreasing for the past three decades, and violent crime has been
generally decreasing for the past two decades. This tells us that an increase in
crime was hardly the reason for the steep increase in U.S. incarceration rates
during this time. Rather, as the National Research Council succinctly states,
"The best single proximate explanation of the rise in incarceration is not rising crime rates, but the policy choices made by legislators to greatly increase
the use of imprisonment as a response to crime."[7]

Elected legislators determine which behaviors constitute criminal activity
and establish the sentencing ranges for crimes. Yet legislators are but one element of the U.S.'s politicized criminal justice system, perhaps the most politi-

cized in the world. We vote for prosecutors at the state and local level. We vote for sheriffs in all but a few states. In many states, we vote for judges, although state and federal legislators have increasingly removed, even eliminated, the sentencing discretion of trial judges and have also restricted appellate judges' power to hear certain criminal appeals. It may be politically impossible to be too "tough on crime" when running for political office, and it can be a significant liability if a political candidate is portrayed as "soft" on crime.

Politics do not occur in a vacuum; they are informed by social conditions. American political leaders adopted a policy of mass incarceration due to three principal factors: the baby boom, the War on Drugs, and the shift away from efforts to rehabilitate prisoners in favor of "get tough" approaches. We look at each.

The Baby Boom

Many policymakers sought to change how American prisons operated because of a significant increase in crime in the 1960s and 1970s. Some of this increase was due to social strife during an era of cultural upheaval and urban unrest. More significant, however, was the post-World War II baby boom. The U.S. Census Bureau defines this period as falling between the years 1946 and 1964, a period when the annual birth rate was at or above twenty per 1,000 people (the annual birthrate today is about thirteen births per 1,000 people).[8] During the baby boom, seventy-six million Americans were born; in the 1960s and 1970s, Boomers comprised more than a third of the American population.[9]

As social scientist James Q. Wilson put it in 1976, "The population today is more youthful than at any other time in this century, and since young people are disproportionately criminals, it is not surprising that prisoners are growing in numbers faster than society generally."[10] Crime tends to be a young person's game, as forty-four percent of those imprisoned are under the age of thirty-five, and over seventy-eight percent of prisoners released at the age of twenty-four or younger are arrested for a new crime within three years of leaving prison.[11] Many criminologists describe the crime problem of the second half of the twentieth century as being at least partly a youth problem. The number of property crimes per 100,000 people more than doubled between 1960 and its peak in 1980, with 1,726.3 property crimes estimated per 100,000 people in 1960, 3,621 per 100,000 in 1970, and 5,353.3 per 100,000 people estimated in 1980.[12] The incidence of violent crimes quadrupled from 1960 until its peak in 1991, with 160.9 violent crimes per 100,000 Americans reported in 1960, 363.5 per 100,000 in 1970, and 758.2 per 100,000 reported in 1991.[13]

Figure 1.2. The Baby Boom
(1946–1964)

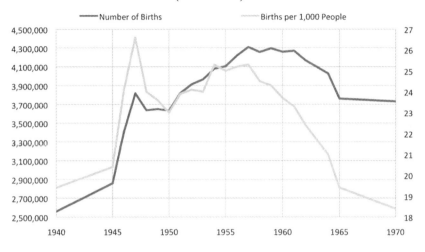

Figure 1.3. Violent Crimes
(per 100,000 people)

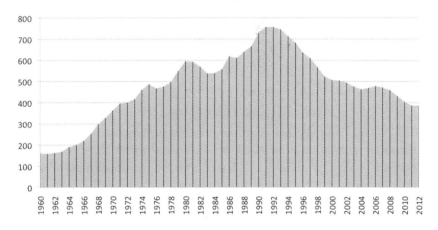

Figure 1.4. Property Crimes
(per 100,000 people)

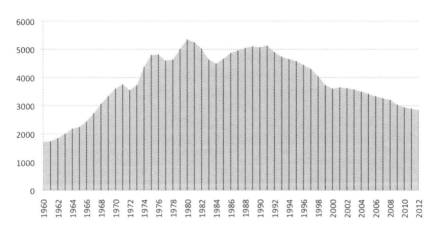

For dramatic effect, let us focus on just the 1960s, looking at the total number of reported crimes rather than crime rates:[14]

These charts tell us that Americans had cause to be alarmed about the rising incidence of crime during this period. Understandably, they looked to local, state, and federal government for solutions, or at the very least, a response.

Figure 1.5. Violent Crimes
(1960–1970)

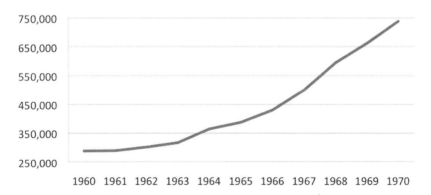

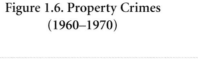

Figure 1.6. Property Crimes
(1960–1970)

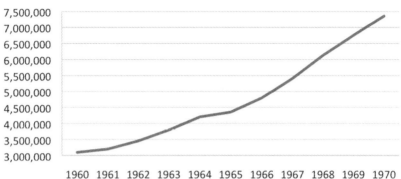

In 1967, soon-to-be presidential candidate Richard M. Nixon wrote an article for *Reader's Digest* entitled, "What Has Happened to America?" Nixon asked his readers, "Why is it that in a few short years a nation which enjoys the freedom and material abundance of America has become among the most lawless and violent in the history of the free peoples?"[15] His answer:

> The shocking crime and disorder in American life today flow in large measure from two fundamental changes that have occurred in the attitudes of many Americans.
>
> First, there is the permissiveness toward violation of the law and public order by those who agree with the cause in question. Second, there is the indulgence of crime because of sympathy for the past grievances of those who have become criminals.
>
> Our judges have gone too far in weakening the peace forces as against the criminal forces.
>
> Our opinion-makers have gone too far in promoting the doctrine that when a law is broken, society, not the criminal is to blame.[16]

Nixon announced his candidacy for the presidency a few months after the *Reader's Digest* article was published. Law and order was a central theme in Nixon's successful presidential campaign. The Lyndon B. Johnson administration created the Law Enforcement Assistance Administration (LEAA) within the Justice Department as part of the Omnibus Crime Control and Safe Streets

Act of 1968; Nixon assured generous funding for the LEAA during his presidency. The LEAA distributed federal tax dollars to the states in block grants that generally allowed the states to spend the money as they saw fit, although in 1970, Congress did require that twenty percent of LEAA money be directed specifically to corrections.[17] By federal fiscal year 1973, the LEAA had distributed $2.4 billion.[18] LEAA funding peaked at $886 million in fiscal year 1975; between fiscal years 1969 and 1980, the LEAA received about $7.5 billion in funding. (When Paxson first started teaching criminal justice, old-timers in the field referred to this period as "the good old days.") Nevertheless, crime continued to rise during this period, and many observers criticized the LEAA as a failure. The Carter administration decided to discontinue LEAA funding, and the Reagan administration declined to restore it.[19]

While spending on law enforcement increased in response to rising crime rates, there was also a major policy shift in the latter part of the last century, as the U.S. Bureau of Prisons and many states effectively gave up on rehabilitation as a goal of incarceration. While other states continued to pursue rehabilitation, many did so with less emphasis. Criminologists often point to two individuals, Robert Martinson and James Q. Wilson, for this shift.

Giving Up on Rehabilitation

Robert Martinson earned B.A., M.A., and Ph.D. degrees at the University of California at Berkeley before moving to New York, where he became chair of the Sociology Department of the City College of New York. Working with Douglas Lipton and Judith Wilks on behalf of New York Governor Nelson Rockefeller's Special Committee on Criminal Offenders, Martinson received the most publicity among the three authors for their vast, 1,484-page survey of scholarly studies on criminal rehabilitation that they finished in 1970. Because of the New York government's apparent discomfort with the trio's findings, the report was not published until 1975. That report, published as *Effectiveness of Correctional Treatment: A Survey of Treatment and Evaluation Studies,* reviewed 231 studies conducted between 1945 and 1967, with the authors finding that none of those studies effectively identified a sustainable method of rehabilitating criminal offenders.[20]

Because of the hesitation of New York to publish the report, Martinson took to the pages of the neoconservative journal *The Public Interest* to draw attention to it in 1974. As it turned out, despite the trio's exhaustive efforts, Martinson found that the studies themselves were flawed. Martinson's summary of his group's findings has been quoted many times since:

It is just possible that some of our treatment programs are working to some extent, but that our research is so bad that it is incapable of telling. Having entered this very serious caveat, I am bound to say that these data, involving over two hundred studies and hundreds of thousands of individuals as they do, are the best available and give us very little reason to hope that we have in fact found a sure way of reducing recidivism [reoffending] through rehabilitation. This is not to say that we found no instances of success or partial success; it is only to say that these instances have been isolated, producing no clear pattern to indicate the efficacy of any particular method of treatment. And neither is this to say that factors outside the realm of rehabilitation may not be working to reduce recidivism—factors such as the tendency for recidivism to be lower in offenders over the age of 30; it is only to say that such factors seem to have little connection with any of the treatment methods now at our disposal.[21]

Martinson found himself in demand by popular media, interviewed by Mike Wallace on CBS's "60 Minutes" in 1975 and by *People* magazine in 1976. Both conservative and liberal observers seized on the study, albeit for very different reasons. Conservatives thought that the study confirmed their law-and-order stance, which favored eliminating most correctional treatment programs in favor of long, harsh prison sentences. Liberals (including Martinson) believed that the study demonstrated that American prisons failed so miserably that they should be abandoned. The conservatives' vision became the controlling one, particularly during Ronald Reagan's presidency in the 1980s. As one scholar recently wrote, "The phrase 'nothing works' was and is commonly attributed to Martinson, and to this day he is singularly blamed for quashing the rehabilitation movement of that era in favor of punishment and incapacitation."[22] Another criminologist puts it more concisely, stating that Martinson "had driven the final nail in rehabilitation's coffin."[23] Martinson may have blamed himself as well; he committed suicide by leaping out a window of his Manhattan apartment in 1980.

While Martinson's reputation arose largely from a single study, James Q. Wilson produced his body of work over many decades. Wilson earned his Ph.D. in 1959 at the University of Chicago and taught government at Harvard for twenty-six years, moving on to UCLA, then Pepperdine. Wilson's 1975 book, *Thinking about Crime*, argued that the best way to deter crime was to lock criminals up for extended periods so that they are unable to commit crimes in free society. This is the incapacitation model, which we discuss in detail in Chapter 3. Wilson acknowledged that there were many reasons why people engage in criminal behavior, including external forces beyond individual control, but argued that the paramount reason was rational choice—that people choose to be criminals of their own free will. In *Thinking about Crime*, Wilson stated that

> some persons will shun crime even if we do nothing to deter them, while others will seek it out even if we do everything to reform them. Wicked people exist. Nothing avails except to set them apart from innocent people. And many people, neither wicked nor innocent, but watchful, dissembling, and calculating of their opportunities, ponder our reaction to wickedness as a cue to what they might profitably do. We have trifled with the wicked, made sport of the innocent, and encouraged the calculators. Justice suffers, and so do we all.[24]

As his colleague Mark Kleiman wrote upon Wilson's death in 2012, "James Q. Wilson helped move the discourse about crime and crime control away from the root causes/rehabilitationist orthodoxy of the 1960s and toward the much more punitive turn that has characterized American crime policy since the late 1970s."[25]

Wilson's focus on individual decision-making grounds itself in rational choice theory. This theory is arguably one more of economics than sociology. Sociological theories locate the decision to engage in crime within social contexts; depending on the particular sociological theory and the particular sociologist, social factors may be considered more, or less, significant than personal factors. Rational choice theory is a derivative of the "rational man" of classical liberal economics, and focuses on the decision-making of the individual rather than social factors. There is no question that this theory explains the criminal behavior of many individuals. Paxson remembers a particular defendant he met while serving a stint as a public defender during a sabbatical leave from his teaching job. Paxson's client had taken a tour along the highways and byways of Massachusetts, leaving a trail of worthless checks in his wake over many years. As another, much more seasoned public defender said after looking through the many pages of the client's criminal record, "This guy just doesn't want to work." In this case, the client, a middle-aged white guy who appeared to possess at least average intelligence, had indeed seemed to make the conscious decision to write hot checks rather than put in a forty-hour workweek.

Rational choice theory evolved from the classical school of criminology, relying on the work of the Italian criminologist Cesare Beccaria (1738–1794) and British philosopher Jeremy Bentham (1748–1832). Both men sought reform of the existing criminal justice system, and opposed physical and capital punishment as immoral and vengeful rather than utilitarian. The utilitarian model of corrections focuses on maximizing good for the greatest number of people. Using this model, the incarceration of criminals protects society by removing the offender from the community for some period, and by attempting to teach the offender a lesson to deter future criminal activity.

In discussing criminal justice issues with his students and others, Paxson has found that most Americans he has talked to about crime embrace rational choice theory as the prevailing reason why people commit crimes. To use James Q. Wilson's term, this is the belief that many, if not most, criminals are "calculators." When Paxson first tried to explain rational choice theory to Watson, Watson replied, "But people aren't always rational. Why would any rational person smoke cigarettes?" As Paxson's colleague Michelle Bloomer, a former prosecutor, told him, "If rational choice theory explained criminal activity, then deterrence would work. But it doesn't." While rational choice theory certainly does explain some criminal behavior, it hardly explains all of it. We look at some of the various theories about why people commit crimes, and how those theories inform correctional policies and practices, in Chapter 3.

The War on Drugs

Much of the crime that shook the U.S. during the 1960s and 1970s was outside of federal jurisdiction, leaving the states to attempt solutions. The states traditionally have maintained the police powers to protect the health, safety, morals, and general welfare of their inhabitants. Thus, the states conduct most criminal prosecutions and imprison most of the nation's criminal offenders. However, illegal drugs fall within the U.S. Congress's power to regulate interstate and foreign commerce.

The conundrum that governments of the world have had to confront is whether to focus drug control policy on curtailing supply by pursuing and punishing those who cultivate, manufacture, and distribute illegal drugs, or reducing demand among users through various mechanisms, including education and rehabilitation. As we discuss in Chapter 4, Western European drug policy tends to be hard on drugs, soft on drug users. The U.S.'s approach has generally been to be hard on both. Richard Nixon is credited with being the first U.S. president to declare a war on drugs. He first focused on demand when he declared drugs "public enemy number one" on July 17, 1971, and proposed a Special Action Office of Drug Abuse Prevention, explaining that, "It would not be directly concerned with the problems of reducing drug supply, or with the law enforcement aspects of drug abuse control." Instead, "It would concentrate on the 'demand' side of the drug equation—the use and the user of drugs."[26] Much of Nixon's underlying motivation seems to have been the fact that so many veterans of the Vietnam War had become addicted to drugs. In a cruel irony, too many vets fought the war *while* on drugs.

However, the Nixon administration's focus soon shifted to the supply of illegal drugs. In 1973, the Drug Enforcement Administration (DEA) began operations, as part of a reorganization and consolidation of federal efforts to stem the drug trade. Starting with 1,470 special agents and a $74.9 million budget, the DEA's budget grew to $206.6 million in 1980 and to $769.2 million in 1990. By 2000, the DEA had 4,566 special agents and a $1.587 billion budget. In 2014, the DEA had 5,249 special agents and a support staff of 5,806, with a budget of $2.882 billion.[27] The agency now has 221 domestic offices and eighty-six foreign offices in sixty-seven countries.[28]

In October 1982, Ronald Reagan revived the War on Drugs. While First Lady Nancy Reagan focused on curtailing demand for illicit drugs with her "Just Say No" campaign, her husband and Congress concentrated on supply. On July 17, 1986, the Boston Celtics chose University of Maryland basketball star Len Bias with the second overall pick of the NBA draft. Two days later, Bias was dead of a cocaine overdose. In the wake of local outrage, U.S. Speaker of the House Tip O'Neill, who represented Boston in Congress, saw a chance for the Democrats to gain politically from new anti-drug legislation. The Anti-Drug Abuse Act of 1986, also known as the Len Bias Act, passed shortly before the November 1986 elections. In the rush to get the bill through before the elections, no congressional hearings were held before passage of the bill; while most legislation is the product of both policy and politics, public policy was not part of the equation here. The law reinstated mandatory minimums for drug offenses, originally established in the Boggs Act of 1951 but largely eliminated by the Comprehensive Drug Abuse Prevention and Control Act of 1970. Funding for interdiction programs increased from an annual average of $437 million during Jimmy Carter's presidency to $1.4 billion during Reagan's first term. Yet funding aimed at education and rehabilitation decreased from an annual average of $386 million to $362 million.[29]

The Anti-Drug Abuse Act of 1988 amended the 1986 act and created the Office of National Drug Control Policy, which requires the president to issue an annual National Drug Control Strategy statement. In the first of those statements, President George H.W. Bush advocated for harsh penalties for both suppliers and users of drugs, telling Congress:

> To prevent people from using drugs, drug enforcement activities must make it increasingly difficult to engage in any drug activity with impunity. That deterrent, however, will only remain credible so long as pressure is brought to bear on the entire drug market, dealers and

users alike. That's why we need a national drug law enforcement strategy that casts a wide net and seeks to ensure that all drug use—whatever its scale—faces the risk of criminal sanction.[30]

The report then goes on to state that, "the freedom from fear of prosecution shared by most drug users is what allows dealers to rely on an ever-present market."[31]

Punishing drug users was the theme of Los Angeles Police Chief Daryl Gates's testimony before the U.S. Senate Judiciary Committee in September 1990, with Gates telling the committee that some drug users "ought to be taken out and shot," because "we're in a war" and even casual drug use constituted "treason." Distinguishing between hardcore drug users with physical addictions and casual drug users, Gates said he was talking about the latter group, "those who blast some pot on a casual basis."[32] While many commentators attributed Gates's remarks to hyperbole, others praised Gates for his zeal.

Drug arrests by local, state, and federal law enforcement agencies peaked at 1,889,810 in 2006, accounting for 13.1 percent of all criminal arrests that year.[33] The FBI reported that there were 1,501,043 drug arrests in 2013, about 13.2 percent of all arrests in the U.S.[34]

By design, the War on Drugs' impact on prisons was significant. The U.S. Bureau of Prisons (BOP) tells us that while in 1980, "The BOP's inmate population was 24,252, holding steady from 40 years earlier,"[35] today there are over 208,000 federal inmates, the majority serving sentences for charges relating to

Figure 1.7. Drug Arrests
(including sale and possession)

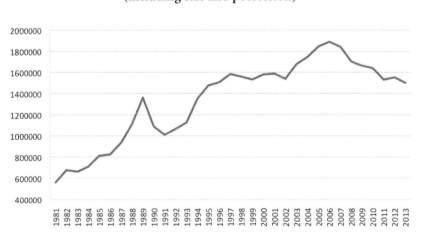

Figure 1.8. Federal Prison Population by Offense
(2013)

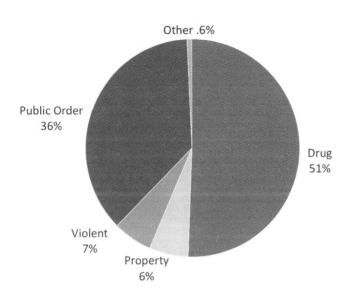

drugs.[36] That was what Watson found to be the case among the 1,900 prisoners he was confined with at the Federal Prison Camp in Beaumont. Despite the popular misconception that federal offenses are worse than state offenses, there are relatively few violent offenders in federal prisons.[37]

The sentence length for federal drug offenders increased from an average of twenty-two months in 1986 to an estimated sixty-two months in 2004. In 2013, federal drug trafficking sentences ranged from an average of thirty-nine months for marijuana related offenses to ninety-six months for crack cocaine related offenses.[38] Combining federal and state prison populations, there were 41,000 people incarcerated for drug offenses in 1982, the year of Reagan's renewed War on Drugs; by 2013, there were over 489,000.[39]

The War on Drugs spurred a particular increase in female incarceration in the U.S. In 1980, females constituted five percent of the total state and federal prison population; by 2013, they had grown to more than seven percent of the total.[40] The female prison population in state or federal prisons stood at over 125,469 in 2012, compared to less than 14,000 in 1980. In 2002, two-thirds of females in federal prisons were there for drug offenses, declining to a little less than fifty-eight percent in 2012.[41] In state prisons, drug convictions account for about twenty-five percent of the females serving time, but drug convictions account for only about fifteen percent of male prisoners.[42]

Figure 1.9. State Prison Population by Offense (2013)

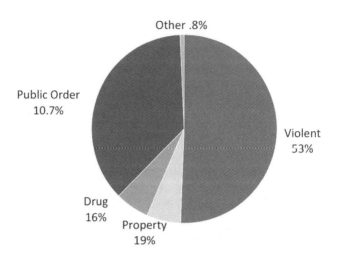

Drug offenders account for a much greater percentage of the federal prison population than they do in state prisons. Yet the majority of U.S. prisoners are held at the state and local level. Among state prisoners, the majority is incarcerated for violent crimes, including assaults, rape, and murder.[43]

Mandatory Minimums

As mentioned earlier, the Anti-Drug Abuse Act of 1986, with broad bipartisan support, re-established mandatory minimum sentences, which had been largely dropped by previous federal sentencing guidelines. By 2000, thirty-six states had instituted mandatory minimum sentences for drug offenses.[44] Federal mandatory minimum sentences also apply to crimes such as identity theft and weapons offenses; in 2010, nearly forty percent of federal prisoners were subject to a mandatory minimum at sentencing.[45]

The Comprehensive Crime Control Act of 1984 created the U.S. Sentencing Commission, tasked with drafting firm sentencing guidelines for federal judges. The act also eliminated parole for civilian offenders convicted of federal crimes after November 1, 1987, required prisoners to serve at least eighty-five percent of their sentence, and anticipated phasing out the U.S. Parole Commission entirely. Congress provided economic incentives to the states to adopt similar sentencing laws.

The Violent Crime Control and Law Enforcement Act of 1994 created the Violent Offender Incarceration and Truth-in-Sentencing (VOI/TIS) Incentive Program. Through this program, the U.S. Justice Department's Bureau of Justice Assistance provided grants to states that adopted sentencing plans that required certain violent offenders to serve at least eighty-five percent of their sentence. More than $2.7 billion was allocated to all fifty states and six territories during federal fiscal years 1996 through 2001.[46] Additionally, by 1999, the *New York Times* found that fifteen states had "taken the politically popular step of abolishing parole boards."[47] The *Times* noted, however, that, "three states, including Connecticut, reinstituted parole boards after eliminating them because the resulting increase in inmates crowded prisons so much that the states were forced to release many of them early."* The *Times* article concluded by citing Allen J. Beck, chief of corrections statistics at the U.S. Bureau of Justice Statistics, who noted that regardless of whether states eliminated parole, time served was increasing across the nation. As we will see in Chapter 4, the U.S. tends to incarcerate people for longer periods than do many other advanced nations for the same types of crimes. According to Charles E. Samuels, Jr., Director of the Federal Bureau of Prisons, the average federal prison sentence today is nine and a half years.[48]

A particularly popular form of mandatory minimum sentence in the 1990s was so-called "Three Strikes and You're Out" laws, which impose mandatory life sentences on those who commit three violent offenses and life with possibility of parole for those who commit three non-violent offenses. By 1997, the federal government and about half of the states had enacted three-strikes legislation.[49] Among the most severe was California's law, signed into law in 1994 in the wake of the murders of eighteen-year-old Kimber Reynolds and twelve-year-old Polly Klaas by repeat offenders.

Although popular with voters in the abstract, in reality, some applications of three-strikes laws have proven to be tragic comedies. For example, in 1995, Leandro Andrade, a father of three, stole five children's videos from a Kmart store in California. A couple of weeks later, he stole four more children's videos from another Kmart. Because of prior convictions for petty theft, burglary,

---

* More recently, after two prisoners on parole committed a particularly atrocious set of crimes in 2007, the *New York Times* published an op-ed article by two professors at Quinnipiac Law School that stated, "Connecticut should follow the lead of the federal government and abolish parole altogether. Criminal sentences should be based on justice, not on predictions about when an offender will no longer be a threat to society." Jeffery A. Meyer and Linda Ross Meyer, "Abolish Parole," *New York Times*, October 28, 2007, http://www.nytimes.com/2007/10/28/opinion/nyregionopinions/28CTmeyers.html?_r=0.

transportation of marijuana, and escape—all non-violent offenses—Andrade's thefts were classified as felonies under California law, and Andrade received two consecutive sentences of twenty-five years to life, one for each count of shoplifting goods with a total value of about $150. Andrade's appeals made their way to the U.S. Supreme Court in 2002. There, the nine members of the Supreme Court held in a five to four decision that because the California law provided for the possibility of parole (after serving fifty years) Andrade's sentence was not grossly disproportionate and thus did not violate the Eighth Amendment's prohibition against cruel and unusual punishment.[50] The dissent pointed out that Andrade, thirty-seven years old at the time of sentencing, had essentially been given a life sentence.

In another California case, Jerry Dewayne Williams received a possible life sentence for his theft of a slice of pepperoni pizza. Responding to critics of the sentence, Los Angeles Deputy District Attorney Bill Gravlin, who prosecuted Williams, said, "The people of California are sick of revolving-door justice, they're sick of judges who are soft on crime. It is wrong to focus on the last offense."[51] (A Google search using the terms "judges" and "soft on crime" yielded over 50,000 hits in June 2015.)

The "Get Tough" Movement

While politicians sought to incarcerate more people for longer periods, they also wanted to make the conditions of confinement less comfortable. New Jersey Representative Dick Zimmer introduced a bill known as the "No Frills Prison Act" in the U.S. House of Representatives in 1995. The law, formally titled "A Bill to Amend the Violent Crime Control and Law Enforcement Act of 1994 to prevent luxurious conditions in prisons" would have banned in-cell televisions, showing of R-rated movies, in-cell cooking devices, bodybuilding or weightlifting equipment, and electronic musical instruments (or the use of any musical instrument for more than an hour a day) and also forbid earned good-time credit. For those prisoners incarcerated for violent crimes resulting in serious bodily injury, the bill would have required that they be housed only in cellblocks that were designated for violent prisoners and "designed to emphasize punishment rather than rehabilitation."[52] The bill failed to become law, even though other U.S. Representatives subsequently reintroduced it in later congressional terms.

However, similar bills were passed into law by several state legislatures. Senator Dave Donley, sponsor of Alaska's "No Frills Prison Act," which became law in 1997, stated, "I feel confident this law will make people think twice before committing a crime in Alaska."[53] Donley's bill may have been good politics, but many prison wardens think that such laws are bad policy. A 1996 study by Sam Houston State University's Criminal Justice Center that surveyed over 600 prison wardens found that, " 'Amenities,' such as cable television, education programs and recreation programs are important for two reasons.... First, they help to soak up idle time and provide constructive activities for inmates. Second, they serve as 'carrots' that can be used to control misbehavior and reward good behavior." "Making prisons tougher makes for great speeches," said Sam Houston criminal justice professor Timothy J. Flanagan, one of the authors of the study, "but ignores the realities of prison administration."[54]

Crime Declined but Incarceration Continued to Rise

Now that we have addressed some of the issues that led the U.S. to mass incarceration, let us look at some of the reasons why (or more accurately, theories why) the crime rate has gone down. The U.S. Bureau of Justice Studies announced in 2008 that the homicide rate had fallen to its lowest rate in four decades. The bureau also found that there was a seventy-seven percent decline in non-fatal violent crime committed by strangers between 1993 and 2010, and a seventy-three percent decrease in non-fatal violent crime committed by offenders known by the victim during this period. Property crimes also decreased; with forty-five percent fewer estimated burglaries in 2012 than in 1980, fourteen percent fewer larceny/thefts, and thirty-seven percent fewer motor vehicle thefts. To summarize, the Bureau of Justice Statistics tells us that the violent crime rate in the U.S. decreased seventy-six percent from 1993 to 2010. Total household property crime during the same period decreased sixty-four percent.[55]

There is hardly consensus on the reasons why the crime rate has gone down so significantly. As a 2015 study by the Brennan Center for Justice at NYU Law School, "What Caused the Crime Decline?" tells us, "Most likely, there is no one cause for such widespread, dramatic change. Many factors are responsible."[56] Just as there are many reasons why the incarceration rate went up, there are many reasons why the crime rate went down. Scholars from various disciplines have offered some other interesting theories about the reason for the recent decrease in crime after several decades of increases. These include theories tied to changes in gun laws, inflation, consumer confidence, and a decrease in alcohol usage. A full analysis of each theory is beyond the scope of this book; the best and most recent compendium of theories that we know of is the Brennan Center's study, which reviews fourteen of the most compelling theories for the decrease in crime. We briefly review a few of those theories here.

Incapacitation

One factor that partially explains the overall decrease in crime over the past couple of decades is the reality that it is impossible to commit crimes in free society while incarcerated. As mentioned earlier, this is the incapacitation effect; the offender in prison for auto theft cannot steal cars while in prison. The window of opportunity for many to engage in crime diminishes during their incarceration. Moreover, not only did the U.S. start locking up a lot more people, it started locking them up for a longer period. A 2012 study by the Pew Charitable Trust's Public Safety Performance Project found that prisoners released in 2009 served an average of nine additional months in custody than those released in 1990. In *Time Served: The High Cost, Low Return of Longer Prison Terms*, the Pew study found a thirty-seven percent increase in time served for violent crimes between 1990 and 2009, a twenty-four percent increase for property crimes, and a thirty-six percent increase for drug offenses. Overall, of the thirty-five states that provided data, the average sentence served rose from 2.1 to 2.9 years, an increase of thirty-six percent. Michigan had the highest average time served, at 4.3 years; South Dakota had the lowest, at 1.3 years.[57]

Those who believe that incapacitation is primarily responsible for the drop in crime tend to defend mass incarceration, arguing that criminals and aspiring criminals finally got the message when the U.S. began imprisoning so many more offenders. However, the Brennan Center's analysis found:

> Increased incarceration accounted for approximately 6 percent of the reduction in property crime in the 1990s (this could vary statistically from 0 to 12 percent), and accounted for less than 1 percent of the decline in property crime this century. Increased incarceration has had little effect on the drop in violent crime in the past 24 years. In fact, large states such as California, Michigan, New Jersey, New York, and Texas have all reduced their prison populations while crime has continued to fall.[58]

End of the Baby Boom

Another explanation for the drop in crime is a demographic one. The baby boom discussed above did come to an end, and Boomers are growing older each day. In 1997, the FBI announced that the 1996 murder rate was the lowest it had been in twenty-five years. CNN cited this report in an article entitled, "Aging Boomers Help Lower Crime Rates," quoting Jack Levin, director of Northeastern University's Program for the Study of Violence, "Part of this is demographic: Many baby boomers are now in their 40s and have mellowed out. They are not committing the high-risk violent and property offenses they did 10 years ago."[59]

More Effective Law Enforcement

An alternative theory for the decrease in crime points focuses on changes in law enforcement. Some point to an increase in the number of police officers as a deterrent to crime; in 1975, there were 211 sworn police officers per 100,000 Americans; in 2001, there were 245.9 sworn officers per 100,000 Americans, an increase of sixteen percent.[60] Another significant change in law enforcement is how policing is done. Technological advances have helped law enforcement agencies compile and analyze data to better anticipate and respond to criminal activity, as well as to better allocate resources. An increase in the number of police officers and advances in police technology both seem to have helped reduce crime over the past few decades, according to the Brennan Center report.[61]

Abortion on Demand

A theory that has generated a significant body of scholarly work received mainstream attention in Steven D. Levitt and Stephen J. Dubner's 2005 bestseller *Freakonomics*. The argument, originally advanced in 2001 by Levitt, an economist at the University of Chicago, and John J. Donohue III, an economist at Stanford Law School, claims, "Legalized abortion appears to account for as much as 50 percent of the recent drop in crime."[62] Donohue and Levitt argue that legalized abortion resulted in a smaller cohort of young males, the demographic group most likely to commit crime, then go on to say that "women who have abortions are those most at risk to give birth to children who would engage in criminal activity."[63] These women include teenagers, unmarried women, and the economically disadvantaged. Donohue and Levitt further argue that abortion allows women to optimize the timing of when they have children, so that they can have children when children are wanted and can be best cared for.

Less Lead in the Environment

Two other economists have advanced another theory for the decrease in crime: the nation's switch to unleaded gasoline. While working as a consultant for the U.S. Department of Housing and Urban Development in the 1990s, Rick Nevin explored the costs and benefits of removing lead-based paint from older residences. The presence of lead paint had become widely recognized as a health hazard to children exposed to it, yet Nevin discovered that the biggest source of children's exposure to lead was leaded gasoline. The baby boom and the suburbanization of America coincided after World War II. Wartime production turned to peacetime production, with Detroit producing millions of new cars for drivers who used the newly built federal highway system to move to the suburbs and raise their growing families. With gasoline plentiful and cheap, the automobiles of this period were gas-guzzlers. Nevin published an article in the journal *Environmental Research* in 2000 that made the case for children being exposed to leaded gas and later criminal behavior.[64] He later published a broader study that reviewed lead and crime data from Canada, Australia, New Zealand, and several European nations, finding trends that replicated the trend he saw earlier in the U.S.[65]

Building on Nevin's work, Amherst College economist Jessica Wolpaw Reyes published a working paper in 2007 through the National Bureau of Economic Research entitled, "Environmental Policy as Social Policy? The Impact of Childhood Lead Exposure on Crime." Reyes tells the reader:

> Childhood lead exposure can lead to psychological deficits that are strongly associated with aggressive and criminal behavior … this article finds that the reduction in childhood lead exposure in the late 1970s and early 1980s is responsible for significant declines in violent crime in the 1990s, and may cause further declines into the future.[66]

Reyes studied differences in data among different American states, which had implemented restrictions on leaded gasoline at different times. In her conclusion, Reyes ties her work to that of Donohue and Levitt:

> This paper shows a significant and robust relationship between lead exposure in childhood and violent crime rates later in life…. The legalization of abortion, as identified by Donohue and Levitt, remains an important and significant factor. Thus, two major acts of government, the Clean Air Act and *Roe v. Wade*, neither intended to have

any effect on crime, may have been the largest factors affecting violent crime trends at the turn of century.[67]

While the leaded gasoline argument began among economists, others have also investigated its possible connection to crime. In a 2012 article published in the journal *Environment International* by toxicologist Howard W. Mielke, a research professor in the Department of Pharmacology at the Tulane University School of Medicine, and demographer Sammy Zahran at the Center for Disaster and Risk Analysis at Colorado State University, the authors found a correlation between children being exposed to lead dust and subsequent violent criminal behavior. After looking at vehicle emission data in six U.S. cities for the period 1950–1985 and subsequent violent crime data in those cities, the authors concluded, "Our findings along with others predict that prevention of children's lead exposure from lead dust now will realize numerous societal benefits two decades into the future, including lower rates of aggravated assault."[68] As some of the researchers and many of their critics noted, there is insufficient data to find a correlation between the U.S.'s move away from leaded gasoline and its decrease in property crime.

Declining Crack Cocaine Usage

The decline in the use of crack cocaine also helps to explain the decrease in crime from the early 1990s on. Crack, although highly addictive, produces an intense yet relatively short "high." It also causes many of its users to be highly agitated. Having a bunch of folks high on crack trying to find the funds to purchase more crack led to a surge in property and violent crime (including homicides) in the early 1990s. For example, Boston saw a surge in homicides from less than 100 in 1988 to more than 150 in 1990.[69] A 1997 study conducted for the Justice Department examined crack usage and homicide rates in eight cities.[70] According to Jeremy Travers, director of the National Institute of Justice, "What we found is that there was a very strong statistical correlation between changes in crack use in the criminal population and homicide rates."[71] By the time the study was released, there had been a marked decrease in crack usage and a general decline in homicide rates. The U.S. Department of Health and Human Services' 1997 National Household Survey on Drug Abuse stated that, "In 1996, there were an estimated 675,000 new cocaine users, compared with about 1.2 to 1.3 million cocaine initiates per year from 1980–1986," and noted that new crack users in 1996 had decreased by more than a third from the year before.[72] In 1999, there were thirty-one homicides in Boston.[73]

Crime Is Going Down;
Does the Public Know That?

Despite the encouraging data on the decrease in crime, many Americans are unaware. A poll conducted regularly by the Gallup organization asks, "Is there more crime in the U.S. than there was a year ago, or less?"[74] Since 2003, a majority of those polled said that they believed (incorrectly) that crime was increasing, including seventy-four percent of those polled in 2009 and sixty-eight percent in 2011. The Gallup organization summarizes the results of the poll succinctly: "This unwarranted pessimism may stem from the imperfect indications of crime that Americans receive from the news and other sources, as well as Americans' overall mood."[75]

The late communication scholar George Gerbner coined the term "Mean World Syndrome."[76] This syndrome affects some of those who are repeatedly exposed to violent mass media, making them perceive the world as more violent than it actually is. Many local television newscasts follow the maxim, "if it bleeds, it leads." Newscasts and the commercial "teases" leading up to them typically focus on violent crimes, car accidents, and other tragedies. On slow news days, previously covered violent crimes are discussed again, labeled "developing stories." Police dramas and action movies also provide fictional albeit frequent and repetitive accounts of violent crimes. Gerbner tells us, "What this means is that if you are growing up in a home where there is more than say three hours of television per day, for all practical purposes you live in a meaner world—and act accordingly—than your next-door neighbor who lives in the same world but watches less television. The programming reinforces the worst fears and apprehensions and paranoia of people."[77]

As we discuss in Chapter 3, many politicians have tapped into this overwrought fear of crime for their own political gain.

The End of Mass Incarceration?

The recession of 2008 and 2009 caused government at the federal, state, and local levels to examine government spending with new vigor. Policy makers and politicians subjected the cost of building and operating more prisons to particular scrutiny. The Pew Charitable Trust's Project on the States reported in 2008 that five states were spending more on prisons than on public higher education, adding that, "During the last 20 years, corrections spending has increased by 127 percent on top of inflation, while spending on higher ed has increased only 21 percent."[78] In 2009, another Pew study found that government spending on corrections was "outpacing budget growth in education, transportation and public assistance, based on state and federal data."[79] State spending on corrections increased from $6.7 billion in 1985 to $53.3 billion in 2012. The U.S. Bureau of Prisons' budget for fiscal year 2010 was over $6 billion.

As we will see in Chapters 3 and 5, much of the mass incarceration movement was driven by conservative politics. The problem for many fiscal conservatives is that mass incarceration has proven to be so costly to taxpayers with so little to show for the money spent. The good news is that some conservatives have recognized the problem. One of the first conservative initiatives to reduce prison spending occurred in Texas. As the state began to address its prison overcrowding in 2007, the Texas Legislature faced the projected need to add 12,000 prison beds by 2012. Rather than spend an estimated $2.7 billion for new construction, the Republican-controlled legislature enacted new laws that allowed prosecutors and judges to provide more alternatives to incarceration to offenders.[80] We discuss some of these measures in Chapter 7.

One group advising the Texas Legislature, the Texas Policy Foundation, went on to found a national organization, Right on Crime. As Right on Crime declares:

> Conservatives are known for being tough on crime, but we must also be tough on criminal justice spending. That means demanding more cost-effective approaches that enhance public safety. A clear example is our reliance on prisons, which serve a critical role by incapacitating dangerous offenders and career criminals but are not the solution for every type of offender. And in some instances, they have the unintended consequence of hardening nonviolent, low-risk offenders— making them a greater risk to the public than when they entered.[81]

Among Right on Crime's signatories are high-profile conservatives, including Newt Gingrich, Grover Norquist, and Jeb Bush.

On the other side of the political spectrum, the Sentencing Project tells us that:

> The United States is the world's leader in incarceration with 2.2 million people currently in the nation's prisons or jails—a 500% increase over the past thirty years. These trends [sic] have resulted in prison overcrowding and state governments being overwhelmed by the burden of funding a rapidly expanding penal system, despite increasing evi-

dence that large-scale incarceration is not the most effective means of achieving public safety.[82]

Prison overcrowding presents safety concerns to both prison inmates and prison staff. The U.S. Justice Department told Congress that in federal fiscal year 2015, federal prisons had inmate populations averaging twenty-eight percent over the rated capacity of facilities; in high security prisons, among the most dangerous, the population was fifty percent over rated capacity.[83] In 2011, the U.S. Supreme Court held in *Brown v. Plata* that overcrowding in California prisons violated prisoners' Eighth Amendment protection against cruel and unusual punishment.[84] The Court upheld a ruling by a panel of three lower court judges that required California to reduce its prison population to 137.5 percent of capacity, which would mean the release or transfer of 46,000 prisoners. At the time of the ruling, California held over 150,000 inmates in facilities designed to house approximately 85,000 inmates.[85]

As California continues to realign its prison population, it is striving to meet the goal of housing no more than 113,720 inmates by February 28, 2016. Part of this reduction is being facilitated through the transfer of some prisoners to out-of-state prisons and other facilities, including county jails and private prisons. Additional reductions are taking place through changes in parole and the development of new alternatives to correction.[86]

The nation has reached a tipping point. In 2013, the U.S. Bureau of Justice Statistics announced that the U.S. prison population had decreased in each of the three previous years. California's prison realignment was responsible for half of the 2012 decrease, but eight states had decreases of more than 1,000 prisoners, and more than half the states reported decreasing prison populations.[87] The *New York Times* quoted Natasha Frost, Associate Dean of Northeastern University's School of Criminology and Criminal Justice, who stated, "This is the beginning of the end of mass incarceration."[88]

Recidivism: The Ultimate Metric

As we have seen, over the past three decades, the nation moved towards locking up more people and locking them up longer, sought to make the conditions of incarceration less comfortable, and made it more difficult to get out of prison early. These measures have cost American taxpayers billions of dollars. Did they work to reduce crime? As we have seen, the U.S. experienced a decrease in violent crime over two decades and a steady decrease in property crime over three decades. However, studies have not found a strong causal link between increased incarceration and this decrease in crime.

The critical test of correctional policies and practices can be summed up in one word: recidivism. In general, recidivism means repeatedly engaging in criminal behavior. In corrections, it means being reincarcerated for another crime after having been released from incarceration for a previous crime. It is this second, more specific definition that we will rely upon through this book, although we note in Chapter 4 that defining recidivism gets tricky when trying to compare one nation's recidivism rate to that of another nation.

A 2014 report by the U.S. Bureau of Justice Statistics found that among more than 400,000 prisoners released in 2005 in thirty states, a little more than two-thirds (67.8 percent) were arrested for a new crime within three years, and a little more than three-quarters (76.6 percent) were arrested within four years.[89] In earlier studies, the Bureau found that 67.5 percent of prisoners released in 1994 were rearrested within three years, as were 62.5 percent of those released in 1983.[90] To summarize this data: the recidivism rate has gone up, not down, since the abrupt shift toward mass incarceration began, and U.S. prisons seem to be successfully deterring future crime among released prisoners at only a rate of thirty-three percent or less. Most of us would label a success rate of one-third as an abysmal failure.

The three-decade increase in incarceration rates in the U.S. can be credited for some of the reduction in crime over the past two decades, as it is now more likely than before the mass incarceration movement that a chronic recidivist is incarcerated. However, the reality is that most prisoners will get out of prison someday, and a prisoner released today is less likely to be rehabilitated than was a prisoner released before the mass incarceration movement began. This is due in part to the work of Robert Martinson and James Q. Smith, which led many correctional agencies to give up trying to rehabilitate in the late twentieth century, seeking instead to punish or merely warehouse prisoners. Some states have begun to move away from the "nothing works" model, but many states remain mired in it.

Conclusion

Steeply rising crime rates in the 1960s and 1970s frightened many Americans. Politicians responded by providing more resources to law enforcement, enacting stricter laws with more severe punishments, and often disregarding prior efforts to rehabilitate criminal offenders in favor of incapacitation through incarceration. The result was a sharp upswing in the nation's incarceration rate, which had been relatively stable for nearly a century. This new phenomenon, mass incarceration, drove the U.S. to incarcerate a higher percentage of its residents than any other nation.

The practice of mass incarceration continued even though crime rates in the U.S. steadily decreased, a trend that social scientists attribute to a variety of causes. However, the recidivism rates of offenders released from incarceration rose. By the early twenty-first century, many observers, regardless of political ideology, have begun to recognize that mass incarceration has proven to be an expensive failure. Because of this recognition of failure, and due to governmental financial exigencies, the U.S. prison population has decreased over the past few years. Finding more effective methods of discouraging criminal behavior and more efficient means of deterring criminals from reoffending remain significant challenges today.

Where Do We Go From Here?

In the next chapter, Watson discusses why he went to prison and what prison was like. He describes his dealings with law enforcement officers, prosecutors, and the trial judge. He talks about some of the inmates he met, as well as some of the staff and administrators. Although Watson was never physically abused while incarcerated, he witnessed not just how ineffective prisons are, but how they can actually cause more harm than good for those serving prison sentences.

Watson hated prison, and has no plans on returning. He is now back home with his family intact, making an honest living. Unfortunately, among released prisoners in the U.S., Watson is an outlier, as a significant majority of prisoners will reoffend, and time spent incarcerated often leads to disrupted and damaged families. This brings us to the title of our book. Watson saw firsthand why American prisons fail. In the chapters that follow, we present a pathology of that failure, and offer some suggestions on how the American correctional system can develop, adopt, and expand successful methods of rehabilitating criminal offenders and place more of them back into society as successful citizens.

Notes

1. "U.S. Prison Population Declined for Third Consecutive Year during 2012," (Washington, DC: U.S. Office of Justice Programs, July 25, 2013), http://ojp.gov/newsroom/pressreleases/2013/ojppr072513.pdf.

2. William J. Sabol, Heather C. West, and Matthew Cooper, "Prisoners in 2008," *Bureau of Justice Statistics Bulletin*, (Washington, DC: U.S Bureau of Justice Statistics, December 2009, revised June 30, 2010), http://www.bjs.gov/content/pub/pdf/p08.pdf.

3. "One in 100: Behind Bars in America 2008," (Washington, DC: Pew Charitable Trusts, February 28, 2008), http://www.pewtrusts.org/en/research-and-analysis/reports/2008/02/28/one-in-100-behind-bars-in-america-2008.

4. Jeremy Travis, Bruce Western, and Steve Redburn, eds., introduction to *The Growth of Incarceration in the United States: Exploring Causes and Consequences* (Washington, DC: National Academies Press, 2014): 2.

5. Adam Lipak, "Inmate Count in U.S. Dwarfs Other Nations," *New York Times*, April 23, 2008, http://www.nytimes.com/2008/04/23/us/23prison.html?pagewanted=all&_r=0.

6. "Interactive Map," The Sentencing Project, accessed June 27, 2015, http://www.sentencingproject.org/map/map.cfm.

7. Travis, Western, and Redburn, 3.

8. Sandra L. Colby and Jennifer M. Ortman, "The Baby Boom Cohort in the United States: 2012 to 2060," (Washington DC: U.S. Census Bureau, May 2014), http://www.census.gov/prod/2014pubs/p25-1141.pdf.

9. Ibid., 6; National Center for Health Statistics, "Table 1-1. Live Births, Birth Rates, and Fertility Rates, by Race: United States, 1909–2000," (Atlanta: U.S. Centers for Disease Control), accessed June 27, 2015, http://www.cdc.gov/nchs/data/statab/t001x01.pdf.

10. James Q. Wilson, "Who Is in Prison?" *Commentary*, November 1, 1976, http://www.commentarymagazine.com/article/who-is-in-prison/.

11. E. Ann Carson, "Prisoners in 2013," (Washington, DC: U.S. Bureau of Justice Statistics, September 30, 2014), http://www.bjs.gov/content/pub/pdf/p13.pdf; Alexia D. Cooper, Matthew R. Durose, and
Howard N. Snyder, "Recidivism of Prisoners Released in 30 States in 2005: Patterns from 2005 to 2010," (Washington DC: U.S. Bureau of Justice Statistics, April 2014), http://www.bjs.gov/content/pub/pdf/rprts05p0510.pdf.

12. "Estimated Crime in United States—total; Crime rate per 100,000 population; Property crime," (Washington DC: Federal Bureau of Investigation), accessed June 27, 2015, http://www.ucrdatatool.gov/Search/Crime/State/RunCrimeStatebyState.cfm.

13. "Estimated Crime in United States—total; Crime rate per 100,000 population; Violent crime," (Washington DC: Federal Bureau of Investigation), accessed June 27, 2015, http://www.ucrdatatool.gov/Search/Crime/State/RunCrimeStatebyState.cfm.

14. "Estimated Crime in United States—total; Violent Crime;" "Estimated Crime in United States—total; Property Crime," (Washington DC: Federal Bureau of Investigation), accessed Jun 27, 2015, http://www.ucrdatatool.gov/Search/Crime/State/RunCrimeStatebyState.cfm.

15. Richard M. Nixon, "What Has Happened to America?" *Reader's Digest*, October 1967, 49–54, 49–50.

16. Ibid., 50.

17. Nancy E. Marion, *A History of Federal Crime Control Initiatives, 1960–1993*(Greenwich, CT: Praeger, 1994): 80–81.

18. "LEAA Activities July 1, 1972 to June 30, 1973," (Washington, DC: U.S. Law Enforcement Assistance Administration, 1973): 1, https://www.ncjrs.gov/pdffiles1/Digitization/147380NCJRS.pdf.

19. Robert F. Diegelman, Federal Financial Assistance for Crime Control: Lessons of the LEAA Experience, 73 J. CRIM. L. & CRIMINOLOGY 994, 996 (1982).

20. Douglas Lipton, Robert Martinson, and Judith Wilks, *Effectiveness of Correctional Treatment: A Survey of Treatment and Evaluation Studies* (New York: Praeger, 1975).

21. Robert Martinson, "What Works? Questions and Answers about Prison Reform," *The Public Interest* 35 (Spring 1974): 22–56, 49.

22. David Farabee, *Rethinking Rehabilitation: Why Can't We Reform Our Criminals?* (Washington, DC: American Enterprise Institute, 2005): xvi.

23. Francis T. Cullen, "Rehabilitation: Beyond Nothing Works," in *Crime and Justice in America 1975–2025*, ed. Michael Tonry, (Chicago: University of Chicago Press, 2013): 299–376, 300.

24. James Q. Wilson, *Thinking About Crime* (New York: Basic Books, 1975): 235–236.

25. Mark Kleiman, "Wilson, Loury, and the Varieties of 'Broken Windows,'" *Washington Monthly*, May 14, 2012, http://www.washingtonmonthly.com/ten-miles-square/2012/05/wilson_loury_and_the_varieties037323.php.

26. Richard M. Nixon, "Special Message to the Congress on Drug Abuse Prevention and Control," June 17, 1971, http://www.presidency.ucsb.edu/ws/?pid=3048.

27. "DEA Staffing & Budget," (Washington, DC: U.S. Drug Enforcement Administration), accessed June 27, 2015, http://www.justice.gov/dea/about/history/staffing.shtml.

28. "Office Locations," (Washington, DC: U.S. Drug Enforcement Administration), accessed June 27, 2015, http://www.justice.gov/dea/about/Domesticoffices.shtml.

29. Leif R. Rosenberger, *America's Drug War Debacle*, (Brookfield, VT: Ashgate Publishing, 1996): 26.

30. George H.W. Bush, "National Drug Control Strategy," (Washington, DC: Office of the President, 1989): 16, https://www.ncjrs.gov/pdffiles1/ondcp/119466.pdf.

31. Ibid., 17.

32. Ronald J. Ostrow, "Casual Drug Users Should Be Shot, Gates Says," *Los Angeles Times*, September 6, 1990, http://articles.latimes.com/1990-09-06/news/mn-983_1_casual-drug-users.

33. "Table 29, Estimated Number of Arrests United States, 2006, 'Crime in the U.S.,'" (Washington, DC: Federal Bureau of Investigation), accessed July 7, 2014, http://www.fbi.gov/about-us/cjis/ucr/crime-in-the-u.s/2006.

34. "Table 29, Estimated Number of Arrests United States, 2013, 'Crime in the U.S.,'" (Washington, DC: Federal Bureau of Investigation), accessed June 27, 2015, http://www.fbi.gov/about-us/cjis/ucr/crime-in-the-u.s/2013.

35. "Before Looking Ahead, You Must Look Behind," (Washington, DC: Federal Bureau of Prisons), accessed June 27, 2015, http://www.bop.gov/about/history/timeline.jsp.

36. "Statistics," (Washington, DC: Federal Bureau of Prisons), accessed June 27, 2015, http://www.bop.gov/about/statistics/population_statistics.jsp.

37. Carson, 17.

38. "Quick Facts: Drug Trafficking Sentences," (Washington, DC: U.S. Sentencing Commission), accessed June 27, 2015, http://www.ussc.gov/sites/default/files/pdf/research-and-publications/quick-facts/Quick_Facts_Drug_Trafficking_2013.pdf.

39. "Fact Sheet: Trends in U.S. Corrections," (Washington, DC: The Sentencing Project): 3, accessed June 27, 2015, http://sentencingproject.org/doc/publications/inc_Trends_in_Corrections_Fact_sheet.pdf.

40. Carson, 5; Margaret Werner Cahalan, "Historical Corrections Statistics in the United States, 1850–1984," (Washington, DC: U.S. Bureau of Justice Statistics, December 1986): 65, https://www.ncjrs.gov/pdffiles1/pr/102529.pdf.

41. E. Ann Carson and Daniela Golinelli, "Prisoners in 2012; Trends in Admissions and Releases, 1991–2012" (Washington, DC: U.S. Bureau of Justice Statistics, December 2013), http://www.bjs.gov/content/pub/pdf/p12tar9112.pdf.

42. Carson, 15.

43. Ibid.

44. Ellen Perlman, "Terms of Imprisonment," *Governing*, April 2000, http://www.governing.com/topics/public-justice-safety/Terms-Imprisonment.html.

45. "Report to Congress: Mandatory Minimum Penalties in the Federal Criminal Justice System," (Washington, DC: U.S. Sentencing Commission, October 2011): 148, http://www.ussc.gov/Legislative_and_Public_Affairs/Congressional_Testimony_and_Reports/Mandatory_Minimum_Penalties/20111031_RtC_Mandatory_Minimum.cfm.

46. "Report to Congress: Violent Offender Incarceration and Truth-In-Sentencing Incentive Formula Grant Program," (Washington, DC: U.S. Bureau of Justice Assistance, February 2012), https://www.bja.gov/Publications/VOITIS-Final-Report.pdf.

47. Fox Butterfield, "Eliminating Parole Boards Isn't a Cure-All, Experts Say," *New York Times*, January 10, 1999, http://www.nytimes.com/1999/01/10/us/eliminating-parole-boards-isn-t-a-cure-all-experts-say.html.

48. Statement of Charles E. Samuels, Jr., Director of the Federal Bureau of Prisons before the U.S. House of Representatives Committee on Appropriations Subcommittee on Commerce, Justice, Science and Related Agencies Federal Bureau of Prisons FY 2014 Budget Request, April 17, 2013, 3, http://appropriations.house.gov/uploadedfiles/hhrg-113-ap19-wstate-samuelsc-20130417.pdf.

49. John Clark, James Austin, and D. Alan Henry, "'Three Strikes and You're Out': A Review of State Legislation: Research in Brief," (Washington, DC: U.S. National Institute of Justice, September 1997), https://ncjrs.gov/pdffiles/165369.pdf.

50. Lockyer v. Andrade, 538 U.S. 63 (2003).

51. Eric Slater, "Pizza Thief Gets 25 Years to Life: Crime: Judge Cites Five Prior Felony Convictions in Sentencing Jerry Dewayne Williams under 'Three Strikes' Law. Defense Attorney Says He Will Appeal 'Excessive Punishment,'" *Los Angeles Times*, March 3, 1995, http://articles.latimes.com/1995-03-03/local/me-38258_1_jerry-dewayne-williams.

52. No Frills Prison Act of 1999, H.R. 370 106th Congress (1999), http://www.gpo.gov/fdsys/pkg/BILLS-106hr370ih/html/BILLS-106hr370ih.htm.

53. "'No Frills Prison Act' Becomes Law," Alaska Republicans, accessed June 27, 2015, http://www.akrepublicans.org/pastlegs/prsb001053097.htm.

54. "National Survey Shows Prison Wardens Support Amenities" Sam Houston State University, February 2, 1996, http://www.shsu.edu/~pin_www/T@S/1996/wardens.html.

55. Janet L. Lauritsen and Maribeth L. Rezey, "Measuring the Prevalence of Crime with the National Crime Victimization Survey," (Washington, DC: U.S. Bureau of Justice Statistics, August 29, 2013), http://www.bjs.gov/content/pub/ascii/mpcncvs.txt.

56. Oliver Roeder, Lauren-Brooke Eisen, and Julia Bowling, *What Caused the Crime Decline?* (New York: Brennan Center for Justice, NYU Law School, 2015): 3, https://www.brennancenter.org/sites/default/files/analysis/What_Caused_The_Crime_Decline.pdf.

57. Pew Center for the States, *Time Served: The High Cost, Low Return of Longer Prison Terms*, (Washington, DC: Pew Charitable Trusts, June 2012): 3, 13.

58. Roeder, Eisen, and Bowling, 4.

59. "Aging Baby Boomers Help Lower Crime Rates," CNN Interactive, October 4, 1997, http://www.cnn.com/US/9710/04/crime/index.html?_s=PM:US.

60. Brian Reaves, "Number of full-time sworn law enforcement officers, annual percent change in employment, and officers per 100,000 residents in the United States, 1975–1998," (Washington, DC: U.S. Bureau of Justice Statistics, updated January 23, 2003),

http://www.bjs.gov/content/data/lwenfemp.csv.

61. Roeder, Eisen, and Bowling, 41, 78.

62. John J. Donohue III and Steven D. Levitt, "The Impact of Legalized Abortion on Crime," *The Quarterly Journal of Economics* 116, no. 2 (2001): 379–420, 379.

63. Ibid., 381.

64. Rick Nevin, How Lead Exposure Relates to Temporal Changes in IQ, Violent Crime, and Unwed Pregnancy," *Environmental Research* 83, no. 1 (2000): 1–22.

65. Nevin, "Understanding International Crime Trends: The Legacy of Preschool Lead Exposure," *Environmental Research* 104 (2007): 315–336.

66. Jessica Wolpaw Reyes, "Environmental Policy as Social Policy? The Impact of Childhood Lead Exposure on Crime," (Cambridge, MA: National Bureau of Economic Research, 2007): abstract, http://www3.amherst.edu/~jwreyes/papers/LeadCrime.pdf.

67. Ibid., 35.

68. Howard W. Mielke and Sammy Zahran, "The Urban Rise and Fall of Air Lead (Pb) and the Latent Surge and Retreat of Societal Violence," *Environment International* 43 (August 2012): 48–55.

69. Matt Carrol, "Homicides Decrease in Boston for Third Straight Year," *Boston Globe*, January 1, 2013, http://www.bostonglobe.com/metro/2013/01/01/homicides-track-fall-boston-for-third-straight-year/KKOmMsHDQcyS89vrBGtVUO/story.html.

70. Pamela K. Lattimore, James Trudeau, K. Jack Riley, Jordan Leiter, and Steven Edwards, "Homicide in Eight U.S. Cities: Trends, Context, and Policy Implications," (Washington, DC: U.S. Office of Justice Programs, December 1997), https://www.ncjrs.gov/pdffiles1/ondcp/homicide_trends.pdf.

71. Fox Butterfield, "Drop in Homicide Rate Linked to Crack's Decline," *New York Times*, October 7, 1997, http://www.nytimes.com/1997/10/27/us/drop-in-homicide-rate-linked-to-crack-s-decline.html.

72. Substance Abuse and Mental Health Services Administration, "1997 National Household Survey on Drug Abuse: Preliminary Results," (Washington, DC: U.S. Department of Health and Human Services, updated February 5, 2009), http://www.samhsa.gov/data/nhsda/nhsda97/nhsda984.htm.

73. Carrol.

74. Lydia Saad, "Most Americans Believe Crime in U.S. Is Worsening," Gallup Well-Being, October 31, 2011, http://www.gallup.com/poll/150464/americans-believe-crime-worsening.aspx.

75. Ibid.

76. George Gerbner, "Reclaiming Our Cultural Mythology," *The Ecology of Justice*, Spring 1994, http://www.context.org/iclib/ic38/gerbner/.

77. Ibid.

78. Scott Jaschik, "Prison vs. Colleges" *Inside Higher Ed*, February 29, 2008, http://www.insidehighered.com/news/2008/02/29/prisons#sthash.IcOQSWgE.dpbs.

79. Solomon Moore, "Prison Spending Outpaces All but Medicaid," *New York Times*, March 2, 2009, http://www.nytimes.com/2009/03/03/us/03prison.html?_r=0.

80. Brooke Rollins, "Rollins: Criminal Justice Reform—Texas Style," *Austin American-Statesman*, October 6, 2013, http://www.mystatesman.com/news/news/opinion/rollins--criminal-justice-reform-texas-style/nbFD7/.

81. "Statement of Principles," Right on Crime, accessed June 27, 2015, http://www.rightoncrime.com/the-conservative-case-for-reform/statement-of-principles/.

82. "Incarceration," (Washington, DC: The Sentencing Project), accessed June 27, 2015,

http://www.sentencingproject.org/template/page.cfm?id=107.

83. "FY 2016 Performance Budget Congressional Submission, Federal Prison System Buildings and Facilities," (Washington, DC: Federal Bureau of Prisons): 3, accessed June 27, 2015, http://www.justice.gov/sites/default/files/jmd/pages/attachments/2015/02/02/federal_bureau_of_prisons_bop_bf.pdf.

84. Brown v. Plata, 563 U.S. ____ (2011).

85. "Year at a Glance 2011," (Sacramento: California Department of Corrections and Rehabilitation, 2012), accessed July 22, 2014, http://www.cdcr.ca.gov/News/docs/2011_Annual_Report_FINAL.pdf.

86. California Department of Corrections and Rehabilitation, "Three-Judge Court Updates, July 2014 Status Report Exhibit B," (Sacramento: California Department of Corrections and Rehabilitation, July 15, 2014), http://www.cdcr.ca.gov/News/docs/3JP-July-2014/July-2014-Status-Report-Exhibit-B.pdf.

87. Erica Goode, "U.S. Prison Populations Decline, Reflecting New Approach to Crime," *New York Times*, July 25, 2013, http://www.nytimes.com/2013/07/26/us/us-prison-populations-decline-reflecting-new-approach-to-crime.html?pagewanted=all&_r=0.

88. Ibid.

89. Cooper, Durose, and Snyder.

90. Patrick A. Langan and David J. Levin, "Recidivism of Prisoners Released in 1994," (Washington, DC: U.S. Bureau of Justice Statistics, June 2002), www.bjs.gov/content/pub/pdf/rpr94.pdf; Allen J. Beck and Bernard E. Shipley, "Recidivism of Prisoners Released in 1983," (Washington, DC: U.S. Bureau of Justice Statistics, April 1989), http://www.bjs.gov/content/pub/phttp://www.bjs.gov/content/pub/pdf/rpr83.pdfdf/rpr83.pdf.

Chapter 2

George Goes to Jail

Not Your Typical Jailbird

Who is most likely to end up doing time in an American prison? If you said someone who is male, young, poor, undereducated, and black or Hispanic, you're right. The U.S. Bureau of Justice Statistics tells us that almost ninety-one percent of those incarcerated are male, and that nearly sixty percent of prisoners are black or Hispanic.[1] The FBI reports that more than half of those arrested are between the ages of sixteen and twenty-nine.[2] Among the most common and most sought-after programs in U.S. prisons are those that grant GEDs and high school diplomas. This brings up the issue of how social inequality leads to racial disparities in the criminal justice system, which is beyond the scope of this book, but if you're interested, we recommend Michelle Alexander's *The New Jim Crow: Mass Incarceration in the Age of Colorblindness* and Bryan Stevenson's *Just Mercy*.

Our protagonist in this chapter, George Watson, shares only one characteristic with the stereotype of a convict. He's male. Otherwise, he's white, has three college degrees, and got into trouble with the law for the very first time at the age of fifty-four. He's happily married. He doesn't even have a tattoo. Let's meet Watson and find out how it all hit the fan.

George Edwin Hill II was born in Amarillo, Texas, three weeks after his father died in the Korean War. His mother soon decided to move to Dallas and start a new life. A year and a half later, she married the man George would come to know as his dad, Jack Watson, and George became George Hill Watson.

After growing up in Dallas, Watson went on to major in psychology at Washington University in St. Louis, where he decided he wanted to become a psychology professor. Human behavior fascinated him and he was excited by the thought of sharing that knowledge with students as well as doing original research in the field. He moved on to the University of Texas at Dallas and received an M.S. in Developmental Psychology, focused on cognitive development and language acquisition in early childhood.

Watson's work in cognitive development and language acquisition started him thinking about how to take advantage of that information in devising a better education system, as well as helping parents understand how best to help their children develop and learn at home and in school. With this in mind, rather than continuing and obtaining a Ph.D. in developmental psychology, the most logical step, Watson entered the doctoral program in Early Childhood Education for the Handicapped at the University of Texas at Austin.

Watson found himself in the wrong place at the wrong time. Many graduate programs today combine psychology and education; some also include courses in social work. However, when Watson began his doctoral program, he found that the faculty in graduate education departments rarely collaborated with psychology faculty. In fact, they looked down on the psychology professors as being too abstract and theoretical and completely unable to deal with the realities of the classroom.

Watson continued with his studies in the education department as well as taking graduate level classes in the psychology department, but grew discouraged after three semesters. Watson's brother moved in with him to attend law school and the two began having conversations about his brother's legal studies. Watson's disillusionment with his education studies, his conversations with his brother, plus the fact that his father had always touted the benefits of a law degree, even for those who never intended to practice law, moved him to go to law school. His dad spoke from experience as a lawyer who never practiced law but worked instead as a commercial real estate broker.

Watson graduated from law school in 1983 and began working as a commercial real estate broker in Dallas, following his father's example. Yet he missed Austin, so he moved back in 1989 and became involved in the flourishing local music scene as a music publisher. There he met and married Holly, a songwriter, who had two young children from a previous marriage. Watson continued working as a real estate broker until 1997, when he decided to look for something that did not require so much driving around. With so many contacts in the real estate business, he fell into practicing real estate law. A sole practitioner, he worked out of his home, without any assistants. Watson handled a fairly constant flow of real estate closings.

If you've ever purchased real estate, even something as relatively simple as buying your own home, you know that this involves a pile of paperwork. There are between fifteen and thirty different documents, running from 100 to 150 pages of legalese. In Texas, the process starts when someone drops off a contract with a closing attorney such as Watson. The closing attorney then gathers the information that the title insurance company needs to start their title research and turns in an order to them. This includes a legal description of the property; identification of the buyer, seller, and purchase price; and if there is a loan, the estimated loan amount. The turnaround time is anywhere from four to eight weeks. The closing attorney waits for the title company to generate the title commitment (guaranteeing to insure good title), for the buyer to obtain financing, and for lien holders to send payoff statements. The day of the closing, the mortgage companies typically send their documents and closing instructions to the closing attorney within three hours prior to the closing. The closing attorney then prepares the closing statement, which can take an hour or more. At this point, the closing attorney is scrambling to get everything ready for the closing. Many attorneys rely on paralegals to fill out and gather the documents; Watson had no staff, so he did this himself.

Although Watson was paying his bills and enjoying a steady income, he was by no means getting rich. The Texas Board of Insurance issues a fee schedule for title insurance; for example, in 2015, a $100,000 title insurance policy cost $875.[3] Title companies typically give the closing lawyer about half that, plus a $100 escrow fee per party to the sale.

A Knock at the Door

Watson's front door peephole had always humorously distorted the way people looked, transforming the UPS driver and the neighbors into caricatures. Then two men in suits carrying briefcases appeared on Watson's front porch in the spring of 2007. The peephole could not temper their apparent hostility.

Watson stared through the peephole, wondering who the hell these two guys were. He noticed that they stood close to the door, not several steps back like door-to-door salespeople. Watson had been practicing law out of his house in Austin for several years and had seen all types of people at his door. Facing legal issues, they often appeared apprehensive. These two guys didn't fit in that category; they looked angry.

Watson figured the best way to deal with the interruption in his morning's work was to send these two on their way, so he opened the door.

"Mr. Watson?"

"Yes?" Watson is polite that way. No "Yeah?" or "Who's Asking?" from him.

Both men pulled out badges and identified themselves. One was an FBI agent and the other worked for the IRS's criminal division. "We would like to talk to you," the FBI agent said. Watson invited the men in, clueless as to why they were there. It turned out Watson was clueless about a lot of things.

Watson led the agents into the dining room. He removed some doll clothes from the table and chairs. His two stepchildren now grown, Watson and his wife were sorting through the clothes to give them to Goodwill. As innocent as the setting was, the ensuing conversation wasn't. "Don't worry, Mr. Watson. We're not going to arrest you when we're through talking." Wow, thought Watson. The one thing that he didn't think about, even though he was a lawyer, was that he should refuse to talk to them until he obtained counsel.

Despite what we see on television and in the movies, most lawyers don't handle criminal cases. There's very little money to be had from most of them, as the average criminal doesn't have much income. In fact, many lawyers rarely step into a courtroom; their practices are focused on contracts and correspondence rather than prosecutions and lawsuits. Watson was one of these lawyers.

The agents had been investigating mortgage fraud, the dumbest crime in the world. It leaves a long and wide paper trail, with the participants' names appearing repeatedly, so refusing to talk would have been useless. Besides, Watson's natural inclination is to be helpful; he answered all their questions, unaware they already knew the answers and that their sole purpose in coming to his house was to try to get him to admit that he had knowingly broken the law.

"We want to talk to you about some real estate closings you handled," said the FBI agent, pulling a chart out of his briefcase with a flourish. Watson saw a lot of red ink with a few black splotches here and there, but that did nothing to explain the presence of these men in his dining room. The agent continued, "These are real estate closings that you handled for the investors listed here. The addresses printed in red are properties that have been foreclosed. Would you please explain to us the steps you went through when you handled real estate closings for these investors?"

The majority of the addresses were printed in red, and the fact that so many had been foreclosed on was news to Watson. The closings had taken place over a ten-year period and many of the names and addresses did not look familiar. Watson explained, "These investors sometimes bought properties, made improvements to them, and sold them. Other times they 'flipped' the properties, owning them for a short while before selling them to someone else. And other times, the investor bought and sold the property at the same time—simultaneous closings."

"Tell us about the simultaneous closings."

"Like I said, that's when an investor buys the property from the original seller at the same time he sells it to the next guy. It's done all the time. There are hundreds of books and seminars on how to do this. Don't you guys ever watch late-night infomercials?"

"Where did the end buyers in the flips get their down payment from?"

"Usually the buyers had their down payment money, and sometimes the investor would use some of his profit to make the down payment for the buyer."

"That's illegal!"

"What's illegal? People give or lend money to family and friends all the time to help them buy a home."

"Come on, Mr. Watson," said the FBI agent, "You're a smart man. You knew what you were doing was illegal."

"No, I didn't, because it wasn't. Like I said, people lend or give money to other people all the time for down payments on houses."

"Where did you go to law school?" asked the FBI agent.

"The University of Texas."

"That's a really good law school, right? I'm sure that they taught you how to do closings." The two men, who specialized in prosecuting white-collar criminals, had to know that "really good" law schools focus on legal theory—how to *think like* a lawyer—and don't teach anything as mundane or practical as how to perform a real estate closing—how to *be* a lawyer. Watson had graduated from law school and passed the state bar exam without knowing anything about real estate closings. What he knew about closings he had later learned on his own.

The FBI agent did most of the talking. "We can't make any promises but if you admit, right now, that you knew you were doing something illegal, things will probably go better for you."

Holly had been listening in the next room. She paced into the dining room, and said, "George is a good person and if he says he doesn't know anything, then he doesn't."

The FBI agent rolled his eyes and laughed. "That's what they all say. We just recently put another lawyer in a federal penitentiary whose wife said the same thing." The IRS agent, mostly silent thus far, threw back his head and snorted in laughter.

Still, the FBI agent and the IRS agent didn't get what they wanted—a statement of guilt that could be used against Watson at trial. They left angry and frustrated. They also left behind two devastated people.

Watson closed the door behind the agents, in the process closing the door on life as he and his family had known it.

Accused

Holly asked, "Are you going to go to prison?"

"I doubt it. I haven't done anything wrong. I can't believe how rude those guys were."

Holly replied, "I can't even believe they were here at all. Do you think they're coming back?"

"No. They asked for a lot of files. That's no problem; as far as I know, there's nothing incriminating in them." *Incriminating.* A word that Watson had never before associated with himself. Nevertheless, a word that would loom large over the next few years. Watson considered himself a good person and liked to think that most people saw him that way as well.

Watson spent the next few days having imaginary conversations with the FBI and IRS agents. That they had laughed at his wife, and at him, had really angered him. "I'll tell you something that I don't understand," he said to Holly one day at the kitchen table. "They didn't read my *Miranda* rights to me before interrogating me. I thought they had to do that. Tell you that you don't have to answer questions without an attorney present and all that stuff."

"Why didn't they?"

"I don't know. I don't know anything about criminal law." The University of Texas School of Law, Watson's attendance at which having been used as a weapon against him by the FBI agent, required students to take only one criminal law course when he was there. Watson had approached the course as a requirement rather than one of personal interest; it was one of several courses that he wanted to get a good grade in, remember a little of during the state bar exam, and then allow himself to forget. Despite his attraction to law, Watson hated conflict. One of the things that drew him to real estate law, which accounted for about half of his legal practice, was that people are usually in a good mood at closings. Rare is the area of the law where that is the case.

Watson found himself accused of white-collar crime. Edwin H. Sutherland coined the term in a speech he delivered as president of the American Sociological Society in 1939. Sutherland described white-collar crime as a "crime committed by a person of respectability and high social status in the course of his occupation."[4] More recent uses of the term de-emphasize the criminal's socioeconomic status. Today, the FBI describes white-collar crime as:

> those illegal acts which are characterized by deceit, concealment, or violation of trust and which are not dependent upon the application or threat of physical force or violence. Individuals and organizations commit these acts to obtain money, property, or services; to avoid the payment or loss of money or services; or to secure personal or business advantage.[5]

Watson barely knew the man who turned out to be the ringleader of the mortgage fraud gang. Cornelius Robinson, a middle-aged Austin resident, was married to Silvia Seelig, a licensed real estate agent, and his co-conspirator. Working with at least fourteen others, including two bank employees and a number of people acting as straw buyers beginning in 1999, the team would buy a house and immediately or soon after sell it for a higher price to the straw buyer, sometimes even flipping the house again for another profit. The documented financial status of the straw buyers was fraudulent, based in part on falsified verification of income and bank accounts. Robinson and Seelig would make monthly payments to the mortgagees on behalf of the straw buyers for a brief period to avoid attracting suspicion from lenders. After a while, they would stop making payments, the straw buyers would go into default, and the banks holding the mortgages would foreclose. The conspiracy involved at least thirty-three properties in the Austin and San Antonio area, nineteen financial institutions, and over $4.5 million in claimed losses.[6]

Over the course of about ten years, Watson had handled fifty-five real estate closings for the husband and wife team. Of those closings, only eleven were the subject of his prosecution. Watson had charged the same amount for those eleven that he charged for any other real estate closing, usually just a little more than $600. In hindsight, Watson thought to himself that if he'd had any suspicions about these particular real estate sales, he could have easily refrained from taking the work, as he had plenty of business otherwise. But he hadn't had any suspicions at the time.

Lawyers that advertise heavily tend to have the types of clients that don't know any lawyers personally. Watson knows plenty of lawyers, but he couldn't think of any that specialized in criminal law. The criminal attorney section of the yellow pages was something that he had never paid attention to before. The words there—jail, bond, felonies—were frightening. Watson made some calls. After a life spent trying to do the right thing, he had to tell a stranger that he was in trouble with the law, facing felony charges.

Watson found a lawyer who specialized in defending these types of cases. Watson asked him about taking the case to trial. After doing some calculations, the lawyer said, "If we go to trial and lose, your prison sentence will probably be between twenty and twenty-five years." This was a well-informed guess; Cornelius Robinson was convicted at trial and given a twenty-seven-year sentence. His expected release date is 2032.[7] Altogether, Watson was indicted on twenty-six counts, some of which could have resulted in up to thirty years in prison. The fact that he was a lawyer made it unlikely that he would enjoy much leniency at sentencing. Watson knew at that moment that he was going to have to try to make a deal with the prosecutor.

There are many Americans who believe that the criminal justice system should get rid of plea bargaining. However, this would place even more burdens on an already overloaded court system. More importantly, the belief that plea bargaining allows criminals to receive less punishment than they deserve is unfounded. In fact, the word "bargaining" here is a misnomer. A criminal defendant has as much bargaining power with a prosecutor as a driver has with a rental car agency. In law, this is called an adhesion contract; the stronger party dictates the terms and the weaker party is forced to adhere to them. Prosecutors possess so much more bargaining power than defendants do that defense lawyers regularly counsel their clients to plea bargain even when they know their client is innocent. We examine plea bargaining in more detail in Chapter 5.

Certainly, an aggravating factor was Watson's occupation. Lawyers accused of white-collar crimes fare poorly at trial, as lawyers are not considered worthy of sympathy in general, and even less so when they are accused of a crime. Watson understood his value to the prosecutor as a defendant. A lawyer accused of participating in a long-term mortgage fraud conspiracy epitomized what many Americans felt was the root cause of the mortgage crisis raging through the country at the time, with the mortgage foreclosure rate in the U.S. of one percent in 2005 more than tripling to 3.3 percent in 2008.[8] Watson's status was reflected in the indictment, which had his name listed third among the sixteen defendants, after Robinson and his wife Seelig. Unluckily, Watson held *no* value to the prosecutor as a government witness. Since he hadn't participated in the machinations of the fraud conspiracy, he couldn't offer any significant testimony against the more culpable members of the group.

White-collar criminals often receive harsher treatment by the criminal justice system than you might think. In federal fiscal year 2008, of the 11,128 fraud cases brought to U.S. District Court, over 9,800 cases saw guilty pleas entered. (As we discuss in Chapter 5, over ninety-seven percent of all federal criminal cases end in plea bargains rather than trials.) Of the relatively few that went to trial, jurors convicted 376 defendants and acquitted only forty-six.[9] The FBI tells us that of the 1,220 mortgage fraud cases it handled in the 2011 fiscal year, 1,089 resulted in convictions.[10]

United States v. George H. Watson

Watson and the others with whom he was accused of conspiring were indicted in January 2008. Watson took his lawyer's advice and pleaded guilty in March. Between the time the federal agents had come to Watson's door and Watson pleading guilty, he had already felt punished. Unable to engage in any legal activities related to real estate while awaiting trial, Watson's law practice suffered. Having fallen behind on his bills, Watson walked out one morning to an empty driveway, his car repossessed during the night. He and Holly began to prepare to put their home up for sale, sell most of their possessions, and move Holly and the few things they had left into her parents' home in San Antonio.

Sentencing took place on June 19, 2008, in what is now the former federal courthouse in Austin. When the day of sentencing came, Watson's legs shook as he walked up to the podium where his lawyer was standing in court. The charge to which he had pleaded guilty was read, and then the prosecutor made a few comments. The four people who appeared in court to speak on Watson's behalf were next. They described him as the kind of person Watson thought he was: honest, kind, and not the sort of person who would intentionally engage in criminal behavior.

Then Watson read his statement, known in law as an allocution. He apologized for anything that he had done wrong. He ended by stating that he had not realized he was doing anything wrong when he was working on those closings and, had anyone explained that to him, he would have stopped immediately. The judge squirmed in his chair and seemed fidgety. Clearly, he had already made his decision.

When the judge began to speak, Watson felt like they were the only two people in the world. Watson wondered how he had gotten himself into a position where another human being could have so much control over his life. Looking up from his papers, the judge's eyes met Watson's. "I sentence you to fifty-seven months in prison and five years' probation."

Watson bent over and put his hands on his knees to keep from falling down. The court clerk hurried over, pulled a chair up, and encouraged Watson to sit down. Although Watson's unsteadiness drew the clerk's sympathy, it seemed to have the opposite effect on the judge. He berated Watson: "A sixteen-year-old boy would have known better." "Deciding to practice law was the biggest mistake you ever made in your life." "Prison camp is just a country club anyway."

In addition to the prison term and probation, Watson was ordered to pay restitution of $448,000. A few months after he was sentenced, the Texas State Bar disbarred him. When he finished his prison sentence, Watson would be unable to practice law until he completed the five-year probationary period. Even then, regaining his law license would require him to go before a state judge and make his case for why he should get his license back. One thing Watson knew: he would *never* handle another real estate closing.

As it turned out, the sentencing judge did Watson one favor. His sentencing order recommended that Watson be admitted into the Residential Drug Abuse Program (RDAP), based on alcohol dependency. This 500-hour program is prescribed by federal law (18 U.S.C. § 3621 (e)). Under this law, successful participation in RDAP, which is restricted to prisoners convicted of nonviolent offenses, reduces a federal prisoner's sentence by one year.[11] In addition, a federal prison can grant a sentence reduction of up to fifty-four days for each year of "good time." As a result, Watson was able to anticipate actually serving approximately three years rather than fifty-seven months.

Preparing for Prison

When they returned home from the sentencing hearing, Holly was the first to begin sorting through household possessions, deciding what would be kept, given away, sold, or disposed of. Before long, friends began showing up with food, as if someone had died. Vans and cars were filled, and plans were made for everyone to return a week later with U-Haul trucks. Conveniently, a friend of Watson's stepdaughter was already planning a garage sale for that weekend, and offered to let Watson and Holly bring things over to sell. They had to take every opportunity to sell or give away their belongings. It was mid-June, and Watson might have to report to prison as early as the end of July.

After everyone had left, Watson and Holly stayed busy planning what to do with their household goods—and their household—to distract themselves as much as anything. They wound down around midnight.

Slipping under the covers next to Holly, Watson lay there thinking about the awful yet simple truth that this daily blessing would soon be out of reach. For years. Soon, he would be in a cell with who-knows-what kinds of people. To paraphrase Arlo Guthrie, mother rapers … father stabbers … father rapers.

Having helped lots of people buy homes (although, unfortunately, helping some criminals buy homes, too) Watson had generally thought of moving as a joyous event. Joy wasn't what he felt as he continued to pack up part of his home for a garage sale. Having lost the car (how *did* that repo man tow that car so quietly?), Watson felt his sense of independence and self-sufficiency slipping away.

The garage sale was successful. The front yard of Watson's stepdaughter's home was covered with tables, bookshelves, and blankets, all well stocked with everything from plates, glasses, and Christmas decorations to furniture, small appliances, and bedding. There were also massive amounts of clothing, and more furniture, spilling out of the garage and down the driveway to the street. If it wasn't growing out of the ground, it was for sale. It was heartening to see desperately needed cash coming in, but Watson's resolve waivered at times as he witnessed so much of his and Holly's life dissolve into the shimmering heat waves of the Texas summer. The bargain hunters thinned out in the afternoon.

Watson counted the proceeds from the sale: $720. They could eat, buy more packing supplies, and keep the electricity on.

Watson and Holly put their home up for sale and the timing was miserable. The great recession had started the previous winter and by July 2008, real estate was in serious trouble. Then again, real estate was the source of Watson's predicament to begin with.

Walking up the street from the mailboxes one day in July, Watson thumbed through the envelopes. He found a letter from the Federal Bureau of Prisons. He found Holly in the utility room and held the envelope before him. "The BOP letter came."

"Go on and open it."

He opened it reluctantly. "It's bad enough getting a letter from the IRS that says you owe them money. But getting a letter from the BOP saying that you owe them fifty-seven months of your life is just … too weird."

Watson hoped that he would serve his time at the Federal Prison Camp (FPC) in Bastrop, Texas, less than a two-hour drive from San Antonio. The reality was that the Bureau of Prisons could send him to any FPC in the country. He was told to report to the FPC in Beaumont, Texas, more than 500 miles roundtrip from San Antonio. Watson was disheartened by the reality that it would be very difficult for Holly to take time away from her old and frail parents to come and see him. (In fact, she never was able.)

Watson was to report to prison on September 12, 2008. On Labor Day weekend, he was drawn to frequent news updates on the path of Hurricane Ike, which was predicted to make landfall near Beaumont just about the same time Watson was supposed to report to the FPC there. His situation made him myopic. He wasn't concerned about the devastation that Ike would bring; he was hoping that it would give him a few more days of freedom. Indeed, wisdom acquired from Hurricane Katrina led authorities to demand an evacuation of the area near FPC Beaumont. For Watson, however, there was no reprieve. He was told to report instead to the Bastrop County Jail and await transfer.

George Goes to Jail

Bastrop County lies southeast of Austin and serves in part as an exurb of that booming city. The county suffered horribly during wildfires late in the summer of 2011, with two deaths and the loss of nearly 1,700 homes. More recently, in the spring and summer of 2015, Bastrop County was the center of resistance to the federal government's Jade Helm 15 military training exercise, with some residents fearing that the government was preparing to impose martial law. Signs appeared in the county, stating "No Gestapo in Bastropo." The county seat is the City of Bastrop, where the county jail is located.

The jail, opened in 1990 with several subsequent additions and renovations since, can hold 432 male and female inmates, with an average daily capacity of 290. Most of these inmates are awaiting trial, being either unable to make bail or having been denied bail. Other inmates are serving sentences of a year or less for misdemeanor convictions. The jail is a maximum-security facility because as a typical jail, its inmate population varies from those awaiting trial for relatively minor offenses to others being held for rape and murder. There is also a fluid population of prisoners who, like Watson, await transfer to state or federal facilities. Texas houses approximately 150,000 people in its state prisons, with another 64,000 held in county jails.[12] Based on its population of 26,956,958,[13] Texas's incarceration rate is 793 per 100,000 people. As discussed in Chapter 1, the U.S. has the highest incarceration rate of any nation, currently estimated at 698 prisoners for every 100,000 people;[14] Texas's incarceration rate is 13% higher than the national rate. This doesn't include those in federal prisons or privately operated facilities in the state.

The Bastrop County sheriff has also contracted with the U.S. Marshal's Office and the Federal Bureau of Prisons to hold federal prisoners; thus, Watson's brief stay there. In 2013, Bastrop County generated about $2 million in revenue through these contracts, with an average of approximately 100 beds taken by federal prisoners.[15]

When Watson arrived in Bastrop, he just wanted to be settled somewhere, anywhere. The efforts of the summer to empty his home and move Holly in with her parents, combined with anxiety about being imprisoned, had exhausted him. His exhaustion trumped his fear.

A corrections officer (C.O.) escorted him into the facility. They came to an intersecting hallway. In one corner there were large windows providing Watson his first view of a jail cell, or in this case a "tank." It was a stark room of cement and cinder blocks, metal tables and stools, and a TV. As he feared, some scary looking men populated the room.

Watson and the C.O. turned right, walked toward the end of the hall, and stopped in front of a large metal door with a small, thick window in it. The C.O. said something into his walkie-talkie and the door slid open, revealing a long, stark hallway. On the near end of the hall on the right was another metal door and on the left were cells with the classic metal bars.

"Go find an empty cell."

Watson looked at her and looked back at the hallway, feeling like a child on the first day of school. He was anxious about proceeding by himself but had no choice. He slowly walked down the hall looking into each cell, feeling like the floor might drop out from under him at any second. The first three were occupied, but the fourth was empty and Watson stopped and stared blankly into it. He looked back at the C.O. and she motioned him in. He walked into the cell, heard her talk into her walkie-talkie, and the metal door at the end of the hall thunderously rolled and banged shut.

He looked around. It was a one-man cell! He had feared being crammed into a cell with two or three other dangerous, dreadful people climbing over each other, sharing a toilet, and enduring endless hours of claustrophobic boredom. He had been given a reprieve of sorts.

One side of the cell was a stainless steel wall. The other had a small desk surface with a metal stool attached to it. Next to that was the sleeping area. It was five feet off the ground and reachable only with the aid of metal steps and a handle welded onto the side of the sleeping platform. At the back of the cell was a toilet with a sink built into the space where the water tank on a toilet would normally be.

Tired as he was, he wanted to explore his surroundings, including meeting the other prisoners—the really scary part of this new environment. There were eight single-man cells in his tank, so there were seven strangers he needed to learn to live with under stressful circumstances.

"No use putting it off," he told himself as he walked down the hall and into the dayroom. There were five men watching news about Hurricane Ike. A couple of them nodded hello while the rest stared at the TV. So far, so good, but now what should he do? Did he need permission to sit down? Should he shake hands and introduce himself?

There were two beat-up metal tables with four round metal seats attached to each one. The room was triangle-shaped. At the front were several large windows looking out over a horseshoe shaped desk where a guard sat a few hours a day. He could see three other tanks facing the desk.

At the back of his dayroom were another toilet and sink, and a shower. The shower had a heavy vinyl shower curtain. The curtain and the shower looked really gross. Not knowing what to do, he sat down on a stool and stared at the TV.

"Is this your first time in jail?" one of the young guys asked.

"Yes, I'm sure it's obvious," he said, feeling both awkward and anxious.

"No problem. My name is Hernandez. If you have any questions, let me know." He said this in a pleasant way, as if he was welcoming someone on the first day at a new job.

"How late do they let people watch TV?" Watson asked, wanting to know when the noise level would drop, not really wanting to watch TV.

"One o'clock on Friday and Saturday, and eleven o'clock the rest of the week."

"What happens then?"

"They announce, 'Lights out in fifteen minutes.' You need to be in your cell by lights out. That is when they close and lock the cells, and turn out the lights." Even though he had a cell to himself, the thought of being locked up in it made Watson feel very anxious and claustrophobic.

He sat there for a while, then asked, "Does the jail provide any books or anything to read?"

"There's a book cart they can bring up to the bean hole. There it is." Hernandez pointed out the window to the other side of the horseshoe desk. The cart was about four feet long with three shelves full of books on either side. Watson's eyes locked onto the cart. As an avid reader, those books looked like an island of safety and familiarity in this strange new environment, after being knocked off course by Hurricane Ike.

"What's a bean hole?"

"It's right there." Hernandez pointed at a rectangular slot in the wall below the center window about fourteen inches wide and five inches tall. A locked door closed up the hole. Watson's confused look prompted Hernandez to continue. "When one of the guards comes by, knock on the window to get the guard's attention and ask him to roll the cart over. When he brings it over he will unlock the bean hole door and open it. Then you stick your arm out the bean hole and grab the book you want."

Knocking on the window to get a guard's attention was a scary proposition. However, as he soon learned, prisoners are totally helpless and completely dependent on the guards for *everything*. Food, medicine, mail, books, you name it, the guards have to provide it, and it comes through the bean hole.

Just then, a guard walked into view and Hernandez, sensing Watson's hesitancy, knocked on the window and motioned for the guard to bring the book cart—you couldn't really yell loud enough for the guard to hear unless the bean hole is open. Thanks to Hernandez, the guard rolled the cart over and opened the bean hole.

This really cheered up Watson, knowing that he would have something to read and especially that one of the prisoners was a nice guy who was willing to help him adjust. Watson squatted down to read the titles through the window, then stuck his arm through the bean hole to retrieve the book that he had chosen. It was Russell Baker's autobiography, *Growing Up*, which turned out, thankfully, to be a transporting and inspirational book.

By now, Watson had seen and heard all the hurricane news he could stand and went back to his cell. The sleeping area was really just a cubbyhole, but luckily, there was just enough room to sit cross-legged without hitting his head.

He could still hear the TV but it wasn't too loud. The bed being up so high made it feel a little more spacious and something like a sanctuary.

He decided to brush his teeth before sitting down with the book. The sink being built into the back of the toilet was unpleasant, but he had no choice but to use it. That chore done, he climbed the steps and settled in to read for a while. The book proved to be as distracting as Watson hoped. Soon he heard the "Lights out in fifteen minutes" announcement. When the lights were turned off it was accompanied by a deafening, otherworldly racket as all eight cell doors and the door to the dayroom closed simultaneously.

Standing on the business side of jail cell bars, looking out at nothing but a concrete and cinderblock hallway, he didn't have the energy to panic. He told himself, "They will only be closed while you sleep," and that was enough to keep him calm. He even had the presence of mind to realize how lucky he was to have a cell in the middle of the hall. The nightlights and the worst of the noise were at the end of the halls. Still, no matter how fortunate his cell placement was, he couldn't believe he was actually in jail.

Watson got undressed and used the toilet. Just as he turned to climb up into bed, a female guard came walking down the hallway. He had pulled his underwear up just in time! It turned out a guard came down the hall every evening after lights out to count the prisoners.

Watson thought about the fact that he was older than most of the other prisoners. As he lay in bed, he tried to imagine he was on the train going to his grandparent's house, where he had had to climb up and down out of the upper berth of a bunk bed. It brought him peace and helped him feel that his grandparents were watching over him.

He was in the middle of a surprisingly happy dream when the lights blinked on at 5:30 a.m. He had trouble orienting himself until the PA system blared out, "Thirty minutes to chow." Just as noisily as they had closed the night before, the cell doors and the door to the dayroom opened in unison. The wheels grinding back and forth in their metal ruts were a perfect metaphor for Watson's life as a prisoner in a county jail.

Though still locked in the tank, having the cell opened and being able to move around in the tank reduced Watson's anxiety. Now what? He dressed and went into the dayroom ready for anything. There were already several people in there, many resting their arms and heads on the tables. Everyone looked bored, so Watson found a place to sit at one of the tables and … did nothing. The TVs were not allowed on before eight o'clock.

A short time later, a couple of the other inmates introduced themselves. Watson began to understand that he wasn't going to be bullied, beaten, or buggered. Then the dancing doors routine was set in motion again as all nine doors roared to life, ending in a clanging chorus of metal on metal. The incessant noise would prove to be one of the most difficult aspects of jail to endure.

Soon the breakfast carts rolled into view with trays of food stacked on one cart and milk containers on the other. The guards unlocked the bean hole door and lowered it. It was barely wide and tall enough for the trays to be passed through. Next, very small glasses of what turned out to be powdered milk were passed through. Then the bean hole door was shut and locked. Watson doesn't remember what breakfast was, but does remember eating everything and still being hungry. Hunger was a constant unpleasant fact in jail.

Before long, the carts rolled into view again and the process was reversed. Then … more nothing. They were locked in the dayroom and sitting on the metal stools was beginning to get very uncomfortable. In addition, it was very cold and dressed in just one layer of clothes and with no socks, Watson was very uncomfortable. Not to mention bored. He asked, "When do they open the doors again?"

"Between 7:30 and 8:00," one of the other inmates said, shaking his head.

"So we just sit here for another hour or more?" Watson asked.

"Yeah."

"Any idea why?"

"No."

By this time, two of the other inmates were playing spades and everyone else was sitting around bored or trying to sleep in one way or another. This would be Watson's daily routine for several weeks. Equally bored and depressed, he tried to doze with his head resting on his arms.

Finally, the doors opened abruptly and released them from the dayroom. Watson headed back to his cell. Everyone else did the same, and it appeared to be standard procedure. Since the lights stay on all day, Watson draped a pants leg over his eyes and drifted off to sleep. Then, about eight thirty, all the doors rattled shut. Not knowing the routine, he was afraid they were going to keep him locked up for the rest of the day. Having been in jail less than twenty-four hours, he had no idea what to expect.

"Mop bucket!" a guard yelled out as he rolled a mop bucket and mop into the tank hallway. The dancing doors routine again ensued. One of the inmates took the mop and began to mop the hallway and dayroom. About thirty minutes later the doors closed again, the mop bucket was removed, and then the doors opened again. The whole day would be like this—a heavy metal door slam-a-thon.

A short while later the bean hole was opened and a guard yelled into it, "Razor blades!" If they wanted to shave, the inmates had to go to the bean hole, get a razor blade from the guard, shave, and return it to the guard.

Having shaved and lain back down, Watson thought, "Finally I can rest a little."

"Medical!" A nurse with a rolling cart filled with prescriptions for the prisoners was alerting everyone in the tank that their medicine was there if they wanted it and if they could hear her yelling. Watson soon discovered that some of the medical personnel did not even bother to bend down and yell through the bean hole so they could be heard.

"If you have any medication you need to take you'd better get up there right away," an inmate standing in Watson's cell doorway told him. Watson climbed down from his sleeping area and hurried to the dayroom. Not surprisingly, he had been diagnosed with depression during his legal travails, and his antidepressant medication was really helping him, so he didn't want to miss it.

Back in bed, he thought about his family and recited some affirmations. He also imagined some of his dogs curled up around him and he finally drifted off to sleep. A couple of hours later, "Thirty minutes to chow!" was called out and he went back to the dayroom. By now, some of the other inmates were watching TV again. Watson sat in the same place he had at breakfast. Everyone had their place. Since he was the newest person in the tank, he had the worst chair, directly under the TV and facing away from it. At noon, the doors were shut and they were locked in the dayroom again. After eating and returning the trays, they were stuck in the dayroom for another hour and a half.

Watson talked to some of the others about how he had ended up in jail, learned how they had ended up there, and so on. Before long, his nickname was "Old School" or just "School." He began to relax a little around the others, realizing that since he was twice their age they were not going to harm him.

Watson can't remember what they watched, even though it was the same thing every day. He does remember that they were shows he had never watched before nor will ever watch again. Around a quarter after one, the unseen hand opened all the doors. Feeling like he could breathe again, he went back to his cell and meditated, then read.

At two o'clock, he called Holly. He had to call collect, as no money would be posted into his account for several days. The call was ridiculously expensive, but he had to hear her voice and let her know that he was safe. The phone was in the dayroom. Watson asked one of the others how to place a collect call. The inmate explained the process and Watson made the call.

After talking to Holly, it was time for Watson's first shower in the tank. This was intimidating. The shower was in the dayroom. There was no privacy. In fact, anyone in the hall also had a full view of the shower. Unsure what to do, Watson undressed in his cell and wrapped himself up in a towel. He walked into the dayroom and headed for the shower.

Someone yelled out, "Wait!" which startled him. His nerves were still really shot.

"What?"

"You can't go in the shower without shower shoes on."

"Oh … OK … thanks." He went back to his cell and put his flip-flops on, the only footwear he had. Then he headed back into the dayroom, a little bit embarrassed, but determined to take a shower. Millions of others had done it, and he could do it, too.

As he approached the shower, it was the moment-of-truth. *This is weird … with the shower being in plain view of everyone in the dayroom and out in the hall. They'll … here goes….* He pulled his towel off, pushed the shower curtain aside, stepped into the shower, and pulled the shower curtain closed.

"Aagh! I've been mooned!" one of the young guys yelled out in mock horror, as the two guys in the dayroom laughed loudly.

The other one chimed in, "School, you wear your clothes into the shower and undress in there."

"Oh, sorry about that. It's kind of a tight squeeze."

"Yeah, but you have to do it!" Now they were all laughing. Watson was glad to provide a laugh and even gladder that only two guys were there to witness his maiden voyage into the shower.

The next day went the same as the first until after dinner when one of the guards came around asking if anyone wanted a haircut. Watson had been meaning to get a haircut for several weeks, but never had the time. He and another inmate asked to get a haircut and they were released from the tank to follow the officer.

It felt so good to get out of the tank that he didn't care where they went. He pictured a small replica of a barbershop with maybe two barber chairs in it. They retraced the steps he had taken when he was first led to the tank. The officer then proceeded to the women's holding tank, right across the hall from the men's holding tank that had terrified Watson so badly when he first entered the jail.

An inmate stood next to a folding chair with an electric clipper in his hand. He was not a licensed barber, but hoped to become one when he was released. His only experience was hanging out at his uncle's barbershop and the practice he had obtained giving jailhouse haircuts. It was obvious asking for Watson's hair to be cut the way it usually was would be useless, so he asked to have about an inch cut off. The aspiring barber apparently wasn't too good with measurements. Watson's hair had not been that short since he was ten years old.

Walking back to the tank, Watson told the guard that he had really been scalped. The guard seemed to appraise the haircut carefully, then said it was actually pretty good for a jailhouse haircut. They laughed, and this small interaction about a normal activity like getting a haircut gave Watson a small sense of normalcy and peace. Good haircut or not, it was worth it just to get out of the tank.

The next two days were the same, minus the embarrassing shower blooper or haircut episode. Watson was finally able to buy a phone card. He had been stressed about calling home collect, because of the exorbitant cost, but had no choice as he desperately needed to hear his wife's voice and the voices of his loved ones. A $20 phone card goes fast at thirty cents a minute. Watson knew that counties needed the money, but anything that cuts off prisoners from their families is counterproductive. Nevertheless, he was willing to sacrifice anything to stay in touch with his family. (We discuss prison telephone contracts and pricing in Chapter 6.)

During the next week, he hung out in the dayroom and played chess and cards with some of the guys and began to feel like one of the crew. They were all there on drug charges and didn't seem to understand Watson's explanation of why he was there. They were even more baffled when he told them that he hadn't made any more money from the closings that were illegal relative to the ones that were not. Even jailbirds understand the risk/reward calculus—in their book, if the illegal ones were riskier, Watson should have charged more for them than the legal ones. (We discuss redirecting ex-offenders' entrepreneurial skills toward legal activities in Chapter 7.)

Two days later the cry was raised, "Recreation!" Watson was in his cell reading, but some of the inmates close to the hall door heard the guard asking if anyone wanted to go to the rec yard; they knew he wanted to go so they passed the information down the hall.

Once the dancing doors had completed their thunderous routine, the hall door was opened. Watson joined the dozen other prisoners going to the rec yard. He had started feeling more at ease around the other guys in his tank but now was being thrown in with an even larger group of prisoners. Some looked nice enough while others made him uneasy; he was certain that he stuck out like a jailhouse novice, a tenderfoot among hardened criminals.

They all had to assume the frisking position, with legs spread and hands on the wall over their heads. Next, they were told to line up single file and move out. The criminal conga line stopped at a nondescript door. As the guard opened the door, the sunshine and fresh air caused the line to unravel as inmates spread out to different areas of the rec yard. In reality, the rec yard was not a "yard" at all—there was no grass. It was all concrete and cinderblocks, about sixty feet by sixty feet.

The only sign of nature was formed by the ceiling being pitched in such a way that there was a ten-foot gap between the ceiling and the top of one wall.

This opening was filled with razor wire, but Watson was so happy to see the sky that even having to view it through that shimmering barricade couldn't dampen his enthusiasm. This opening let in fresh air and, at the right time of day, sunshine. Luckily, they were there at the right time of day and the sun was shining in toward the back of the rec area.

There were large patches of sun on the concrete floor and, obeying a signal from deep in his soul, the first thing Watson did was sit in one of those patches and feel those glorious sunbeams on his body. After ten days without sunshine or fresh air, this was a powerful tonic.

He began to walk in circles. Keeping up a good pace in flip-flops was difficult; but anything was better than nothing. Around and around, over and over, even though his world had shrunk, he pushed against those constrictions in every possible way, even if it was just walking in circles. The other inmates stood or sat singly or in small groups talking or doing exercise routines. After about an hour and a half, the guard returned and marched the prisoners back to their cells.

One of the younger prisoners had been transferred and his cell was empty. The next day another young man came in, set his box on the floor in the empty cell, and shouted out, "Who wants to get high?" This scared the hell out of Watson. He was sure they would all get in trouble, even those who didn't want to get high. The kid looked Watson's way and Watson said, "No, thank you." Those who wanted to smoke some pot went into the back cell.

Before long, the whole tank smelled like pot, and Watson briefly wondered if he should tell one of the guards about it so he wouldn't get in trouble, but quickly decided that was a bad idea. The prisoners had thus far left "Old School" alone, and the possibility of being labeled a snitch was a scary one. The smell dissipated quickly and there was only enough pot for two more pot parties so that by the end of the next day, the crisis was over and Watson was greatly relieved.

"I should be 'catching the chains' any day now. It'll be your turn soon." This was about three weeks into Watson's stay at the jail. He was sitting on his bed and the other inmate was sitting on the toilet, a common practice when an inmate had "company." The "chains" sounded menacing. Watson still didn't know where the BOP was going to send him but wherever it was, he hoped it wasn't in chains.

"What kind of chains?"

"The same ones they brought you here in. Ankle chains and handcuffs attached to a chain around your waist. What's really bad is if they fly you somewhere on Con Air."

"What's Con Air?" His federal prison placement still uncertain—Hurricane Ike might have made placement in Beaumont impossible for all he knew.

"Convict Airlines. It's what they call the planes the BOP flies convicts around in. The marshals actually chain you to the floor of the plane."

"And the BOP doesn't tell you when you're going or where you're going?"

"No. One of the guards here will come get you at four in the morning and keep you in the holding tank until the marshals come to get you." (As Watson later found out, the marshals' secrecy is intended to prevent efforts to escape.)

By this time, Watson had adapted fairly well in the county jail and the thought of being flown in chains to who-knows-where was terrifying. He began wondering if just staying in the county jail would be preferable. At the same time, he thought that a federal prison camp had to be better than a county jail. But for the month that Watson spent in jail, he saw no effort to rehabilitate the men around him. This was warehousing at its worst.

Watson Goes to Camp

A few nights later, he heard, "Mr. Watson? Where is Watson?"

"I'm here," he replied, tired after only a few hours of sleep.

"You're leaving today. Be at the door to the hall in ten minutes."

"Okay." He had arranged with another inmate to leave leftover shampoo, stamps, and a phone card in return for calling Watson's wife to tell her what was going on and why Watson wasn't calling her that afternoon. Then he went down and waited by the hallway door.

The guard reappeared and the door opened. They walked into the laundry room. "Set the box over there. Here are your street clothes." Watson was happy to put on the clothes that he had worn in his everyday life. As he dressed, the guard said, "You don't really seem like you belong here. How did you get here?" Watson gave a short explanation, then the guard asked, "Do you have a college degree?"

"Yes." He left it at that.

"So you were the brains of the operation."

"No. Not really. Cornelius Robinson was."

"If you have a college degree, you're the brains. I wish I had gone to college when I had the chance. It's too late now."

"It's never too late," Watson said as he slipped his shoes on, wondering why the shoestrings had been removed. (He learned later that this was an effort to prevent a possible suicide.) "There are all kinds of online programs and night schools. The sooner you start the sooner you'll finish."

"No, it's too late. Follow me."

"Where are we going?"

"To the female holding tank." This was the erstwhile barbershop. By now, the thought of being in there was not nearly as appalling or repulsive as it had been twenty-eight days earlier. But there was also no seating in the tank.

"How long will I be in there?"

"They don't tell us that. We just have to have you dressed and ready by five-thirty."

"Can I have a blanket to sit on?"

"Sure." The guard handed Watson a blanket from a stack by the tank, then unlocked the door, and motioned him in. There were two other prisoners in there, both appearing to have led hard lives. They nodded hello as the guard locked the door. Watson dozed for a little while, then breakfast was delivered. Sitting on the floor in a raunchy, fluorescent-lit holding tank would have ruined his appetite a month earlier. Now he ate everything.

The marshals showed up around six-thirty and chained them up in the usual way, then led them out to a van. After a short while, it was obvious that they were headed back into Austin and not to the Bastrop Prison Camp. Being back in Austin was bittersweet. So close to and yet farther away from a normal life than he had ever been before.

They ended up in the holding cells that were Watson's first experience with being held captive after he had surrendered himself. Over the next hour, the marshals kept pushing more people into the cells until the holding tank was crowded. When the cell was full, they were provided sack lunches.

After several hours, they were loaded onto a bus, and a guard announced they were being taken to the airport. The bus drove directly onto the tarmac about 150 yards from the terminal. Watson looked at the terminal, the scene of many happy comings and goings in his life. Now, he felt the eyes of passengers in the terminal staring down on him and the other convicts. Not far from the bus was a passenger jet, painted solid white. There were two other buses and three U.S. marshals with sunglasses and large guns.

There were about twenty prisoners. They were told to take their shoes and socks off, which were examined and returned. The marshals started calling out names.

Watson answered to his name and a very stern looking marshal looked at him and said, "Mr. Watson?"

"Yes."

"You're going to the Beaumont USP."

"What's the USP?"

"A penitentiary."

"I'm supposed to go into a camp."

"It says USP." Then he called out another name and moved away.

A convict next to him, trying to be helpful, said, "Don't worry, they'll probably just keep you there for a little while for observation."

This failed to calm Watson. Having prepared himself for the relative freedom and safety of a prison camp, he now envisioned a maximum-security facility full of bullies and rapists. A brief distraction was climbing up the stairs to the plane while wearing shackles. He entered the plane and passed a few female prisoners in front, and walked toward about forty male prisoners in the back of the plane. There were men of all ages, many of them hardened and grizzled looking, along with five marshals. The one bright spot is that nobody was chained to the floor of the plane, despite what he'd been told earlier.

They landed at a military base in Houston. Marshals with guns circled the plane. Then names were called out and people started lining up at the front. Watson now had to walk down the stairs in shackles. He and about twenty others boarded a bus and they left the air base.

The bus soon pulled into a Jack-in-the-Box and stopped. One of the guards on the bus went inside and brought back food for the driver and himself. It had been several hours already since Watson had eaten a sack lunch. He could smell the guards' food. Sitting there, shackled and caged in, envious of those able to stop and buy junk food whenever they wanted, drove home the fact that Watson was now a second-class citizen.

They arrived at the Beaumont Federal Correctional Complex in darkness. Because of the "tough on crime" movement of the late twentieth century, there are now more jails and prisons in the U.S. than there are colleges.[16] In addition to about 1,600 state prisons and 3,200 local and county jails, there are 121 federal correctional institutions spread throughout the U.S. housing about 210,000 federal prisoners.[17]

At the Beaumont Federal Correctional Complex, opened in 1998, a circular road surrounds the administration building; around the ring are four penal facilities. Designed to house 5,120 prisoners, in March 2015, all four facilities held more than they were designed for, totaling 5,407 prisoners. Prisoners in the complex range from eighteen to eighty-one years old.[18] USP (United States Penitentiary) Beaumont is a high-security penitentiary surrounded by several fences ringed with watchtowers. Built to house 960 inmates, it had a population of 1,437 in March 2015.[19] FCI (Federal Correctional Institution) Beaumont is comprised of medium- and low-security facilities, each with fences but without watchtowers. FPC Beaumont, the facility where Watson stayed, is a minimum-security facility that doesn't even have a fence around it. The Bureau of Prisons attempts to locate minimum-security facilities next to higher security facilities so that inmates at the minimum-security facility can perform tasks such as janitorial and maintenance work in the higher security facilities where inmate movement is carefully limited.

The bus pulled up first in front of the low-security prison and a few names were called out. Watson was stressed, sure he was headed to the maximum-security prison. Then the guard driving asked the other guard if there were any "campers" on the bus. He checked his records and said there were two, calling the name of Watson and another. Watson was so relieved he started shaking.

On his first day in the camp, Watson met a camp employee whom he would grow to admire, respect, and appreciate greatly. This was Mr. Thomas. Watson asked Thomas if it would be possible for him to call his wife, as he knew she would be very worried, not knowing where he was or what was happening to him. Thomas said yes, he needed to come see him in his office at four o'clock.

Mr. Thomas sat down at a computer and shortly thereafter assigned the new campers to their respective cubes. Watson was getting ready to learn the place he would call home for the next several years. He gathered up his belongings along with a mattress and headed towards a door. He had been told he would be living in a "dorm," but had no idea what that would be like. It evoked images of college dorm rooms with two, three, or four people living in them. Who would his roommates be?

When he opened the door, people were everywhere. Large numbers were sitting at tables outside the dorms and others are walking around. There were buildings situated around a large grassy area and the dorm he was going to was across the way. Cinder blocks, metal roofs, concrete. Some grass and a few trees in the distance would be the most he would see of nature.

When he walked inside, he realized that the dorm was really just a big warehouse, a huge open area with dozens of cubicles made out of six-foot high cinderblock walls. An ant's nest of people. He had been told to report to Unit A number 43. Someone noticed him looking lost and pointed him in the right direction. He arrived at Cube 43 and found a bunk bed, single bed, two ugly metal lockers, and a very obese man snoring ferociously. Before the shock could wear off, another inmate walked up and said, "Follow me." Unsure whether this was allowed, he hesitated.

"You'll never get any sleep here. Luckily there is a vacancy in 51." The inmate led Watson to Cube 51 and pointed to the lower bed of the bunk bed. The other inmate introduced himself and made some notes on a legal pad. Then he left.

Very much alone in a crowd, Watson had to stay busy to keep from falling apart. Human survival instinct kicked in and he made his bed. As he would soon learn, in prison, with everything from your normal everyday life stripped away from you, anything you can call your own is immensely important, including your little bit of real estate—your bed and your locker. Of course, the prison workers could also take this at any time, but if it's all you have, it's huge.

About this time, his cellmate—his "cellie"—walked into the cube and introduced himself. A heavyset and jovial fellow, he gave Watson the basic rundown on camp life. Next, he took Watson around the dorm, introduced him to some other inmates, and scrounged up a pair of tennis shoes and ear buds for an old radio of his that he loaned to Watson. The shoes hardly had any soles, but they would allow Watson to take walks or go jogging and not have to wear the steel-tipped boots that were standard issue.

Another inmate took Watson to a storage room and told him that he and some other inmates tithed by keeping certain items stocked in the locker for new arrivals. He gave Watson a pair of shower shoes and a soap dish. The shower shoes were priceless since Watson would not be able to shop at the commissary until late the following week and no one in their right mind would step into one of the showers without shower shoes on.

Watson still did not have any shorts and so it was time to learn the fine art of dumpster diving. There was a large, blue, plastic "dumpster" in each dorm about four feet deep, eight feet wide, and six feet tall. The dumpster is where people who are leaving put the camp issued clothes they cannot take with them, or other clothes they do not want to take. His cellie rummaged around and fished out a pair of shorts that look like they would fit as well as a sweatshirt. Since Watson did not have any laundry detergent, his new cellie graciously offered to wash them for him.

Without the generosity of these people, Watson does not know what he would have done. It was far more than the shoes and other things they gave him; it was the humanity, the sense of community, the support net. Even so, the wounds inflicted by the criminal justice system were still raw and he had a lot of adjusting to do. His next stop was the psychologist's office, where he broke down crying. She was supportive and kind, and allowed him to sit in her office for a while.

Soon he experienced his first "yard recall," when inmates had to return to their respective dorms. He knocked on the office door of Mr. Thomas, who allowed Watson to call his wife. He was so happy and relieved to hear her voice that he couldn't help himself and started tearing up.

Waiting to go to dinner, he sat on his bed talking to his cellmate about how they ended up in prison. About ten minutes before they started calling people to dinner by dorm, they went and waited in the area in front of the door. He was still adjusting to not being free. They could not leave the building and go eat without being given permission.

"Unit A, come to chow." They were being called first for dinner and the thirty or so people waiting in the hallway began walking as fast as they could to the chow hall. He followed his cellie, trying to keep up. They arrived at and entered the door to the chow hall. He saw more concrete and cinderblocks, and ugly little tables with ugly plastic chairs attached to them. Standing in line, he looked around mentally repeating his now-familiar mantra—"I can't believe this is all I am going to see for the next thirty-two months."

The line moved past a bulletin board with a notice about keeping your shirt-tail tucked in. Watson finally reached the serving line; the only choices he had were to say he did not want something and to ask for the "heart-healthy alternative." He took his tray and proceeded to the area where glasses, iced tea, and water were available. He got some tea and sat down at a table with his cellie.

Two other people soon sat with them and he was introduced. The inevitable question about what he did to end up in prison came up. They explained briefly why they were there and then the conversation turned to things he was ignorant of, but would soon become all too knowledgeable about—the lunacy of the federal prison system in general and the stupefying behavior of many of the prison workers.

After dinner, he went for a walk around the dirt track and then headed for the library. He had always loved perusing library shelves and this small bit of freedom, moving around the library and picking out books, gave him some comfort. He stayed in the library until yard recall at eight-thirty.

He had been in the dorm only a few minutes when he heard the cry, "Mail call!" Watson knew he would not receive any mail that first mail call, since no one knew where he was going until he was already there. Still, he could not tear himself away from watching until all of the mail was delivered.

He turned his attention to showering. Unsure how to proceed and not wanting to recreate his previous embarrassing shower moment at the Bastrop jail, he walked carefully into the bathroom. There was a line of people waiting to shower, in no small part because out of twelve showers, only six worked. He also noticed another thing about his fellow inmates in their state of relative undress that further frightened him. In addition to being muscular, they had a lot of tattoos. He had never seen so many tattoos and found many of them disturbing to look at, either because of the content or quantity, or both.

The next morning, after a depressing breakfast in the chow hall, he took a walk. He found that not seeing any fences around the camp did make the experience more bearable. Being able to walk around the camp, small as it was, did make life much more pleasant.

Watson quickly learned that postage stamps served as currency among prisoners. This is against the rules, but unenforced. Stamps were exchanged for a variety of services, such as haircuts. In addition, some prisoners ran "stores" out of their lockers, selling soft drinks and candy bars to people who want something before their weekly visit to the commissary. Stamps were also used for illegal purposes such as gambling or buying things that had been stolen from food service.

Watson Goes to Work

The Bureau of Prisons operates an inmate work program within its institutions. To the extent practicable, the work program:

(1) Reduces inmate idleness, while allowing the inmate to improve and/or develop useful job skills, work habits, and experiences that will assist in post-release employment; and

(2) Ensures that activities necessary to maintain the day-to-day operation of the institution are completed.

U.S. Bureau of Prisons Program Statement, October 1, 2008[20]

Shortly after breakfast on Tuesday, his fourth day at the camp, he heard, "George Watson, please come to the message center." He walked into the administration building with all kinds of unpleasant thoughts running through his mind. He was glad that he was going to work, as it would keep him busy and help pass the time. But were there rocks to be broken in the hot sun?

"Are you Watson?" Another inmate in his mid-fifties reached out to shake hands. "I'm Forrester and you are going to be working with me at the USP."

"It's nice to meet you. What's the USP?"

"The United States Penitentiary." The USP was the maximum-security prison at the prison complex where the worst, most violent prisoners were kept. This sounded dangerous.

"What do we do there?"

"It's easy; we clean the main lobby at the entrance and the warden's offices."

"It's not dangerous, is it?"

"No. We are never close to the prisoners."

About halfway to the USP the road crossed a large culvert that was full of water. Forrester pulled some slices of bread out of his pocket, tore them into small pieces, and threw them into the water. Several turtles appeared from the depths and ate the bread. Nice, thought Watson. Working at the USP would have some benefits, and besides, anything that seemed like a normal activity that made you feel like a normal person made life a little more bearable

"What are we going to do exactly?"

"We sweep, mop, and dust. We can usually finish in an hour to an hour and a half."

"Then what?"

"We're done for the day. You have the rest of the day free."

"Wow, this is a great job."

"I've worked several different jobs and this is the best because it gives you so much free time. I spend mine working on my appeal. The government screwed me and now they are trying to settle out of court."

They entered the lobby where there was a horseshoe shaped desk and a metal detector. They passed through the detector and Watson was introduced to the staff. There's not much dignity in saying "Howdy" to someone new when you're wearing a prison uniform.

They went to the utility closet and he grabbed a broom and began sweeping. Having finished the entry hall, he went to look for Forrester in the warden's office. He passed through a door into a suite of offices that looked pretty much like any business office. The familiar surroundings helped to take the edge off. But there was no mistaking his station in life. He was wearing janitorial green, although he didn't even have the status of a janitor. He was a criminal performing janitorial duties.

Forrester clearly had the administration's trust and some respect for his ability to do his work, but even he was quick to play the subservient role when spoken to. Watson introduced himself to the warden's secretary, a woman he rarely saw working in the two months he worked as a USP orderly. In fact, he never once saw the warden in his office. He seemed to spend a lot of time traveling around the country looking at other facilities and attending meetings at taxpayer expense.

Back out in the sunshine they headed back to the camp. "How much will I make a month at this job?"

"Eighteen dollars, that's the rate for a Level 4, the lowest level where you are now. The pay scale goes up to $60 for a Level 1."

"That's all? I know we only work about an hour a day, but that is twenty hours a month so we are making less than a dollar an hour." He thought about how his wife had no money and that her parents, living on a fixed income, could not help either. To use his 300 minutes of permitted phone time a month would cost $65. He dreaded only being able to talk to his wife two hours a month. Not to mention this would leave him no money for the commissary.

Watson's experiences at the commissary were rarely pleasant. Everything available was listed on a sheet. He marked which items he wanted and turned in the sheet. Then they started calling names. He frequently had to wait thirty minutes or more. When called, he went into a small room and handed them his ID through a hole like a movie theater ticket window. Beneath that was a chute where the goods slid down. He put them in his laundry bag, signed his ticket, and left.

Figure 2.1. Selections from Federal Corrections Complex
Beaumont Comissary List[21]

clear calculator $4.20	Native American bandanas $4.90
clear alarm clock $7.80	ramen picante chicken soup .30
white shower shoe $4.45	tootie fruities cereal $3.90
mustache scissors $6.70	honey pepper turkey logs $1.90
acne cream $1.60	pork skins $1.65
styling gel $3.00	shoe polish (black or brown) $2.75
toothbrush (medium or soft) .90	playing cards $2.70
soap dish .65	mighty bright book light $12.95
ear plugs .50	missing you card $1.00
sandalwood prayer oil $4.00	English/Spanish dictionary $2.25

Most of the officers who worked at the commissary were decent people. But there were a few, one woman in particular, who were clearly unhappy and loved to yell at the prisoners for nothing. Clearly, these people, surrounded by the misery of others, needed therapy, and probably never should have been hired in the first place.

Watson quickly developed the habit of taking a book to read with him at lunch and dinner. He easily spent an hour a day in line at the chow hall. Those 365 hours a year would allow him to get a massive amount of reading done. One of his main goals was to make sure he accomplished as much as possible while in prison. If he had to be away from his family, at least it would not be wasted time.

After he had been at the camp for about a month, he was standing at the end of the line at dinner when one of the C.O.s who ran food service said, "Where are you working now?"

"I'm a USP orderly."

"How much do you make?"

"Eighteen dollars."

"If you want to work in food service I can make you a grade 2 and pay you $43."

"That sounds great." He had thought there was some unseen hand that controlled all of the work assignments, but apparently, there was some flexibility.

"Come see me in my office when you are through eating."

After dinner, he walked into the kitchen. Never having been in a commercial kitchen before, he treaded gingerly between a large griddle and commercial-size oven. Besides, there were signs all over the entrance into the kitchen area saying "Off Limits," "Do Not Enter Unless Authorized," etc., that were still very intimidating to him. He reached the C.O.'s office and knocked.

He introduced himself and they chatted for a while. Lindsey turned out to be a great guy. He was easygoing and respectful of the people working for him. He was clearly a happy person and not out to make other people miserable, unlike some of the other C.O.s. Watson's job would be in "veggie prep." Yep, chopping onions, potatoes, and so on. Lindsey said it would only take about an hour a day. Watson knew he would miss the walk to the USP, but he really wanted that extra money.

Watson felt he now had replicated the appearance of the typical media depiction of a prisoner as he stood there, chopping vegetables. While the pay was better, it was a terrible job for him. Not because he disliked chopping vegetables; the problem was that the veggie prep room was at the back of the kitchen. This was far from the only window in the kitchen and natural light was important for his mental health. Even that wasn't as bad as the fact that he was locked in the room, and often had to wait for up to half an hour to get in or out.

So far, Watson was doing pretty well, though some days were still rough. He and Holly kept telling each other on the phone that something good was going to come out of all of this. Talking to Holly every other day saved Watson from total depression. Unfortunately, as in the county jail, the FPC's phone calls were expensive.

One thing that Watson noticed was the constant stream of new faces pouring into the camp. This was good news—they really were letting people out so they would have to make room for the newcomers. Another thing he noticed is that several of the new guys were middle-aged. White-collar offenses certainly were the crime *du jour* as far as prosecutors were concerned.

On the weekends, two different movies were shown. Unfortunately, they were rarely anything Watson was interested in watching. At times, he wandered into one of the TV rooms and asked if they could see what was on PBS. He discovered that most of the inmates he asked did not even know what PBS was, and the few who did were not at all interested in watching it.

Watson spent the next two months as a veggie prep worker, including his first holiday season in prison. Thanksgiving, Christmas, New Years. "The most wonderful time of the year," as the song says. The days started to go by more slowly, especially between Thanksgiving and New Year's Day.

In the first part of December, he had his first visit. A friend he had known since he was ten years old came to visit and this lifted his spirits tremendously. It had been hard hearing other inmate's names called every weekend to go to visitation and not having a visit himself. Because of his family's financial situation he knew they would not be able to visit soon, if ever.

A few weeks before Christmas, tobacco was found in their dorm and the camp administrator went nuts. The prisoners were told to stand in their cubes while he yelled and screamed at the top of his lungs as he walked around the dorm. Watson was scared to death. He had never been yelled at in this way in his life and this man had complete control over him. Watson's legs were shaking and he looked around at the other inmates to see how they were handling it. Most were very alert, though not especially alarmed. The administrator finally calmed down and finished by saying the microwaves in their dorm were to be removed as well as the televisions, a favorite tactic of his.

This was Watson's first real exposure to some of the things that are seriously wrong with the federal prison system. Treating inmates like children. Yelling and screaming. Punishing all the inmates in the dorm (about 130 at that time) for the transgressions of two or three. The lack of leadership ability on the part of the camp administrator was often on display. The idea that punishing people and making their lives as miserable as possible is the best way to alter their behavior doesn't work. For one thing, it did nothing to stop the flow of tobacco into the camp.

When one of the inmates pointed out that it really was not fair punishing everyone when most of them had no idea anyone was breaking the rules, the camp administrator yelled, "I'm not stupid and if you don't like it you can go to the hole!" This type of response seemed to be the result of the camp administrator's insecurity and low self-esteem. Instead of inspiring inmates to do better and be better people, he was driving a wedge between himself and the inmates. This only served to further alienate inmates from authority and create an "us versus them" mentality that carries over into the outside world. This is exactly the opposite of what should happen. The corrections system should strive to make people feel like they are a part of society and its rules and regulations, not separate. This is why all BOP employees need to be screened psychologically and need to be trained in leadership skills and therapeutic skills.

Christmas came. It was foggy and drizzling outside. The inmates were told to stay in their cells after yard recall and a cart came around with a bag full of candy and food. Watson was thankful to see something different from what was served in the chow hall and what he could buy at the commissary. Watson had enough money to call Holly every day between Christmas and New Year's Day and that was the best present he ever had.

In January he received what he thought was excellent news. There was an article in *Parade Magazine* about prison overcrowding and how so many more people are put into prison in the U.S. than other countries. Finally! Word would get out to the American public and something would be done about our broken criminal justice system. Maybe Congress would get busy and do something in time to shorten his prison sentence. Boy, was he wrong. Even with a center page spread and an article written by U.S. Senator James Webb, the American public seemed to have completely ignored it.

He lobbied hard for a library job. He really wanted to get out of the veggie prep room, but more than that, he wanted to be where he felt comfortable and where his knowledge of books, love of books, and love of learning could be best put to use. Another big bonus to working in the library was having access to a typewriter with some electronic memory. He had many things he wanted to write, but he was a terrible typist and he knew what he wanted to write would require many revisions.

Keeping Busy

At the beginning of 2009, Watson learned he could become a librarian when another inmate left, which would be toward the end of January. The day arrived and he sat down at his desk in what was one of the most comfortable chairs inmates had access to at the camp. With a typewriter and a locker to keep things in, he was doing as well as he was going to do in prison. And he loved reading and talking about books!

He began typing some of the essays he had written on prison reform. With the articles he had seen in papers and magazines he was sure the time was ripe for prison reform and that someone, somewhere with the power to change things would pay attention to them. Watson was unhappy about being imprisoned, but he also believed that he could help effect some changes in the prison system.

ACE (Adult Continuing Education) classes started and he took three of them. These included electricity (what you need to know to pass the apprentice electrician's test), investing (stocks, bonds, etc., led by Richard Scrushy, the founder of HealthSouth), and commodities investing (something Watson had been interested in for twenty years, but never had the time to really study). These classes were conducted once a week for two hours. They were taught by inmates, and they were quite informative.

He also took some classes in the recreation department, a yoga class, and beginning guitar. Though he had been doing yoga off and on for thirty years, he was always open to learning something new and he knew it would force him to do his yoga at least twice a week. He had also played guitar a little as a teenager and always wanted to start again, so he enjoyed the lessons.

He was now busy six nights a week with classes. In the afternoons, he practiced the guitar. Time started going by very quickly. In March, Watson had a conversation with his yoga instructor about another course the yoga instructor was teaching, "Embracing Reality," sponsored by Counselor Thomas. This course discussed life skills and knowledge that inmates could use to help them succeed once they were out of prison.

Watson and the yoga instructor were talking about why some of the officers acted like bullies, and Watson explained it was due to low self-esteem and insecurity caused by childhood trauma(s). Watson was asked to teach the basics of this information to the students in one of their classes. This is when Watson started writing in earnest. He put together a detailed outline about the origin of self-esteem in childhood, how to recognize it in other adults, and how best to deal with it. He also wrote about how to look for it in yourself.

He was asked by several people to teach the personal development ACE class using the information he had put together for the Embracing Reality class. He taught this class three times over the next eight months. People responded well to it and seemed to get a lot from it.

Watson was extremely busy during this time teaching, writing, playing guitar, reading, exercising, and working in the library. This would be true the entire rest of the time he was in prison—there were never enough hours in the day to do everything he wanted to do. But that was a good thing; it helped the time to go by quickly, and as he had planned, he was bettering himself.

Watson Learns Prison Culture

Watson was able to observe one of the annual rituals of the Bureau of Prisons. It was time to submit budget requests, and apparently, part of that process is accounting for how the money they received last year was spent and whether there was any left over. The "leftovers" also included anything that had been purchased, but not put into use yet. "Put into use" is a BOP term of art. Things that were still in boxes and unopened or unused were *thrown away*. Whether it was a $20 baseball glove or a $2,000 tool of some sort, it was tossed in the dumpster so that the BOP could claim it had spent all the money given to it and needed just as much this year, if not more.

In preparation for an inspection by the American Correctional Association (ACA), the inmates cleaned everything. Watson understood this, but it would seem the ACA would be interested in more than the camp's cleanliness. What about educational opportunities? Efforts at rehabilitation?

Figure 2.2. PrisonOfficer.org Forum[22]

August 25, 2011

Thread: ACA Inspection

ADXCO: "I don't know how often they come around but this place looks like a brand new joint. They are throwing so much money to make this prison look more like a hotel. They have a sheet of questions and what to say for the answer. Talk about RETARDED."

BOPCO87 [identified as FCC Beaumont employee]: "Funny how they throw that money around for dumb **** like an ACA review. They are implementing a[n] augmentation roster here to prevent paying a single cent in overtime. So take the counselors, case managers, and unit secretaries away from the jobs they are already behind on. Talk about having your priorities in line!"

Crosstimbers Okie: "I've been saying the same thing for 19 years. When ACA comes through a state prison, everything is right because everything is ran [sic] by ACA standards on a daily basis. When ACA inspectors go through a federal prison it's like the team of mules you see pulling a wagon in an old western movie. The mules are wearing blinders so that nothing upsets them and so they don't see too much. ACA is a fraud."

The ingenuity of inmates at the prison camp was amazing. Watson saw irons being used to heat up tortillas and other kinds of food. He also saw an ingenious way of fixing the radios that were sold at the commissary. The only electronics that inmates had were those radios and the headsets used to listen to them. Sometimes the volume control or something else would go wrong and needed to be repaired. Unfortunately, the BOP did not provide the tools and materials necessary to make those repairs. As far as they were concerned, you could just buy another one.

Fortunately, one inmate was very good at electrical repairs and very resourceful in coming up with the tools and materials necessary to do so. Since he did not have a soldering iron, he improvised. He took a small shoe polish tin sold in the commissary and filled it with baby oil. He then took a piece of string and inserted it into a hole in the shoe polish. He lit the string and that was his soldering iron.

When he lit the string, he answered one of Watson's lingering questions. When doing laundry, Watson noticed that wire was missing from the lint screens in the dryers. It turns out inmates used them for lighters. Watson thought they were using smuggled lighters to light their smuggled cigarettes. Instead, they took wire from the lint screens and held it to each end of an AA battery. This heats up the wire enough to light a cigarette or, in this case, light the wick in the electronics wizard's workshop. Of course, this was against the rules but, as the ever-disappearing lint screens in the dryers demonstrated, this was widely ignored.

Part of getting used to the prison culture was learning about the individual personalities of the corrections officers. Each had quirks and personalities and needed to be dealt with in different ways. As an example, one evening an officer who had been working for eighteen years for the BOP and only had two years left until retirement, came into the dorm fuming and fussing about something and he kept yelling, "They are really making me mad. They've really done it this time." He went on to explain, finally, that he was mad that inmates from another dorm, who had had their TVs removed for some infraction of the rules, had come into our dorm to watch TV. He went on to threaten the men in Watson's dorm with all kinds of losses such as their televisions, microwaves etc., if they did not do something about these inmates coming into their TV room.

One of the inmates yelled out, "Isn't that the job of the officers? We're just inmates, we have no control over other inmates. That is the officers' job." There was a long pause, then the officer responded loudly, "Okay, well, it'll be okay, it'll be all right, don't worry about it, we'll work it out." Then he left the dorm room and, rumor has it, went to the parking lot, got in his truck, and left even though it was three hours before the end of his shift.

Even though Watson had never smelled alcohol on his breath, several people Watson trusted said that this officer drank frequently before coming to work. However, Watson didn't think it was the drinking alone that was causing his problematic behavior in regards to the inmates. He just did not have the emotional balance necessary to have complete control over other human beings' lives.

This officer was generally easy-going and fairly easy to deal with. But his behavior, like the behavior of so many of the other officers, could be erratic. This made for a lot of unnecessary stress on the inmates. In addition, this was time and energy he could have spent interacting with the inmates in a way that would have had a positive effect on their lives and increased their chances of success when they left prison.

Correctional officers in the Bureau of Prisons earn \$39,400 to \$52,230 annually.[23] Mass incarceration in America assures those interested in becoming correctional officers that there are "MANY vacancies."[24] The job posting at USAJobs.gov states that these positions require competency in oral communication, interpersonal skills, writing, organizational awareness, managing human resources, and of course, stress tolerance.[25] Watson is not sure how well the Bureau of Prisons screens for these competencies.

Bureaucracy Behind Bars

One of the biggest problems, and one of the most difficult things to adapt to in prison, is the feeling of powerlessness, which is compounded by the feeling that nobody cares. Whether it is something fairly minor, or something major, the inmate is pretty much left on his own. Society as a whole just does not really care what happens to inmates, figuring they are just getting what they deserve. Many of the complaints that inmates have about prison life are easily and readily dismissed by people looking in from the outside who believe that prison is not supposed to be fun, it's supposed to be unpleasant, so what should prisoners expect?

The mailroom was a good example. The rules regarding mail, and in particular books being delivered, were enforced erratically the entire time Watson was in prison. Sometimes books in a box would be allowed in and other times they would be sent back. One time Watson was having trouble getting books delivered and the friend who was mailing them to him was growing frustrated. Watson went to the mailroom at the camp and asked what was going on. The officer said he did not remember seeing a package from this particular person and stated that he never sent anything back. He said that the only people who send things back are the people in the complex mailroom.

Accordingly, Watson visited the complex mailroom and told the officer working there about what the officer in the camp mailroom had said. The complex mailroom officer told Watson they never send things back, no matter what comes in they always forwarded to the camp mailroom. If something had been sent back, it had been sent back by the mailroom at the camp.

Watson went back to the camp mailroom and asked the officer in charge about this. He said, "That's not true, I never send anything back, if it was sent back the complex mailroom did it." Watson tended to believe the officer at the camp mailroom, as he had several dealings with him before, and always found him to be fair and helpful. Watson felt that the officer at the complex mailroom just flat-out lied to him.

This was a minor issue, perhaps, but keep in mind that prisoners have very few personal possessions. Therefore, what little they do possess takes on a greatly exaggerated value and importance. Prisoners have only the few clothes they are issued and what they can purchase at the commissary, which is very limited. So, any time a prisoner can get a book in the mail—the only thing they can receive from the outside besides letters and magazines—it is a big deal.

Watson's only recourse was to file a complaint. The complaint process designed by the BOP is a masterwork of bureaucratic finesse. An "Inmate Request to Staff" (BP-8) must be filled out. The BOP has a certain amount of time to respond to it, and then get back to you. If you are not satisfied with the answer, you fill out another form, a BP-9, and then they have more time to respond. If you're still not satisfied, there's the BP-10, and they again have a certain amount of time to respond to you. There are four levels of forms and the last one (yes, you guessed it, the BP-11) goes to the BOP offices in Washington, DC. The process existed, but Watson still had trouble with his mail during the rest of his stay in Beaumont.

By the end of August 2009, Watson was getting close to having been incarcerated for a year. He was beginning to wonder if he was becoming "institutionalized." Like a windshield that gradually gets dirty without you realizing how dirty it is, he was beginning to wonder if his view of the world, of prison, of himself, was becoming clouded and hard to see clearly. Nevertheless, Watson decided that he was not becoming institutionalized, that he was keeping a good head on his shoulders and continuing to think clearly.

Yet there were people around him who had obviously become institutionalized. He saw prisoners who felt that being in prison life was normal and made sense on some level. In addition, those who were institutionalized feared the outside world. Who wouldn't? If you had not been out in the world for ten, fifteen, twenty years or more and you were going to be suddenly thrust out into everyday society, you would be scared to death, too. It's a huge adjustment that many long-term inmates are not able to make, primarily because of the lack of training and preparation that the BOP provides.

Watson had adjusted to the constant interruptions of daily life, both expected and unexpected. When the guards and the administrator came storming angrily into the dorm or chow hall it no longer stressed him out. Watson was used to strange rules and regulations, and not just the infrequent, totally silly occurrences.

Real Men Stay in Prison

Towards the end of August 2009, the camp administrator came into the dorm and asked the inmates to bring extra pairs of pants and shirts to the front of the dorm, as the camp had gotten so crowded that they were running out of "greens" and needed inmates to bring any extra pairs they had to the front. Ostensibly there to collect surplus clothing, the camp administrator began a lecture that indicated not only his own mindset, but perhaps that of the BOP culture in general.

He talked about the Residential Drug Abuse Program (RDAP), a program that gives inmates with drug abuse histories intensive therapy and counseling for nine months. In return for making it through the 500-hour program, which is intellectually and emotionally challenging, the inmates are given a year off their sentence. In Watson's conversations with several people who had completed or were enrolled in the program, it was obvious the program had helped them. These people really needed counseling in order to improve their lives and the lives of their loved ones. (As mentioned earlier, Watson's sentencing judge recommended him for participation in RDAP, and Watson later did so.) The RDAP program was located in Unit G-D. To participate in RDAP, an inmate had to live in Unit G-D, and all of the inmates in that unit were in RDAP, hence the name *Residential* Drug Abuse Program.

The camp administrator told those listening that the RDAP inmates were not *real* inmates. He went on, "They don't need that program, they're just trying to get the year off. You're better than that. It's just bullshit. Real men do all their time. I look up to you guys, you're doing all your time like you're supposed to, not like those G-D inmates." The ridiculousness of this performance had Watson laughing heartily, and he was later able to write down the administrator's "pep talk" word for word.

Perhaps the benefits of the RDAP program, in particular, the reduction in the recidivism rate of its participants, had not been communicated to the camp administrator. Let's assume that's what happened. Certainly, there was nothing to keep him from looking into the program on his own. Why wouldn't he do this? If he knew a program was working, why wouldn't he look into expanding the program, instead of criticizing it? In fact, he would not have to look much further than the Bureau of Prisons' own website, which states:

> The Bureau and National Institute on Drug Abuse combined funding and expertise to conduct a rigorous analysis of the Bureau's RDAP. Research findings demonstrated that RDAP participants are significantly less likely to recidivate and less likely to relapse to drug use than

non-participants. The studies also suggest that the Bureau's RDAPs make a significant difference in the lives of offenders following their release from custody and return to the community.[26]

Watson had observed the camp administrator's bullying behavior repeatedly over thirty months. Unfortunately, some other prison personnel demonstrated similar antipathy. Watson knew that the officers' job was often a tough and unhappy one; their boss's demeanor merely enabled and amplified their bad attitudes.

Not all of the officers working at the prison camp were troublesome or troubled people. One in particular, Ms. Dill, who coordinated food service at various times, was an excellent role model for the inmates. Her demonstrated desire to do her very best for the inmates was inspiring, putting everybody in a better frame of mind and encouraging people to cooperate with her and help her. Watson heard this repeatedly from inmates working in food service as well as the general inmate population.

In an effort to encourage positive behavior towards inmates on the part of the staff, Watson came up with the idea of having a staff recognition certificate. Watson called this simply the "Job Well Done" certificate. At first, Watson tried to get the BOP to officially approve the form and make it available at every federal prison. It would be a formal method of encouraging the staff to behave in ways that would help inmates succeed once released from prison. Just as importantly, it would encourage inmates to look for positive things about the officers' behavior, instead of focusing only on negative aspects.

Watson submitted this form to U.S. Attorney Eric Holder as well as the head of the BOP. Neither responded, and the issue went back to the complex's warden. The warden said that inmates could just use the "Inmate Request to Staff" form, the BP-8. This form was typically used to make complaints or at best, to make simple requests. The whole purpose of the staff commendation form was to help the inmates focus on what the staff was doing well and to help reduce the sense of "us versus them" that poisons the atmosphere of prisons.

Since the BOP turned down this idea, Watson came up with his own form and used it to honor Ms. Dill. Watson had approximately fifty inmates sign it. Most were happy to do so, though a few said initially that they could not imagine saying something nice, especially in writing, about any of the officers. When Watson reminded them how helpful and supportive Ms. Dill had been to the inmates and how she had done her very best to make the food taste as good as possible, they replied, "Yeah, you're right, we should do something for her." Thus, the form did exactly what it was supposed to do: encourage inmates to look for positive aspects of authority. Authority being the people and institutions that enforce the rules and regulations that they all had to live by, including bosses, the police, spouses, and so on.

A few months later, another example of bureaucracy colliding with rehabilitation occurred with the arrival of a new food service director for the complex. In an effort to make his mark, he quickly instituted many changes, the most telling of which was portion control. BOP regulations specify the exact amount of food inmates are to receive at every meal and the complex food director was determined that no inmate was to receive more than that exact amount. This necessitated throwing away large amounts of food that normally would have been served as seconds to those who wanted it or served the next day along with what was being prepared for that day.

This waste of the taxpayer's money went on for several weeks until the inmates at the medium-security prison went on a hunger strike, forcing the medium-security facility into a lock-down, costing the taxpayers even more money. After a few days, common sense prevailed and the food director dropped portion control at all four institutions. Inmates at the prison camp were appreciative of the medium-security inmates for going on the hunger strike and being willing to suffer lock-down in order to put an end to yet another poorly thought-out regulation. Nevertheless, it should not have had to come to that. With prisoners deprived of so many basic creature comforts, messing with something as basic as their food typically meets with strong resistance, as it did in Beaumont.

George Goes Home

Watson moved to Unit G-D in April 2010 to begin the RDAP program. This greatly encouraged him, as he was looking forward to the program itself, and knowing that it was a one-year program, it meant that he likely had only a year left in Beaumont before beginning to the process of going home. He also remembered witnessing inmates from G-D leaving the dorm with their personal items in a box, about to be driven out of the complex and released.

In March 2011, Watson was told that he would be released in May. When the day arrived, he was waiting expectantly to be paged by the Receiving and Discharge Office. When his name was called, he went in and received the rest of the money in his account, a bus ticket, a pullover shirt, and blue jeans about eight inches too long with no pockets. When he got in the van, he realized he hadn't been in a motorized vehicle in thirty-two months. The van driver was too talkative for Watson, who wanted to ride in silence. As the van left the

Figure 2.3. Prison Menu[27]

U.S. Bureau of Prisons National Menu Fiscal Year 2014 Week 3

Tuesday Lunch	Wednesday Dinner
tomato rice soup	minestrone soup
tuna salad	taco salad
or two boiled eggs with salad dressing	or soy taco salad
lettuce leaf	salsa
hearty healthy pasta salad	beverage
steamed broccoli	
wheat bread	
margarine	
fresh fruit	
or dessert	
beverage	

compound, Watson reflected on his first impression of the camp—monotonous. That initial impression had been confirmed daily for nearly three years.

As the bus from Beaumont arrived in Houston, Watson felt like a third-world resident as he looked up at the skyscrapers. A change of buses took him to San Antonio. As he and a fellow ex-camper waited for a cab to the halfway house, the other man was nervous, saying that they were going to be staying in a bad part of town. This bad vibe seemed to have been shared by the cab driver, who appeared anxious as he drove them to the halfway house. Watson thought about the irony of feeling safer in prison than he did at that moment. After the driver dropped them off, he left in great haste.

One of the best things about the halfway house was that Watson was now allowed to have a phone. A friend brought him one, and Watson was no longer limited to five hours a month of talking time. He arrived in San Antonio on a Wednesday, and was finally able to see Holly and his family on Saturday. It was as wonderful as he had hoped it would be.

Although staying in the halfway house was supposed to serve as a means of reintegrating into the community, it did not have a computer to allow residents to look for jobs. The irony of this did not escape Watson. He and some other residents were taken in a van to a Goodwill store downtown. There was a room with several computers for job hunters, and Watson spent many hours there searching for work.

Watson had trouble landing a job. He could only imagine what it was like for those who had spent more time in prison than he had. Many of them, he realized, lacked basic computer skills and were not familiar with the internet. Another impediment was "the box." This is the part of the employment application that asks if the applicant has ever been convicted of a crime. Watson felt himself wince every time he clicked it.

Although San Antonio was where Watson would now live, thanks to his in-laws, who had Holly with them for the prior three years, he would have had an easier time looking for work in Austin, where he had many more connections. Finally, though, a friend in San Antonio who was a lawyer gave Watson a job working as a paralegal. After six weeks at the halfway house, Watson was allowed to move in with Holly and his in-laws. He was then on home confinement for four-and-a-half months. He was monitored by the federal probation office, which called him on his in-laws' landline at all hours of the day to ascertain that he remained at home. Paxson came to visit and took Watson and Holly out to dinner. Watson had to clear that with his probation officer, and could only go to a restaurant with a public address system. Fortunately, he was able to enjoy his enchiladas without being paged.

Watson continued to do some legal work for several years after his release. However, at the time of writing, he remains on probation, and will not be able to petition to get his law license back until he finishes probation. Watson appreciated being able to work, but he needed to make more money. He is currently selling cars in San Antonio. He would be happy to put you behind the wheel of a brand new automobile.

Conclusion

Watson was released from prison after being incarcerated for a period of almost three years. His imprisonment cost taxpayers approximately $64,000.[28] This does not include the cost of prosecuting him, nor other costs external to the prison camp, such as his stay at the Bastrop County, his ride on Con Air, nor his stay at the halfway house. Had Watson been placed in a more secure facility with more correctional officers guarding him, it would have cost taxpayers about $100,000.[29]

Did Watson need to go to prison? According to the U.S. attorney, he did. Was he rehabilitated while in prison? That presumes that he needed rehabilitation. Yet even if he did, Watson immersed himself in activities in Beaumont because of his personal determination not to let his time in prison be a waste of his life; it wasn't because of the guidance of those operating the prison camp. Watson returned to free society in worse shape than when he left it. He lost three years of income production (and contributing to the nation's economy through paying taxes). He missed the funeral of a beloved brother-in-law. He was not able to help his wife care for her failing parents.

Are ex-offenders like Watson common? No; as we pointed out at the beginning of this chapter, Watson falls outside of the most common demographic characteristics of offenders. However, as we will see in the following chapters, Watson's predicament epitomizes an American criminal justice system that is more likely to incarcerate people than that of any other nation.

Notes

1. "National Prisoner Statistics 2009 Midyear Population Report," (Washington, DC: U.S. Bureau of Justice Statistics, 2009), http://bjs.ojp.usdoj.gov/index.cfm?ty=dcdetail&iid=269.

2. "Crime in the United States," (Washington, DC: Federal Bureau of Investigation, 2010), http://www.fbi.gov/about-us/cjis/ucr/crime-in-the-u.s/2010/crime-in-the-u.s.-2010.

3. "Texas Title Insurance Premium Rates," (Austin: Texas Department of Insurance, 2013), http://www.tdi.texas.gov/title/titlerates2013.html. Note that this rate had been in effect since 2013.

4. Edwin Hardin Sutherland, *White Collar Crime*, (New York: Dryden Press, 1949): 9.

5. Federal Bureau of Investigation, *White Collar Crime: A Report to the Public* (Washington, D.C.: Government Printing Office, 1989): 3.

6. "Robinson to Serve 27 Years for Mortgage Fraud Schemes," *Lockhart Post-Register*, September 5, 2008, http://post-register.com/local-news/robinson-to-serve-27-years-for-mortgage-fraud-schemes/.

7. "Inmate Locator," (Washington, DC: Federal Bureau of Prisons), accessed June 23, 2015, http://www.bop.gov/inmateloc/.

8. "Table 1194. Mortgage Originations and Delinquency and Foreclosure Rates: 1990 to 2010," (Washington, DC: U.S. Census Bureau), accessed June 24, 2015, http://www.census.gov/compendia/statab/2012/tables/12s1194.pdf.

9. "White Collar Crime Statistics," (Glen Allen, VA: National White Collar Crime Center, 2009), http://www.nw3c.org/research/site_files.cfm?fileid=2424d489-b40e-47ba-9a9c-f48bdc2f46a4&mode=r. Those who waived juries did better before judges, who convicted 14 defendants and acquitted 20. Recall, however, that the federal judge in Watson's case was known for being particularly tough.

10. "Just the Facts: Mortgage Fraud Statistics," (Washington, DC: Federal Bureau of Investigation), accessed June 29, 2015, http://www.fbi.gov/about-us/investigate/white_collar/mortgage-fraud.

11. "Program Statement: Early Release Procedures Under 18 U.S.C. §3621(e)," (Washington, DC: Federal Bureau of Prisons, March 16, 2009), http://www.bop.gov/policy/progstat/5331_002.pdf.

12. "High Value Data Sets," (Austin: Texas Department of Criminal Justice), accessed June 22, 2015, http://www.tdcj.state.tx.us/tab1_public.html; Texas Commission on Jail

Standards, "Abbreviated Population Report for 5/1/2015," http://www.tcjs.state.tx.us/docs/AbbreRptCurrent.pdf.

13. "State and County Quick Facts," (Washington, DC: U.S. Census Bureau), accessed June 22, 2015, http://quickfacts.census.gov/qfd/states/48000.html.

14. "World Prison Brief," (London: International Centre for Prison Studies), accessed June 22, 2015, http://www.prisonstudies.org/country/united-states-america.

15. "Jail Bureau," (Bastrop, TX: Bastrop County Sheriff's Office), accessed June 22, 2015, http://www.bastropsheriff.org/page.php?id=13.

16. Christopher Ingraham, "The U.S. Has More Jails Than Colleges. Here's a Map of Where Those Prisoners Live," *Washington Post*, January 6, 2015, http://www.washingtonpost.com/blogs/wonkblog/wp/2015/01/06/the-u-s-has-more-jails-than-colleges-heres-a-map-of-where-those-prisoners-live/.

17. James J. Stephan, "Census of State and Federal Correctional Facilities, 2005," (Washington, DC: U.S. Bureau of Justice Statistics, 2008), http://www.bjs.gov/content/pub/pdf/csfcf05.pdf; "FY 2016 Performance Budget, Congressional Submission, Federal Prison System," (Washington, DC: Federal Bureau of Prisons): 2, http://www.justice.gov/sites/default/files/jmd/pages/attachments/2015/02/02/27._federal_bureau_of_prisons_bop_se.pdf.

18. "PREA Audit Report," (Washington, DC: U.S. Bureau of Justice Statistics, March 2015), http://www.bop.gov/locations/institutions/bmp/BMX_prea.pdf.

19. Ibid.

20. "Inmate Work and Performance Pay," (Washington, DC: Federal Bureau of Prisons, October 1, 2008), http://www.bop.gov/policy/progstat/5251_006.pdf.

21. "Commissary List," Federal Correctional Complex Beaumont, Texas, January–June 2012, http://www.bop.gov/locations/institutions/bmp/BMX_CommList.pdf.

22. "ACA Inspection," Prison Officer.org, August 25, 2011, http://www.prisonofficer.org/main-control/14801-aca-inspection.html.

23. "Correctional Officer," USA Jobs, accessed June 22, 2015, https://www.usajobs.gov/GetJob/ViewDetails/395855300.

24. Ibid.

25. Ibid.

26. "Substance Abuse Treatment," (Washington, DC: Federal Bureau of Prisons), accessed June 26, 2015, http://www.bop.gov/inmates/custody_and_care/substance_abuse_treatment.jsp.

27. "National Menu FY 2014," (Washington, DC: Federal Bureau of Prisons), accessed June 28, 2015, http://www.bop.gov/foia/national_menu_lun_din.pdf.

28. Nathan James, "The Federal Prison Population Buildup: Overview, Policy Changes, Issues, and Options," (Washington, DC: Congressional Research Service, 2015): 15.

29. Ibid.

Chapter 3

What Were They Thinking? Why People Commit Crimes and How America Punishes Them

In Chapter 1, we discussed the current state of the American prison system. Watson described how he ended up in prison and what his prison experience was like in Chapter 2. In this chapter, we survey some historical and contemporary explanations for criminal behavior (criminology) then look at how penal institutions have attempted to prevent and discourage criminal behavior (a subset of criminology called penology) and conclude with a brief history of American prison facilities.

Why Do People Commit Crimes?

How do we keep people from committing crimes? How do we prevent criminal offenders from reoffending? Most societies approach these questions by first asking, "Why do people commit crimes?" To some people, the obvious answer is that criminals are people who are greedy, who lack compassion and empathy, and who are perhaps just plain evil. Even if we choose to use this over-reductive argument (and we don't) the question remains: can we fix the problem? Politicians, the police, corrections officials, academicians, and even criminals themselves have long held competing theories about the causes of crime and how to prevent or reduce criminal behavior. These theories form the core of criminology.

In 1959, C. Ray Jeffery (1921–2007) traced "The Historical Development of Criminology" in the *Journal of Criminal Law and Criminology* and identified its three principal components, arguing that, although grounded in sociology, criminology is interdisciplinary in nature.

Criminology involves three different types of problems:

(1) The problem of detecting the law breaker, which is the work of the detective, the police officer, the medical specialist, the chemist; in other words, the field of criminalistics.

(2) The problem of the custody and treatment of the offender once he is detected and legally judged to be guilty, which is the work of the penologist.

(3) The problem of explaining crime and criminal behavior, which is the problem of scientifically accounting for the presence of crime and criminals in a society.... The explanation of criminal behavior is of interest to the sociologist, the psychologist, the psychiatrist, the anthropologist, and the biologist.[1]

In this book, we focus on Jeffery's second and third criminological problems.

Criminology 101

Academic specialization in many fields of knowledge as we know them today began in earnest in the 1800s. The French philosopher Auguste Comte (1798–1857) often receives credit for coining (or at least popularizing) the term "sociologie" in 1838.[2] The University of Chicago created the first sociology department in the U.S. in 1892. Chicago graduate Edwin Sutherland (1883–1950) published one of the first criminology textbooks in the U.S. in 1924 entitled simply, *Criminology*.[3] He was an important figure in the American shift to sociological explanations for criminal behavior, opposing earlier European theories of crime that tended to focus on individual and biological theories. Sutherland and his former Indiana University doctoral student and co-author Donald Cressey (1919–1987) provided one of the most commonly used definitions of criminology:

> Criminology is the body of knowledge regarding crime as a social phenomenon. It includes within its scope the process of making laws, of breaking laws, and of reacting toward the breaking of laws.... The objective of criminology is the development of a body of general and verified principles and of others types of knowledge regarding this process of law, crime, and treatment.[4]

The early theories emphasize individual decision-making, biological characteristics, and the psychological or psychiatric characteristics of those who engage in criminal activity. Each of these early criminological theories received new scholarly adherents after their initial influence had lapsed. The latter schools of thought emphasize social structures, social processes, and social conflict rather than individualistic causes, and as is true in many academic disciplines, these theories have grown increasingly complex. We now look at some of the most influential theories of criminology.

Preclassical Theory

Early explanations of behavior that deviated from social norms typically attributed deviance to evil, supernatural forces. As was seen in the Salem witch trials of the late seventeenth century, the belief that witchery, demonic forces, and the like controlled human actions was common among the people of the time. Torture and executions were prescribed for a wide variety of crimes upon the belief that if the accused were truly innocent, God would intervene.

Classical Theory

Much of the basis of classical criminological theory lies in Italian philosopher Cesare Bonesana, the Marchese di Beccaria's *Essays on Crimes and Punishments*, published in 1764. Beccaria (1738–1794) rejected the then-common practice of torture and argued that punishment should be proportionate to the crime. Beccaria also argued that punishment should be public when possible, in order to provide a general deterrent against crime among others in society. In this advocacy for deterrence, Beccaria established his place in the Enlightenment. This seventeenth and eighteenth century movement questioned traditional authority and argued for the betterment of humanity through analysis and reason.

Rather than focusing on crime as a sin, which Beccaria believed was an issue best left to the Church, he stated that governments should focus on justice. Based on this argument, as well as his emphasis on preventing crime rather than punishing it after it occurs, Beccaria is often seen as one of the founders of both criminology and criminal justice systems. His statement that, "in the eye of the law, every man is innocent whose crime has not been proved,"[5] is the basis of the Anglo-American principle of innocent until proven guilty.

Although Beccaria's emphasis on rationalism was met with condemnation by the Catholic Church (which excommunicated him), his work proved influential on new European legal codes and informed the laws of the U.S. The British philosopher Jeremy Bentham (1748–1832) embraced Beccaria's advocacy of a rational and humane legal system. Bentham began with the premise that potential criminals calculate the risks of committing crimes before doing so, conducting a cost/benefit analysis of criminal activity. This is classical rational choice theory.

Classical Theory and Rational Choice

Criminal justice practices grounded in rational choice theory focus on the criminal act and how to make that act less attractive to the individual. Under this theory, the criminal justice system attempts to affect the potential criminal's thought processes and deter that person from committing a crime. In the case of those who do commit crimes, the role of the correctional system is to deter future offenses. As Bentham stated it,

With respect to a given individual, the recurrence of an offense may be provided against in three ways:

1. By taking from him the physical power of offending.
2. By taking away the desire of offending.
3. By making him afraid of offending.[6]

As we discuss later in this chapter, the first goal in Bentham's list is incapacitation, while the latter two fall within the goal of deterrence.

Rational choice theory, as the name says, claims that human behavior can be seen as the product of rational decision making. British sociologist John Scott's frequently cited essay "Rational Choice Theory" tells us, "What distinguishes rational choice theory from other forms of theory is that it denies any kinds of action other than the purely rational and calculative. All social action can be seen as rationally motivated, as instrumental action, however much it may appear to be irrational or non-rational."[7]

The basic assumptions of rational choice theory are that humans freely choose how to behave, that human beings behave rationally, and that these behavioral choices are based on a profit/loss analysis (reflecting the origins of rational choice theory in economics) or pleasure/pain analysis of different behaviors in different situations. To respond to those who rationally choose to engage in criminal activity, the belief is that the criminal justice system in general and correctional agencies in particular can deter bad choices by making it clear that an illegal act will result in some form of punishment, and that deterrence can be effected by manipulating the swiftness, severity, and certainty of punishment.

Besides being an easy (we claim oversimplified) explanation for human interactions, what other factors contributed to the rational choice theory becoming the dominant theory about human behavior for our criminal justice system? One factor is our country's history. The U.S. was founded upon the principle that people should be free to choose for themselves in all areas of their lives and neither a monarch nor any other government authority should be able to tell them what to do. These civil liberties are enshrined in our Constitution and are deeply engrained in the American psyche.

This quest for freedom lies at the most fundamental level of American belief. For example, a week after the attacks of September 11, 2001, President George W. Bush, trying to explain the cause of the attacks to Congress and the American people, referred to them as attacks on freedom thirteen times.[8] At a much less significant but daily level, Americans so deeply embrace the ideal of freedom that the phrase "freedom of choice" is a ubiquitous advertising slogan today. Of course, sometimes this choice is a hollow one, as one has the freedom to choose between Coke or Pepsi, Democrats or Republicans, plastic or paper, debit or credit.

A second factor is the American reverence of rugged individualism. This is the belief that we are in control of ourselves, and thus are worthy of having freedom to choose. With this freedom, however, comes responsibility. In many ways, the American philosophy of government in general and the criminal justice system in particular give us, to quote the old saying, "just enough rope to hang ourselves." As American philosopher John Dewey (1859–1952) put it:

> The more comprehensive and diversified the social order, the greater the responsibility and the freedom of the individual.… His responsibility is greater because there are more demands for considering the consequences of his acts.… In its external aspect, responsibility is *liability*. An agent is free to act; yes, but—. He must stand the consequences, the disagreeable as well as the pleasant, the social as well as the physical. He may do a given act, but if so, let him look out. His act is a matter that concerns others as well as himself, and they will prove their concern by calling him to account; and if he cannot give a satisfactory and credible account of his intention, subject him to correction.[9]

Is rational choice theory a valid explanation for human behavior? Even a cursory look at our culture and ourselves tells us that it is not. Companies would not spend billions of dollars a year on advertising if rational choice theory explained the bulk of human behavior. Such spending would be a waste of money; it would be better to just lay out the facts about your product and let the consumer make a logical, Spock-like decision.

Is using tobacco products a rational decision? Staying in an abusive relationship? Buying products you cannot really afford? Eating food that is bad for you? In the world of finance and economics from which the rational choice model arose, there is a lack of support for rational choice theory in terms of there being clear metrics for rational decision making. Looking at the number of bankruptcy filings (over one million in 2013[10]) as well as this young century's multi-billion dollar mortgage debacle reveals this to be true.

This leads us back to the question, "What were they thinking?" Without understanding the internal context in which a person's decision are made, we are not in a position to help them make better decisions. Merely saying, "You better start making more rational decisions or you will end up in prison again," is of no use to a person who has little or no understanding of how and why he makes the decisions he does. For those who consistently make bad decisions, the best advice may be to undergo cognitive behavioral therapy—helping a person understand the origins of one's emotions and how those emotions are affecting one's thinking. We examine cognitive behavioral therapy and other therapeutic practices in Chapter 7.

Fortunately for most of us, our lack of understanding about why we behave the way we do leads, at worst, to things like weight gain, a closet full of clothes we never wear, a bigger pickup truck than we really need, bruised emotions, or perhaps bankruptcy. But what about people whose choices land them in prison? Rational choice theory says they consciously, logically chose to break the law. Does this mean the rational choice theory holds true for criminal acts, even though it does not hold true for noncriminal acts? The answer is no. All human behavior is a function of a person's emotional and mental state; without understanding that, we can no more understand and control illegal behaviors than we can legal behaviors. We argue that rational choice theory adequately explains neither legal nor illegal behavior.

In their 2008 book *Nudge: Improving Decisions About Health, Wealth, and Happiness*,[11] behavioral economists Richard H. Thaler (b. 1945) and Cass R. Sunstein (b. 1954) offer a critique of rational choice theory and argue instead that people often make decisions, even important ones, based on irrational biases and emotions. The authors advocate for a systemic acknowledgement that humans are not always rational, and that government and other social institutions should provide what they label "choice architecture," allowing individuals to make decisions for themselves among well-defined choices. In Chapter 7, we discuss how choice architecture can inform criminal justice policy.

Positivist Theory

Positivist theory arose in the early 1800s. Those who embraced positivism sought to apply what they considered scientific methods to social problems. They generally disputed the classical school's belief that free will and rational choice explained criminal behavior. Cesare Lombroso (1835–1909) an Italian physician, who gained the most acclaim among those advocating for biological positivism, argued that criminality was characteristically an inherited trait. Lombroso claimed that criminality could be inherited directly from criminal parents, or indirectly through insanity, alcoholism, and sexually transmitted diseases. Lombrosco coined the term "atavism" to describe criminals as primitive humans who have not evolved as the rest of humanity has. As his proof, Lombroso, studied the corpses of criminals and claimed that criminals shared certain physical traits that he labeled "atavistic anomalies." These included the size of teeth, ears, jawlines, and most importantly, the size of the skull.

Lombroso's theories soon fell out of favor among European criminologists, especially in the wake of British physician Charles Goring's *The English Convict*, a study of over 3,000 prisoners published in 1913 that found, "the physical and mental constitution of both criminal and law-abiding persons, of the same age, stature, class, and intelligence, are identical. There is no such thing as an anthropological criminal type."[12] Yet Goring (1870–1919) still believed that there was a correlation between criminal behavior and the physical and mental conditions of those who commit crime:

> But, despite this negation, and upon the evidence of our statistics, it appears to be an equally indisputable fact that there is a physical, mental, and moral type of normal person who tends to be convicted of crime: that is to say, our evidence conclusively shows that, on the average, the criminal of English prisons is markedly differentiated by defective physique—as measured by stature and body weight; by defective mental capacity—as measured by general intelligence; and by an increased possession of willful anti-social proclivities.[13]

Goring's conclusions are confusing and seemingly contradictory. Let's use one of his examples: "tall persons are relatively immune from conviction for rape."[14] Here, he seems to be telling us that not all short people are rapists, but among those people who are rapists, they are more likely to be short than tall.

Of course, the racial aspects of this line of thought can be troublesome, and there was indeed a correlation between positivist criminology and the eugenics movement, which advocated for human engineering by preventing the mentally, physically, and morally weak from procreating. In his 1890 book *The Criminal*, Havelock Ellis (1859–1939) a British physician and eugenicist, after describing the cranial and cerebral characteristics of criminals, as well as the criminal's face and hair, told readers:

> Perhaps the most general statement to be made is that criminals present a far larger proportion of anatomical abnormalities than the ordinary European population. Now this is precisely the characteristic of the anatomy of the lower human races: they present a far larger proportion of anatomical abnormalities than the ordinary European population. It is true that our knowledge of the anatomy of the lower

human races is still incomplete, but the evidence so far as it goes is perfectly clear.[15]

Accordingly, eugenicists warned against race mixing, specifically of whites with non-whites, which was one of the impetuses behind anti-miscegenation laws forbidding white people from marrying those of other races. Anti-miscegenation laws continued to exist in a number of states well into the twentieth century and were occasionally enforced until the U.S. Supreme Court declared them unconstitutional in 1967.

The 1927 U.S. Supreme Court case *Buck v. Bell* may have been the peak of eugenic criminology. The case concerned the constitutionality of a Virginia statute that allowed the state to forcibly sterilize those who were determined to be "feeble minded," or intellectually disabled. In an eight-to-one decision, the court ruled that the Virginia law was constitutional. The decision, written by Oliver Wendell Holmes, stated that, "It is better for all the world, if instead of waiting to execute degenerate offspring for crime, or to let them starve for their imbecility, society can prevent those who are manifestly unfit from continuing their kind."[16] In the wake of *Buck v. Bell*, several states adopted forcible sterilization statutes similar to Virginia's, and forced sterilizations were not uncommon in the U.S. for more than a decade after the case was decided.

If there is an upside to biological positivism, it is the positivists' belief that a criminal is biologically predetermined to engage in criminal activity. This led positivists to focus on the criminal rather than on the crime when determining punishments for criminal activity. Positivist criminology generally opposed determinate sentences, which are essentially "one size fits all." Positivism also stressed rehabilitation efforts that took into account the biological and cognitive traits of each individual offender. As Havelock Ellis began his chapter entitled "The Treatment of the Criminal," "If, as now scarcely admits of question, every truly criminal act proceeds from a person who is, temporarily or permanently, in a more or less abnormal condition, the notion of 'punishment' loses much of its foundation. We cannot punish a monstrosity for acting according to its monstrous nature."[17] While some applications of positivist theory seem antiquated and barbaric, positivism also promoted important correctional practices that include probation, parole, and indeterminate sentences.

Sociological Theories

Unlike classical and positivist theories, which focus on individualistic explanations for criminal behavior, sociological theories argue that people's place in the social structure determine their behavior.

Social Conflict Theories

Although Karl Marx (1818–1883) wrote relatively little about crime, Marxist theories inform the work of social conflict theorists. The central conflict here is the class struggle between capitalists and labor, or more simply, between the haves and the have-nots. According to conflict theorists, laws are written to protect the interests of the haves against the interests of the have-nots. Consequently, American laws, beginning with the Constitution, give more attention to protection of private property than they do to basic human rights. (Fittingly, in the late nineteenth century, the U.S. Bureau of Indian Affairs attempted to suppress the potlatch, a long-held tradition among Native Americans in the Pacific Northwest by which those who had accumulated wealth gave it away in elaborate rituals.)

Marxist theories also look at the effects of alienation of individuals from their environment; as human beings become objectified as labor in capitalist societies, this further leads to the alienation of individuals from each other. While some Marxist theorists see criminals as victims of a ruthless capitalist system, others acknowledge that the working class is more likely to be victimized by crime than is the ruling elite.

Strain Theory

Relying on the pioneering work of French sociologist Émile Durkheim (1858–1917), American sociologist Robert K. Merton (1910–2003) developed strain theory, a sociological theory that argues that those who cannot (or perceive that they cannot) obtain traditional goals through traditional methods will often seek nontraditional methods. The strain on the individual is caused by the gap between culturally approved goals and the individual's ability to attain those goals. As an explanation for the criminal activity of some individuals, strain theory touches on both conformity (the desire to have what we have been socialized to want, such as nice clothes and a new car) and deviance (using criminal means to get those clothes and car). This is exacerbated in the U.S., where incredible displays of wealth and luxury are regularly shown in popular media and visible to all, including those who lack the education, intelligence, talent, or social connections necessary to acquire such luxury. In addition, the American dream typically portrays hard work as the means to get what one wants in life; if one fails to get one wants, the blame is placed on the individual, not on social limitations and inequities in America.

Today, many Americans go to college in order to get the type of job that will allow them to buy a decent house in a safe neighborhood, drive a reliable car, and have enough money left to take the kids to Disney World at least once before they leave home. This is hardly greedy; in fact, it's the American norm. This is fine if one is intelligent enough to make it through college or has another sought-after skill.

Let's use a worst-case scenario. A young man has never met his father; Watson points to research that finds that children who have a parent absent because that parent is incarcerated are more likely to be more at risk for criminal behavior than children who don't have a parent in prison.[18] This young man's mother is a drug addict and abused drugs during her pregnancy; according to an article published in the *Journal of the American Medical Association*, 16.2 percent of pregnant teens and 7.4 percent of pregnant women between the ages of eighteen and twenty-five use illegal drugs.[19] The result is often babies born addicted to drugs and suffering from Neonatal Abstinence Syndrome related to drug withdrawal upon leaving their mothers' uterus. Other babies are victims of Fetal Alcohol Syndrome, which the National Institutes of Health identify as a leading cause of birth defects and developmental disabilities.[20]

Starting life with cognitive disabilities and the lack of a stable home life, this young man will nevertheless likely be acculturated to want what most of us want: a nice place to live, good transportation, and some walking-around-money in one's pocket. Using the vocabulary of strain theory, this individual may innovate—rather than using traditional means of attaining what is culturally desirable, he may resort to a non-traditional means, i.e., crime, to do so.

Social Learning Theory

Albert Bandura (born 1925) a Stanford psychologist, popularized social learning theory in the 1960s. Social learning theory maintains that the learning process takes place in social contexts and that learning occurs through observing or experiencing rewards and punishments. Prior to Bandura's work, Edwin Sutherland presented a social learning theory of criminology in 1939. Sutherland, discussed previously in this chapter and in Chapter 2, was the leading American criminologist of the twentieth century. His work was solidly embedded in sociological theory, emphasizing social and environmental factors that affect behavior rather than criminals' personal characteristics. Sutherland advanced one of the most influential social learning theories, differential association theory, which argues that criminal behavior is learned from interaction with others, particularly within intimate personal groups. This learning includes techniques of committing crime, whether complicated or simple, as well as the motives, rationalizations, and attitudes. Sutherland sums up the principle of differential association as when a person becomes delinquent because of an excess of definitions favorable to violation of law over definitions unfavorable to violation of the law. Sutherland goes on to state that although criminal behavior is an expression of general needs and values, it is not explained by those general needs and values, because noncriminal behavior is an expression of the same needs and values.[21] (Similarly, strain theory points to traditional goals pursued through illegal means.)

Other criminologists used Sutherland's work as the theoretical roots of their later social learning theories. As Ronald L. Akers (born 1939) and Wesley G. Jennings (born 1980) explain, "social learning theory is presented as a more comprehensive explanation for involvement in crime and deviance compared with Sutherland's original theory; thus, any such support that it offered for differential association theory provides support for social learning theory, and findings that support social learning theory do not negate/discredit differential association theory."[22]

Akers's differential reinforcement theory incorporates Sutherland's differential association theory and psychological learning theory, and states that behavior is reinforced through rewards and discouraged through punishment. For young criminals, much of this can be described by the old expression "falling in with the wrong crowd." Because differential reinforcement theory argues that young criminals undertake a risk/benefit analysis before choosing to engage in criminal activity, this contemporary theory supports classical rational choice theory.

Integrative Theories

The more recent trend in criminological theory combines multiple theories to explain crime, rather than relying on a single "simple" theory. As integrative theorist Gregg Barak tells us, "the traditional or one-dimensional accounts, models, and explanations of crime and/or punishment that have tended to divide human beings and society into biological, cultural, psychological, or sociological entities, at best, are [only] partially correct.... [B]y the turn of the twenty-first century, the integrative paradigm had become the newly emerging paradigm in criminology and penology."[23] For example, many integrative theories combine biological (nature) and sociological (nurture) theories. Similarly, an integrative theory can combine both experiences during childhood and adolescence (differential association theory) with experiences that occur later in life (differential reinforcement theory) to attempt to explain criminal behavior.

Multifactor Theory

One of the more influential integrative theories of criminology is multifactor theory, developed by Sheldon (1896–1980) and Eleanor (1898–1972) Glueck, a married couple who both worked at Harvard Law School and were prolific researchers and authors. Through interviews with large groups of incarcerated men and women, as well as juvenile delinquents, they developed a theory of criminal behavior that was holistic, embracing psychological, emotional, physical, and environmental factors. In essence, shortcomings in these factors can lead to criminal activity, yet policy makers and governmental and nongovernmental agencies can address many of these shortcomings to reduce the number of people who initially engage in crime as well as prevent recidivism. Of particular importance on the issue of recidivism, the Gluecks conducted longitudinal studies, interviewing their subjects at several different times over a period of years, as demonstrated in the titles of two of their books, *One Thousand Juvenile Delinquents* and *Juvenile Delinquents Grown Up,* published in 1934 and 1940 respectively.

In 1950 the Gluecks produced a "Social Prediction Table" that examined five factors that they argued affect the propensity of a male child to become a juvenile delinquent: discipline by the father, supervision by the mother, affection of the father, affection of the mother, and family cohesiveness. Five years later, they introduced a table that ignored the father and focused on just three factors: supervision by the mother, discipline by the mother, and cohesiveness of family. Looking at those factors for each boy studied, the Gluecks assigned a "weighted failure score." For example, if Junior scored 200 or above on the three-factor table, the Gluecks estimated that he had an eighty-nine percent chance of becoming a delinquent. While their prediction table has not proven to be particularly accurate, the Gluecks's pioneering work has been useful for the later efforts of others in prediction studies.[24]

Life Course Theory

In the 1980s, Harvard social scientist Robert J. Sampson (born 1956) and John Laub (born 1953) now at the University of Maryland, began using data collected by the Gluecks on hundreds of disadvantaged males born in the Boston area during the Great Depression to analyze the life experiences of those men since then. With an emphasis on nurture over nature, life course theory argues that people are unique individuals yet share some common experiences. Some of those experiences mark trajectories or turning points that affect the person's likelihood of engaging in crime. Unfortunately yet commonly, these experiences can occur when the person is quite young, such as growing up in a dysfunctional household. Life course theory also looks at negative experiences that may cause those who have engaged in criminal behavior to continue to do so (persist) or positive experiences that cause them to stop (desist).

What criminologists have long realized is that there is no single explanation for criminal behavior, and the complexity of the most recent theories arises in part from their multidisciplinary approach. Criminological theory today "has roots in wider disciplinary inquiry," embracing sociology, social psychology, psychology, economics, political science, philosophy, biology, and anthropology, among numerous other areas of inquiry.[25]

Having briefly surveyed some of the theories of why people commit crimes, we next look at some of the prevailing reasons why society punishes criminal offenders.

Why Do We Incarcerate?

We are told from early in our lives that few things are more important than our freedom and liberty. When the government decides to take away a person's liberty and remove that person from free society, it is based on the determination that the person presents a danger to others. Society and government attempt to promote a number of goals through incarceration. These include incapacitation, retribution, specific and general deterrence, treatment, rehabilitation and reformation, and reentry with reintegration. Rather than being mutually exclusive, these goals can be (in our minds, should be) pursued concurrently.

Incapacitation

While incarcerated, prisoners have great difficulty in committing crimes against free members of society; they are incapacitated from doing so. Incapacitation does not necessarily protect inmates and correctional officials during the period of incarceration. Some inmates commit violence against others in correctional facilities and may victimize other inmates through theft, extortion, and fraud. Some inmates are able to engage in criminal conspiracies with co-conspirators who are not in prison.

Generally, however, the drug dealer who sold illegal drugs in a school zone, the burglar who broke into homes and offices, and the robber who held up banks are unable to ply their trades while locked up. Thus, incarceration successfully serves its primary goal of incapacitating criminals. However, the cost of incarceration is high, with inmates unable to contribute to the support of their families and themselves. In 2010, the estimated cost of incarceration in U.S. state prisons averaged $31,286; in several states, the average cost to house a prisoner annually exceeded $50,000.[26] Five states, Vermont, Michigan, Oregon, Connecticut, and Delaware, spent more on prisons in 2008 than they did on their public colleges and universities.[27] In 2011, it cost New Jersey $44,000 to incarcerate a prisoner; tuition at New Jersey's prestigious and private Princeton University was $37,000 that year.[28]

Because many inmates enter prison in poor health due to substance abuse and other personal welfare issues, and because prison life itself is highly stressful, correctional expenditures for medical care are significant. Thirty-five of the forty-four states that participated in a Bureau of Justice Statistics study reported an increase in per capita medical costs from 2001 to 2008, with five reporting increases of 100% or more.[29] Compounding the problem is the aging of the American prison population. Because of prisoners' pre-existing conditions and the stress of prison, many correctional agencies consider prisoners 50 years and older to be elderly. Despite the popular belief otherwise, many prisoners serving life sentences die in prison, with expensive geriatric care paid for by us, the taxpayers.

Beyond its cost, another problem with incapacitation is its long-term ineffectiveness. The common formula for incapacitation of criminal offenders is custody, confinement, and control. The cheapest way to incarcerate people is to warehouse them, keeping them in their cell for as many hours a day as possible. Anytime inmates move out of their cells, additional supervision is required, and personnel costs represent by far the largest share of correctional budgets, with payroll and employee benefits typically comprising sixty to seventy percent of correctional spending.[30] Thus, educational and training programs, behavioral therapy (which includes therapy for substance abuse, self-esteem, and anger management) and work programs are often viewed as too expensive, especially by the general public and the politicians they elect.

Incapacitation works during the period of incapacitation, but we need to look at the long term—does locking somebody up for some period of time make that person less likely to commit crimes upon release? A complicating factor here is that removing somebody from free society for a while makes it even harder for that person to readjust to free society, to find employment, and to attain a comfortable situation in the community. After all, the last time prisoners were in free society, they screwed up. That's why they went to prison; are we making them better able to function in free society after incarceration than they were before incarceration?

Deterrence

Deterrence takes two forms. General deterrence uses the punishment of criminals as a reminder to the rest of us that if we break the law, we are subject to punishment as well. A simple example: assume that you are traveling down the highway one morning. You have not been paying much attention to your speed, so it's a safe bet that you're speeding. Up ahead on the right side of the road, you see a police cruiser with its lights on. A few yards in front of the cruiser, you see a car with a noticeably unhappy driver. When you see the police car's lights, you instinctively take your foot off the accelerator and softly tap the brakes. You do not want to be the next motorist pulled over for speeding. Perhaps you monitor your speed more carefully as you continue your journey. Perhaps you travel under the speed limit until you can no longer see the police car's lights, and then resume your previous speed. Witnessing another motorist being punished for speeding makes you more careful about your own speed, at least for a while. This is general deterrence—witnessing the punishment of others had an effect on your own behavior.

Specific deterrence is directed at the criminal. Society hopes that the punishment a criminal endures will deter that person from committing more crimes in the future. Let us take a brief look at the ultimate specific deterrent: the death penalty. If somebody commits a heinous murder in a state that executes those who commit heinous murders, that person may be executed, which is certainly a specific deterrent to further heinous murders by that individual. But does a state's use of the death penalty provide a general deterrent to other people in that state who are contemplating committing hideous murders?

Paxson lives in Massachusetts; Watson lives in Texas. Texas has used the death penalty more times than any other state, having executed over 500 people since 1976. Massachusetts has not had an execution since 1947, and currently does not have a law providing for the death penalty. The FBI reports that the murder and non-negligent manslaughter rate in Texas in 2012 was 4.4 per 100,000 people. In Massachusetts, the rate was 1.8 murders and non-negligent manslaughters per 100,000 people.[31]

We don't mean to say that the cultural, economic, and geographic situations in Massachusetts and Texas are similar. Texas has a poverty rate higher than the national average and some of the poorest counties in the nation while Massachusetts's poverty rate is lower than the national average.[32] Texas is among the lowest states in terms of economic mobility; Massachusetts is among the highest,[33] while at the same time Texans demonstrate higher geographic mobility than the national average, while Massachusetts residents demonstrate less.[34] Texas has the lowest percentage of adults twenty-five or older with a high school diploma among all fifty states, while Massachusetts leads the nation in adults twenty-five or older with baccalaureate and advanced degrees.[35] The point is that the propensity of Texas to execute killers hasn't made that state a safer one than Massachusetts, which hasn't executed in more than half a century. Moreover, the difference in the homicide rates between Texas and Massachusetts isn't based on how those two states punish criminals, but on the social conditions that contribute to criminal activity—conditions that no punishment nor any prison can fix.

Life's experiences provide much of the basis for general deterrence. (Many of us begin discussing particularly troubling periods in our lives with the phrase, "Well, I learned a lot.") There is no question that knowledge of the consequences of our actions affects our behavior. This helps explain why crime is more likely to be committed by younger people, who are less likely to consider consequences due to immaturity and inexperience. We don't let people drive until they are sixteen, drink alcohol until they are twenty-one, or, typically, rent a car until they are twenty-five. (Nevertheless, all fifty states allow, and in some situations require, juveniles accused of crimes to be tried in adult courts under certain circumstances.[36])

In our brief survey of criminological theories earlier in this chapter, we devoted much of that discussion to an attempt to debunk rational choice theory. This is because in Paxson's more than twenty-five years of teaching criminal justice courses, he has found that the great majority of his students attribute criminal behavior to rational choice theory—that people make a conscious and considered decision to engage in crime. As Paxson's dean, a former prosecutor, has told him, if rational choice theory adequately explained the bulk of criminal activity, then punishment would work as a general and specific deterrent. But, as we can see from our nation's high recidivism rates (with nearly two-thirds of current prisoners having served sentences for other crimes in the past) our current correctional system does not successfully deter criminal behavior.

Retribution

Retribution is known as "an eye for an eye," or "just deserts." The fancy phrase for this is "societal vengeance." In sociological terms, members of a society reinforce social norms by punishing those who violate them. Deviance is acting outside the norms, or acting in a way that is considered socially unacceptable. Not all deviant acts are treated as criminal wrongs. A man wearing a dress isn't against the law, but it may cause others to ostracize him. Noisily passing gas in a crowded elevator won't win you any friends, but it's not a crime. When legislatures determine that deviance is not merely a nuisance, but decisively or potentially harmful to society, deviance is criminalized by legislation.

Criminal law distinguishes between crimes that are *mala prohibita* and *mala in se*. Crimes that are considered *mala prohibita* are prohibited largely for the purpose of social order rather than for moral reasons. For example, for several decades it was against the law to give someone a tattoo in Massachusetts. This law was passed in the wake of a hepatitis epidemic. Years later, as widespread knowledge about the need for hygienic practices arose during the AIDS epidemic, Massachusetts lawmakers rescinded the tattoo prohibition. Laws that prohibit the sale and possession of marijuana are also based on the concept of *mala prohibita*. Selling marijuana remains a crime in most states, but this is no longer true throughout the country.

On the other hand, *mala in se* offenses are morally wrong; they are evil. Rape, murder, and mayhem fall within this category. While humans in general and Americans in particular may have divergent views of whether certain acts should be crimes, acts that fall within the category of *mala in se* are nearly universally despised. For example, most Americans did not personally know somebody who died in the terroristic bombing of the Murrah Federal Building in Oklahoma City in 1995, nor did most Americans personally know somebody who died in the attacks of 9/11. Nevertheless, most Americans wanted those responsible for those acts held accountable.

Speaking again about the death penalty, a majority of Americans consistently respond that they favor the use of the death penalty in certain situations. When asked, "Are you in favor of the death penalty for a person convicted of murder?" a majority of those polled by the Gallup organization have consistently answered affirmatively since 1976. Since 2001, a majority of Americans have also answered that they find the death penalty morally acceptable.[37] Thus, while we cannot say with certainty that the death penalty serves the goal of general deterrence, it does serve the goal of retribution in the U.S.

Notice that retribution isn't a means of correction. What's best for the prisoner in terms of helping that person become a law-abiding member of society is ignored. Retribution punishes the offender with the goal of appeasing society—the punishment of the individual is simply a means of achieving what is perceived to be a greater social good. As discussed in Chapter 1, the writings of Robert Martinson and James Q. Wilson in the last quarter of the twentieth century caused many to give up on shaping criminals into better people, focusing instead on warehousing them.

Rehabilitation, Reformation, and Reentry with Reintegration

Rehabilitation

We talk about these goals together not because they're alliterative, but because, when done well, they operate synergistically, providing additional energy to the other goals.

Rehabilitation is changing the way people think: the way they think about themselves and those around them. Part of the rehabilitative process is overcoming negative self-fulfilling prophesies; if a person thinks that s/he is a loser, that person will act like a loser. Paxson has met several people with "Born to Lose" tattoos, and others with teardrop tattoos. One thing those folks had in common was that they were indeed losers. Obviously, the challenge is to get this type of person to have a more positive outlook about their abilities and their prospects in life. If one's perception is that he is a loser, adding the extra handicap of a criminal record only exacerbates the problem.

Another challenge is overcoming a person's belief in an external locus of control, which is a fancy way of saying the belief that they have little or no control of the outcome of events in their lives. The key here is to help that person understand that consequences are often the result of one's actions, which means that person does have some control of the outcome, whether positive or negative.

Julian B. Rotter (1916–2014) was the most influential scholar of locus of control theory. Rotter taught psychology at the Ohio State University and the University of Connecticut. In 1954, he published *Social Learning and Clinical Psychology,* in which he argued that personality is essentially the interaction between a person and the environment.[38] Rotter's 1966 monograph, "Generalized Expectancies for Interval Versus External Control of Reinforcement" introduced the Internal-External Locus of Control Scale.[39] People characterized as having an external locus of control attribute much of what happens to them in life as the product of fate or luck. Those characterized as having an internal locus of control attribute their experiences as the function of their behavior.

Paxson had a client in Cambridge, Massachusetts, whose probation officer wanted to have his probation revoked and have the client incarcerated. Paxson's conversation with the client went something like this:

> Paxson: "Your probation officer wants you to come in to see her every Tuesday morning at ten o'clock. You don't have a job, so you should be able to fit that in your schedule. You don't have a car, but the pro-

bation office is just two blocks from the Green Line trolley stop, and you've got a trolley pass, so transportation isn't a problem. Now, she wants you to take a pee test every week to check you for drugs. Of course, you want to pass the test to stay out of prison. What do you say?"
Client: "I'll try."
Paxson: "You've got to do more than try. You've got to stay clean and show up on time every Tuesday morning."
Client: [blank look and silence]

Some correctional officials believe that the only thing that really helps rehabilitation is the aging process. Many criminals "age out" of crime, weary of the stress of the lifestyle (crime is a highly stressful occupation) and tired of being locked up. In this sense, incarceration does contribute to rehabilitation, as for every year a prisoner is incarcerated, the prisoner grows a year older. One of the more deliberate ways of trying to rehabilitate criminals is the reformation process.

Reformation

Reformation seeks to change the criminal's situation in life. If a criminal lacks marketable skills, s/he can be offered adult basic literacy training, vocational training, completion of high school with either a diploma or a GED, and perhaps college course credits. The correlation between lack of education and incarceration is significant. A study conducted for the U.S. Bureau of Justice Statistics found that, "About 41% of inmates in the nation's state and federal prisons and local jails in 1997 and 31% of probationers had not completed high school or its equivalent. In comparison, 18% of the general population age 18 or older had not finished the 12th grade."[40]

If a criminal has marketable skills but is using them for criminal purposes those skills can be redirected into legal activities. For example, many drug detailers are self-employed business people with a thorough understanding of supply and demand and marketing. Because many employers are hesitant to hire job-seekers with criminal records, some ex-offenders find it best to seek self-employment upon release. To facilitate this, some governmental and private organizations have established entrepreneurial training programs for ex-offenders.

If drug or alcohol abuse contributes to an offender's criminal activity, this can be addressed through a variety of relatively effective programs. If a criminal struggles with anger management issues, therapy can address them. Reformation takes place through these and other processes (which we discuss in more detail in Chapter 7) with the goal of contributing to the rehabilitation process. The high school dropout who thinks that s/he is a loser can become a graduate; the person with a dependency on harmful drugs or alcohol can stop being dependent.

Reentry with Reintegration

The vast majority of prisoners are serving less than life sentences and will be released from prison. Reentry is the process of getting a prisoner ready to return to free society. Spending twenty or more hours in a cell each day hardly replicates real life. In real life, people have to work to support themselves, find a place to live, manage a household (cleaning, laundry, cooking), and interact with others in a variety of environments. Reentering prisoners suffer from several disadvantages. First, all reentering prisoners have criminal records that make finding suitable employment and adequate housing more difficult. Many reentering prisoners also lack adequate education, job skills, and employment histories. A significant number of reentering prisoners have health and substance abuse problems.

Prison industries offer a chance for prisoners to earn some money and learn marketable skills. However, many labor organizations and industry groups oppose prison industries that compete against private sector businesses. Commercial enterprises fear being undersold due to the relatively cheap cost of prison labor, with many prisoners earning less than a dollar an hour. Accordingly, many prison industries provide goods and services primarily to government agencies. These include traffic signs, agricultural products, office furniture and supplies, janitorial supplies, vehicle maintenance, uniforms (for both law enforcement and the people they arrest), and of course, license plates. In some states, prison industries may provide goods and services to not-for-profit organizations. According to the Federal Bureau of Prisons, "Inmates who worked in prison industries or completed vocational and apprenticeship programs were 24% less likely to recidivate and 14% more likely to be gainfully employed."[41] However, due to heavy lobbying by some industry groups, members of Congress occasionally draft bills to limit and restrict prison labor. This led to the creation of the Prison Industry Enhancement Certification Program, by which the U.S. Bureau of Justice Assistance certifies that local or state prison industry programs fall under exemptions from federal restrictions on prison industries.

Work release allows the prisoner to earn wages, interact with others, and function within the context of having bosses and coworkers. Many of the "get tough" prison programs effectively infantilize prisoners, warehousing them in their cells rather than having them participate in cooking their food, washing their laundry, performing general maintenance of their environment, or working in a trade or occupation. The Federal Bureau of Prisons often places minimum-security federal prison camps adjacent to more secure facilities so that the prisoners at the minimum-security facilities can work in the more security facilities in a variety of capacities. Furloughs are also helpful to help prisoners transition back into the real world while still subject to conditions of release and supervision.

Many criminals have never held a "real job." They get out of bed when they want to, eat when they want to, and engage in criminal activities when the need for money presents itself. They often grew up in households with parents either unable to find or sustain suitable employment, or in households where criminal behavior was common among household members.

Americans who lack a college education are finding it increasingly difficult to find suitable employment in the post-industrial U.S. Reentering prisoners with criminal records find it even more difficult. However, when New York governor Andrew Cuomo announced in February 2014 that he wanted to spend $1 million of the state's $2.8 billion budget on providing college courses for state inmates, objections to Cuomo's plan were loud and swift. Some state legislators posted a "Hell No to Attica University" petition online. Three members of Congress from New York introduced a bill they called the "Kids before Cons" act that would forbid the use of federal dollars for higher education for incarcerated criminals. While the majority of New York legislators who opposed Cuomo's plan were Republicans, there was also opposition among Democrats. The first Democratic legislator to oppose Cuomo's plan publicly told reporters, "I feel a certain obligation to protect the public money and in my district I understand that this is not a popular sentiment. I have an obligation to represent the taxpayers."[42]

Within six weeks of his announcing the plan, Cuomo stated that he was no longer pursuing it. One of the more ridiculous criticisms of Cuomo's plan came from his opponent in the 2014 gubernatorial election, Rob Astorino, who said, "Maybe our 10-year-old son, we should sit him down and explain how to rob a bank."[43] (We're betting that Astorino would have decided against giving his son that talk, even if Cuomo's proposal proved successful.)

At the federal level, Pell Grants for both state and federal prisoners were eliminated in the Violent Crime Control and Law Enforcement Act of 1994, signed into law by Democratic president Bill Clinton. U.S. Senator Jesse Helms reflected congressional sentiment in his exclamation, "You may teach inmates how to fix automobiles. You may teach them how to write, certainly how to read. But a college education free of charge? Such a policy is an outrage."[44] Nevertheless, numerous college programs operate in American prisons today, supported through a complex mix of public and private funding. We discuss education's role in rehabilitation in more depth in Chapter 7.

The final, and most critical, state of reentry is reintegration: the release of the offender from the restrictions (as well as the support) of the corrections system. To facilitate this process, some correctional agencies have established programs such as the Hampden County (Massachusetts) After Incarceration Supports Program (AISS). The AISS identifies some of the challenges that ex-offenders face as they attempt to reintegrate into their community: "The majority of ex-offenders when released are faced with many problems ranging from lack of support, addiction, no place to live, no money, no job, no food, no clothes, no proper identification, no license, lack of confidence, fear of failure, inappropriate modeling by family/friends, constant temptation to return to criminal lifestyle, etc."[45] Successfully overcoming these obstacles proves challenging to both the ex-offender and the agencies that support them.

Restorative Justice

Restorative justice gained popularity in the 1990s thanks to the work of Howard Zehr and others. Zehr distinguishes retributive justice, which conceives of crime as being an offense against the state, which restorative justice, which conceives of crime as being an offense against people. Zehr outlines three basic principles of restorative justice, stating that a restorative justice response to crime:

1. Acknowledges and repairs the harm caused by, and revealed by, wrongdoing (restoration);
2. Encourages appropriate responsibility for addressing needs and repairing the harm (accountability);
3. Involves those impacted, including the community, in the resolution (engagement).[46]

We don't like using impact as a verb, but we would like to point out that restorative justice, when successful, serves two important purposes: it helps victims recover their (economic and psychological) losses after a crime, and it helps the offender recognize the consequences of the offender's actions on others. In cases where the victim bears a loss, the criminal cannot only restore that loss at least in part but also learn how that loss affected the victim. (Somebody steals your camera at the airport while you are returning from a family reunion. The camera can be replaced, but the last picture of you and your late, beloved Aunt Edna can never be.)

Of course, depending on the crime, many victims will not want to confront the criminal afterward, although Zehr discusses how restorative justice methods can be used even in cases of violent crime. In those cases, Zehr states that the offender is most likely to participate in the process while incarcerated and will not receive benefits such as good time, parole, etc., for participating. Thus, the offender who agrees to participate does so without creating the perception that the offender is merely trying to game the system. Zehr also discusses using a panel of victims who suffered similar types of offenses as those committed by the prisoner to have the prisoner hear about the impact those offenses have had on their lives. This reduces the stress of the victim having to face his or her actual assailant.[47]

A History of U.S. Prisons

In American criminal justice literature, histories of U.S. prisons tend to focus on two topics: the design and condition of the facilities, and the programs and daily routines inside those facilities. While it becomes most apparent how the underlying philosophies of corrections inform programming at a particular prison, the layout (or at least, the original layout) of a prison also reflects that prison's underlying philosophy. We identify some of the major paradigms of American prisons below. By paradigms, we mean a common way of thinking about something (epistemology) or doing something (praxis). Paradigms frequently shift over time, and this is certainly true of American prisons.

Imprisonment was relatively uncommon during the nation's early days. Capital punishment was used for a wide variety of crimes. During the colonial period, people were executed for murder, piracy, rape, treason, concealing birth, burglary, arson, counterfeiting, slave revolt, horse stealing, attempted rape, and attempted murder, among other crimes.[48] Executions were often staged in public. Those who were not executed would be fined, whipped, or branded. In small communities where residents were likely to know each other, public forms of humiliation were common, using the pillory or stocks, in which the offender's body was confined with the head and hands placed through holes in a wooden beam and passing townspeople could insult, spit upon, or throw rocks and other objects at the offender.[49] The primary emphasis during the colonial period was on retribution—punishment for the sake of appeasing others in the community. Secondary was general deterrence—public punishments were intended to deter others from committing crimes.

Colonial jails held people awaiting trial and also held debtors, as imprisonment for debt was common at the time. Vagrants and others seen as public nuisances could be sent to workhouses or houses of correction, where they were required to engage in hard labor and could be subject to whipping if they proved disruptive. If a prisoner had supportive family or friends with means, the prisoner could eat well and wear decent clothing. On the other hand, if the prisoner lacked such resources, time spent in a jail or workhouse was wretchedly miserable. These buildings were overcrowded, squalid, and often unbearably hot in the summer and frigid in winter.

The Pennsylvania System

After American independence, Pennsylvania was the first state to adopt methods of incarceration that were unlike previous colonial practices, due largely to the influence of Quakers and their (at the time) very progressive ideals. The Eastern Penitentiary opened in Philadelphia in 1829. Prisoners were kept apart from each other at all times, and were required to remain silent. This was perhaps the world's first institutionalized effort to change the future behavior of its prisoners. The term "penitentiary" arose from the belief that each prisoner would silently reflect on his past offenses and would seek penance for them, and that it would be best to isolate prisoners from the corrupting influences of each other and the outside world.

The Auburn System

New York abolished capital punishment for all offenses except murder and treason in 1796. This created a need for prisoner housing. The first state facility was built at Newgate at what is now West 10th Street in New York City's Greenwich Village. Although its Quaker warden Thomas Eddy attempted to use humanitarian methods to rehabilitate prisoners, the facility quickly grew overcrowded. At the second New York state prison, the Auburn Penitentiary in the Finger Lakes region, the administration modified the Pennsylvania system of separation with what became known as the Auburn system, also known as the congregate system. At Auburn, prisoners worked and ate together (albeit under enforced silence) and slept in solitary confinement at night. Although it seems to be only common sense today, the Auburn system was revolutionary in that it categorized offenders based upon the nature of their crimes and upon their behavior while incarcerated. Auburn also introduced the striped uniform and the lockstep method of marching that moved prisoners together in silence. Prison sentences were typically determinate sentences—a fixed period of years, with the entire sentence to be served. The Pennsylvania and Auburn systems represented the leading paradigms for American prisons in the nineteenth century.

In 1831, Alexis de Tocqueville and Gustave de Beaumont were sent by the French government to tour the U.S. and examine its prison reform efforts. News about the Pennsylvania separate system and the Auburn congregate system had reached Europe, and the French political climate at the time was such that both men thought it best to leave home for a while. The pair visited numerous prisons and political leaders; during their nine-month tour, they traveled through seventeen of the then twenty-four states, and met the sitting president, Andrew Jackson, as well as former president John Quincy Adams.

The first English translation of Beaumont and Tocqueville's *On the Penitentiary System in the United States and Its Application in France* was published in Philadelphia in 1833, with Beaumont doing much of the writing, relying on Tocqueville for gathering facts. They found the conditions they witnessed in Louisiana disturbing. "The place for convicted criminals in New Orleans cannot be called a prison: it is a horrid sink, in which they are thronged together, and which is fit only for those dirty animals found here together with the prisoners."[50]

However, the pair also encountered some correctional practices that they believed should be emulated in France. They were particularly impressed during their visit to the Eastern Penitentiary in Philadelphia in 1831, and lauded its policy of solitary confinement and complete silence among inmates:

> Thrown into solitude [the prisoner] reflects. Placed alone, in view of his crime, he learns to hate it; and if his soul be not yet surfeited with crime, and thus have lost all taste for any thing better, it is in solitude, where remorse will come to assail him … Can there be a combination more powerful for reformation than that of a prison which hands over the prisoner to all the trials of solitude, leads him through reflection to remorse, through religion to hope; makes him industrious by the burden of idleness.[51]

Eleven years after Beaumont and Tocqueville's appraisal of American prisons, Charles Dickens published his *American Notes for General Circulation*. Dickens also visited several American prisons, including the Eastern Penitentiary, but unlike the earlier French visitors, Dickens was horrified, writing:

> In the outskirts, stands a great prison, called the Eastern Penitentiary: conducted on a plan peculiar to the state of Pennsylvania. The system here, is rigid, strict, and hopeless solitary confinement. I believe it, in its effects, to be cruel and wrong.* In its intention, I am well convinced

---

* Some 170 years later, the use of solitary confinement remains a controversial yet common practice in American correctional facilities. This practice includes some juvenile and mentally ill offenders. In May 2014, U.S. Representative Cedric Richmond of Louisiana introduced a bill to develop and implement national standards for the use of solitary confinement in U.S. prisons, jails, and juvenile detention facilities. The bill was referred to the

that it is kind, humane, and meant for reformation; but I am persuaded that those who devised this system of Prison Discipline, and
those benevolent gentlemen who carry it into execution, do not know
what it is that they are doing. I believe that very few men are capable
of estimating the immense amount of torture and agony which this
dreadful punishment, prolonged for years, inflicts upon the sufferers.[52]

Ultimately, the failure of the policies and practices instituted at the Eastern
State Penitentiary were not due to the isolation of prisoners but overcrowding. This forced the doubling up of prison cells and the end of solitude. Single-
bunk cells simply proved a luxury that states could not afford.

Southern Prisons in the Second Half of the Nineteenth Century

The Southern system of corrections achieved its worst notoriety in the wake
of the Civil War. The first "Black Code," or legislation designed to limit the
rights of newly freed slaves, was enacted in Mississippi in 1865. Part of the law
stated that, "all freedmen, free Negroes, and mulattoes in this state over the
age of eighteen years found on the second Monday in January 1866, or thereafter, with no lawful employment or business, or found unlawfully assembling
themselves together either in the day or nighttime ... shall be deemed vagrants."[53] Although the statute only permitted incarceration for up to ten days,
the fine was up to $150; because the fine could not be paid, the debt had to be
worked off.

The convict leasing system often placed prisoners in quickly and crudely
erected work camps. This helped alleviate prison overcrowding, as many prison
facilities had been damaged or destroyed during the war. Leased prisoners were
used to help rebuild much of the infrastructure. As African-American author
and civil rights activist Ida B. Wells (1862–1931) said of the system:

The Convict Lease System and Lynch Law are twin infamies which
flourish hand in hand in many of the United States. They are the two
great outgrowths and results of the class legislation under which our
people suffer to-day. Alabama, Arkansas, Florida, Georgia, Kentucky,
Louisiana, Mississippi, Nebraska, North Carolina, South Carolina,
Tennessee and Washington claim to be too poor to maintain state con-

---

House Judiciary Subcommittee on Crime, Terrorism, Homeland Security, and Investigations,
where it died without being passed into law.

victs within prison walls. Hence the convicts are leased out to work for railway contractors, mining companies and those who farm large plantations. These companies assume charge of the convicts, work them as cheap labor and pay the states a handsome revenue for their labor. Nine-tenths of these convicts are Negroes.[54]

Wells cited the work of author George Washington Cable. Cable read a paper at the 1883 National Conference of Charities and Correction in Louisville, stating that under the convict lease system, "the possession of a convict's person is an opportunity for the state to make money; that the amount to be made is whatever can be wrung from him."[55] The economics of the convict lease system certainly favored the former slaveholder. As one contemporary observer at the Louisville conference put it, "Before the war we owned the negroes. If a man had a good nigger, he could afford to take care of him; if he was sick, get a doctor. He even might get gold plugs in his teeth. But these convicts: we don't own 'em. One dies, get another!"[56] As Michelle Alexander points out in her 2012 book *The New Jim Crow: Mass Incarceration in the Age of Colorblindness*, "Black people found themselves yet again powerless and relegated to convict leasing camps that were, in many ways, worse than slavery."[57] Not coincidentally, in Florida the supervision of prisoners was assigned to the Commissioner of Agriculture in 1877.[58]

Several Southern states came to depend on convict leasing as an important revenue stream. Historian Blake McKelvey tells us in *American Prisons: A History of Good Intentions* of an Alabama warden's advertisement of 1880 offering, "three grades of prisoners for contract, asking $5.00 per month for the 'full-hands,' $2.50 for 'medium-hands,' and nothing but their keep for 'dead hands [the sick and the elderly],' thus borrowing some well-known terms from slave traditions."[59] Sasha Abramsky notes in *American Furies: Crime, Punishment, and Vengeance in the Age of Mass Imprisonment*, "The resource-heavy Quaker system worked only by limiting prison admission to those convicted of the most serious crimes; the [convict leasing] system, by contrast, functioned best by sweeping up lower-level offenders *en masse* and then trading away their labor."[60] Convict leasing continued in most Southern states until the 1920s.

The National Prison Association and the Evolution of Prison Reform

In 1867, two members of the Prison Association of New York, Enoch Cobb Wines and Theodore William Dwight, published *Report on the Prisons and Reformatories of the United States and Canada*. Wines (1806–1979) was a Congregational minister. Dwight (1822–1892), grandson of a president of Yale, later became the founding dean of Columbia University's law school. Wines and Dwight visited prisons in eighteen states and found "there is not a state prison in America in which the reformation of the convicts is the one supreme object of discipline."[61] Their work informed the National Prison Congress held in Cincinnati in 1870; the National Prison Association, established at the conference, elected Ohio governor and future U.S. president Rutherford B. Hayes as the association's first president. Wines served as the association's first secretary and later organized the first international prison conference, the International Penitentiary Congress of London, held in 1872. The National Prison Association's Declaration of Principles emerged from its 1870 conference. The association defined punishment as "suffering inflicted on the criminal for the wrong done by him, with a special view to secure his reformation" and explained, "The treatment of criminals by society is for the protection of society. But since such treatment is directed to the criminal rather than to the crime, its great object should be his moral regeneration. Hence, the supreme aim of prison discipline is the reformation of criminals, not the infliction of vindictive suffering."[62]

The Reformatory

In his paper presented at the 1870 conference in Cincinnati entitled "The Ideal Prison System for a State," Zebulon Reed Brockway (1827–1920), then the superintendent of the Detroit House of Corrections, advocated for a classification process that evaluated an entering prisoner's chances for reform based on prior offenses and academic and vocational training needs. Under Brockway's model, prisoners would engage in industrial and agricultural activities together and would have access to a library, academic classes, and religious services. Brockway also called for indeterminate sentences that would allow prison officials to detain a prisoner for as long or as short a period deemed necessary to prepare the prisoner for successful reentry, and proposed parole as an intermediate means of reentry. Brockway has been called the "father of prison reform" and the "father of American parole."

Brockway was able to implement many of his proposals when he became the first superintendent of New York's Elmira Reformatory in 1876. As its name tells us, the Elmira prison reflected the shift from the penitentiary paradigm to the reformatory. Rather than treating all prisoners equally, the reformatory model sought to classify prisoners based on their likelihood of future criminal activity. It was also perhaps the first correctional institution in the U.S. to offer formal educational opportunities to prisoners. Prisoners entering Elmira were first-time offenders who were thirty years old or younger. They participated in a prison band, competed in athletic leagues, and published a prison newspaper, *The Summary*. However, the Elmira Reformatory had little success among many of its prisoners; tellingly, a chapter of Brockway's autobiography is devoted to Elmira's "Difficult Prisoners"[63] and the reformatory resorted to corporal punishment. By 1895, Brockway was known by some as Paddler Brockway, and the *Buffalo News* accused him of "wholesale and retail cruelty."[64] For his part, Brockway's autobiography discusses, "the aid of some physical collision that suddenly disturbs the [prisoner's] existent prevalent objectionable mood," namely, "the slap, or spanking,—offensively named 'paddling,'... chosen for this remedial use because of its safe, easy, accurate adjustment."[65] Despite its shortcomings, the Elmira Reformatory under Brockway's leadership is recognized as the first correctional facility in the U.S. aimed at the rehabilitation of prisoners.

The reformatory period marked the first American effort to design prisons and programming specifically for females. While female prisoners in many states remained in traditional custodial facilities, often in separate parts of male prisons, women's reformatories were intentionally separate facilities. Advocates for women's reformatories sought to teach female offenders to be genteel and domestic—in essence, to be ladylike. These facilities were viewed as particularly appropriate for younger offenders, although younger black females were more likely to be placed in custodial facilities. Separate facilities for female prisoners remained the exception, not the norm, in many states well into the twentieth century.

The Three Prisons Act of 1891 authorized the federal government to establish its first prisons; previously, federal civilian prisoners were contracted out to state and local facilities. In 1895, the U.S. War Department transferred control of the military prison at Ft. Leavenworth, Kansas, to the Justice Department. A second, newly built federal prison opened in Atlanta in 1902, followed by a third in an existing facility on McNeil Island in Puget Sound, Washington, in 1904.

The Twentieth Century's Big House

The early twentieth century saw a shift to "big house" prisons. Prisoners were often kept busy during the day, working in roadbuilding chain gangs, working in the fields, or performing other jobs within the facilities. While much of this work was monotonous, it did keep prisoners busy, and more importantly, the use of corporal punishment greatly diminished during the early twentieth century in most prisons, save for those in the South. Many facilities also dropped the practice of the lockstep march, allowing prisoners to move freely within the prison yard.

During the first half of the 1900s, many states began to embrace more individualized treatment of prisoners. Prisoners received incentives for good conduct. "Good time" rewarded prisoners with reduced sentences for good behavior while incarcerated. Indeterminate sentences became the norm in many states; rather than serving a sentence determined often arbitrarily by a trial judge, prisoners remained incarcerated for a period deemed appropriate for the individual by corrections authorities. The typical indeterminate sentence saw the judge provide a minimum period of incarceration with the prison board determining the maximum period based on the prisoner's behavior during incarceration. By 1925, forty-six out of the forty-eight states had instituted the use of parole, allowing supervised early release of prisoners who had proven themselves worthy.[66] Probation, first implemented in Massachusetts in the mid-1800s, and adopted by other states afterward, provided a supervised alternative to incarceration, and the National Probation Act of 1925 allowed federal courts to institute the practice.

Despite a burgeoning reform movement, many correctional facilities remained hellish. In this 1923 book, *Crucibles of Crime: The Shocking Story of the American Jail*, federal prison inspector Joseph F. Fishman describes the typical jail of the period:

> An unbelievably filthy institution in which are confined men and women serving sentence for misdemeanors and crimes, and men and women not under sentence who are simply awaiting trial. With few exceptions, having no segregation of the unconvicted from the convicted, the well from the diseased, the youngest and most impressionable from the most degraded and hardened. Usually swarming with bedbugs, roaches, lice, and other vermin; has an odor of disinfectant and filth which is appalling; supports in complete idleness countless thousands of able bodied men and women, and generally affords ample time and opportunity to assure inmates a complete course in every kind of viciousness and crime. A melting pot in which the worst elements of the raw material in the criminal world are brought forth blended and turned out in absolute perfection.[67]

Fishman distinguished jails from penitentiaries, with jails holding people until trial or for relatively short periods of incarceration, while penitentiaries held prisoners for longer sentences, but described similar conditions in both types of facilities. He found cells with no plumbing and prisoners relying on slop buckets instead. Fishman described New York's Sing Sing Prison, "When I was last there, in the latter part of January, 1922, the cellhouse was freezing cold. You could 'see your breath' when you talked. I was very uncomfortable, even with my overcoat on."[68]

The early years of the big house era saw an increasingly industrialized model of incarceration, with prisoners engaged in the manufacture of many items used in the prison and other items being sold in the marketplace. This industrialization was based on the same principle that underlies the convict lease system—a prison should pay for itself. However, as the Great Depression raged through the U.S. from the late 1920s onward, politicians grew concerned with prison industries' ability to undersell civilian enterprises. The Ashurst-Sumners Act of 1935 banned most prisoner-made goods from transport in interstate and foreign commerce. As a result, most prison industries focused on supplying governmental entities with items such as road signs and license plates.

The federal government's Public Works Administration arose as part of Franklin Delano Roosevelt's New Deal to fight the Great Depression. In addition to schools, libraries, bridges, and roads, the agency also built, expanded, or renovated prisons at the local, county, state, and federal level. Examples include the Federal Prison at Terre Haute, Indiana, the Georgia State Prison, and the Bronx County (New York) Jail.

The Federal Bureau of Prisons

Sanford Bates became the first director of the Federal Bureau of Prisons (BOP) in 1930. Prior to that time, federal prison wardens operated their prisons almost autonomously. Bates earned his law degree at what is now Northeastern University in 1906, served in the Massachusetts Legislature, and became the first commissioner of the Massachusetts Department of Correction in 1919. In Bates's first month as director of the BOP, all of its employees were transferred into the Civil Service system, replacing the previous political patronage system. In 1934, Bates implemented a system for classifying prisoners, the first of its kind in the U.S. This classification system attempted to incorporate a risk assessment of each prisoner, assigning prisoners to facilities with varying degrees of security, with the highest risk individuals sent to Alcatraz beginning in 1934. That same year saw the beginning of the Federal Prison Industries program, operating today as UNICOR, manufacturing goods with the federal government as its own customer.

Predictably, the economic pressures of the Great Depression, which began in 1928, coupled with some overlapping years of the lawlessness of Prohibition, repealed in 1933, led to a new peak in incarceration rates in the U.S. during the 1930s. Fifteen new federal correctional facilities opened during Bates's seven-year tenure as director. Although Bates stepped down as director of the Bureau of Prisons in 1937, he remained in charge of the Federal Prison Industries program until 1972.

Prisons Evolve into Correctional Institutions

The first modern correctional institutions appeared in the 1940s and 1950s. There were fewer deprivations and rules at these facilities than in the big house prisons. Recreational facilities and libraries became common, and educational and vocational programs were often offered, although many prisoners still spent much of their day in their cells or wandering around the prison yard. The evolving paradigm is reflected in the American Prison Association changing its name to the American Correctional Association in 1954, and the mid-century trend of prisons being renamed as correctional institutions.

The treatment model of incarceration, also called the medical model, first proposed earlier in the century began to take root in many of the world's prisons in the 1950s. This model advocated for treatment of the biological and psychological conditions that led prisoners to commit crimes. Rather than merely warehousing prisoners and perhaps trying to keep them occupied with busy work, correctional officials increasingly emphasized practices that relied on professional, specialized expertise and individualized programs. In many advanced nations, the treatment model of incarceration continues to evolve and serves as the basic philosophy of their correctional systems.

"Nothing Works" and Mass Incarceration

By the 1970s, American political leaders had grown skeptical of the treatment model and the highly publicized work of Robert Martinson and James Q. Wilson helped end the treatment model in the U.S. and the beginning of the mass incarceration movement, as discussed in Chapter 1.

The "nothing works" movement led to a rapid expansion of prison capacity in the U.S. The number of state prisons grew from 592 in 1974 to 1,023 in 2000. Texas built 120 prisons between 1980 and 2000. Among the top ten states in prison construction during that period, the number of prisons grew from 195 to 604.[69] At the federal level, the Bureau of Prisons increased its number of facilities from seventy in 1989 to 119 in 2014.[70] With the current abundance of prisons, modern facilities tend to be specialized.

Prisons Today

Podular (or modular) design represents the most recent prison paradigm. A reaction against the earlier big house design, inmates live in a collection of smaller, relatively self-contained facilities. Inmates are classified based on risk-assessment, including the risk of escape and the risk of reoffending upon release. Based on these assessments, prisoners are assigned to pods centered on the particular programming and security levels offered in each pod. These facilities tend to have a central atrium with cells arranged along the sides of the atrium. Inmates typically eat in the atrium area of their particular pod, and attend educational and therapy programs there as well. Inmates who are in work release programs will typically share the same pod, as would inmates involved in substance abuse treatment programs, etc. The pods are typically not arranged as rectangles. Triangular designs, in particular, isosceles triangles, are common. This geometry facilitates direct supervision by corrections officers, who can monitor the cells of the pod from a post at the base of the triangle. These officers work within the atrium in direct contact with the prisoners. Because the number of cells within a pod is relatively small, officers are likely to know inmates by name and are likely to be familiar with inmates' traits. Corrections officers in podular facilities rarely carry keys—commonly, doors are opened and closed electronically from a central station staffed with officers monitoring multiple cameras throughout the facility.

For prisoners considered particularly dangerous, the freedom of movement provided in a podular design is impractical. More secure facilities, called "control unit prisons," place prisoners in what is essentially solitary confinement. While some have argued that solitary confinement amounts to cruel and unusual punishment, advocates of control unit prisons state that the measures used are administrative rather than punitive. Advocates further state that placing the "worst of the worst" prisoners in control unit prisons allows other prisons to relax some security measures.

Federal prisons today are organized based on risk-assessment. Prisoners considered to be the least at risk for escape and possessing the best opportunity for reintegration are housed in federal prison camps. Prisoners incarcerated for particularly serious crimes are placed in federal penitentiaries. Between these two are federal correctional institutions. Those considered the highest-risk offenders are placed in administrative security facilities—these include the "supermax" prisons. As we discussed in the previous chapter, federal penitentiaries often have an adjacent federal prison camp, with camp inmates working in service occupations (such as janitorial work and food services) inside the more secure facilities where inmates spend most of their time in their cells.

Because of the paradigm shifts that prison programming and design have undergone over the past two centuries, and because there is rarely political pressure to modernize correctional facilities, there is a wide variety of prisons in use in the U.S. today. Some prisons still use facilities that were built in the nineteenth century; a single prison site often includes part or all of the original nineteenth century structure with various additions and satellite buildings that have been built over the years since. Often, despite the best intentions of the federal and state agencies that build prisons, the facilities become overcrowded, resulting in dangerous conditions for both staff and prisoners, and a decline in programming as facilities and staff are overwhelmed.

Conclusion

The history of humanity has long included human beings who deviate from the social norms of their particular societies and perhaps from the norms of human civilization in general. Many of the earliest explanations for deviant behavior focused on sin caused by demonic forces. The classical school embraced rationalism and attributed crime to conscious decisions made by those who elected to engage in crime. Biological, psychological, and sociological theories followed. Toward the end of the twentieth century and continuing today, contemporary criminology embraces increasingly complex theories grounded in a wide range of disciplines.

American correctional systems have long focused on deterrence and retribution—deterring the offender and others from future offenses, and assuring society that those who offend are punished. Rehabilitation is a more recent goal that, although out of favor during the "nothing works" period of the late twentieth century, remains a stated goal of many correctional agencies. Today there is increasing attention on preparing ex-offenders for reintegration into free society.

Despite the fact that deviant behavior has occurred throughout human civilization, prisons as we know them arose only since the founding of the United States. Because there is little political pressure to renovate or replace aging correctional facilities, the current inventory of facilities includes some that are more than 100 years old. This means that existing facilities have been built based on a variety of shifting correctional paradigms.

In the next chapter, we examine some of the correctional paradigms of other nations, comparing and contrasting them to American correctional theories and practices.

Notes

1. Clarence Ray Jeffery, *The Historical Development of Criminology*, 50 J. Crim. L. & Criminology 3 (1959): 3.

2. Auguste Comte, *Cours de philosophie positive: Tome 3, La philosophie chimique et la philosophie biologique*, (Paris: Bachelier, 1838).

3. Edwin H. Sutherland, *Criminology* (Chicago: University of Chicago Press, 1924).

4. Edwin H. Sutherland and Donald R. Cressey, *Principles of Criminology,* 6th ed., (Philadelphia: Lippincott, 1960): 3.

5. Cesar Beccaria, *Dei delitti e delle pene,* 1764, translated by E.D. Ingraham as *An Essay on Crimes and Punishments* (Philadelphia: H. Nicklin, 1819): 47.

6. Jeremy Bentham, *The Rationale of Punishment* (London: Robert Heward, 1830): 20.

7. John Scott, "Rational Choice Theory," in *Understanding Contemporary Society: Theories of the Present,* ed. Gary Browning, Abigail Halcli, and Frank Webster, (London: Sage, 2000): 126–127.

8. "Text: President Bush Addresses the Nation," *Washington Post,* September 20, 2014, http://www.washingtonpost.com/wp-srv/nation/specials/attacked/transcripts/bushaddress_092001.html.

9. John Dewey and James H. Tufts, *Ethics,* (New York: Henry Holt and Company, 1908): 436.

10. "Table F., U.S. Bankruptcy Courts–Bankruptcy Cases Commenced, Terminated and Pending During the 12-Month Periods Ending December 31, 2013 and 2014," (Washington, DC: U.S. Courts), http://www.uscourts.gov/uscourts/Statistics/BankruptcyStatistics/BankruptcyFilings/2014/1214_f.pdf.

11. Richard H. Thaler and Cass R. Sunstein, *Nudge: Improving Decisions about Health, Welfare, and Happiness,* (New York: Penguin, 2008).

12. Charles Goring, *The English Convict; A Statistical Study* (London: His Majesty's Stationery Office, 1913): 370.

13. Ibid.

14. Ibid., 371.

15. Havelock Ellis, *The Criminal,* (New York: Scribner and Welford, 1890): 208–209.

16. Buck v. Bell, 274 U.S. 200, 206 (1927).

17. Ellis, 233.

18. "Incarceration and the Family: A Review of Research and Promising Approaches for Serving Fathers and Families," (Washington, DC: U.S. Department of Health and Human Services, Office of the Assistant Secretary for Planning and Evaluation Administration for Children and Families/Office of Family Assistance, September 2008): 4-2, http://aspe.hhs.gov/sites/default/files/pdf/75536/report.pdf.

19. Stephen W. Patrick, Robert E. Schumacher, Brian D. Benneyworth, Elizabeth E. Krans, Jennifer M. McAllister, and Matthew M. Davis, "Neonatal Abstinence Syndrome and Associated Health Care Expenditures," *Journal of the American Medical Association* 307, no. 18 (May 9, 2012): 1934.

20. Michael J. Cannon, Yvette Dominique, Leslie A. O'Leary, Joseph E. Sniezek, and R. Louise Floyd, "Characteristics and Behaviors of Mothers Who Have a Child with Fetal Alcohol Syndrome," *Neurotoxical Teratol* 34, no. 1 (January–February 2012): 90–95.

21. Edward H. Sutherland, *Principles of Criminology,* 4th ed., (Philadelphia: Lippincott, 1947): 6–7.

22. Ronald L Akers and Wesley G. Jennings, "Social Learning Theory," in *21st Century Criminology: A Reference Handbook,* ed. J. Mitchell Miller, (Thousand Oaks, CA: Sage, 2009): 324.

23. Gregg Barak, "Integrative Theories, Integrating Criminologies," *Critical Criminology,* accessed June 30, 2015, http://critcrim.org/critpapers/barak_integrative.htm.

24. Kurt Weis, "The Glueck Social Prediction Table—An Unfulfilled Promise," 65 J. CRIM. L. & CRIMINOLOGY 397 (1974): 404.

25. Werner J. Einstadter and Stuart Henry, *Criminological Theory: An Analysis of Its Underlying Assumptions*, 2nd ed. (New York: Rowman and Littlefield, 2006): 28.

26. Christian Henrichson and Ruth Delaney, "The Price of Prisons; What Incarceration Costs Taxpayers," Center on Sentencing and Corrections, (New York: The VERA Institute of Justice, January 2012, updated July 20, 2012): 10, http://www.vera.org/pubs/special/price-prisons-what-incarceration-costs-taxpayers.

27. "One in 100: Behind Bars in America 2008," (Washington, DC: Pew Center on the States): 16, accessed June 27, 2015, http://www.pewstates.org/uploadedFiles/PCS_Assets/2008/one%20in%20100.pdf.

28. Brian Resnick, "Chart: One Year of Prison Costs More Than One Year at Princeton," *The Atlantic*, November 1, 2011, http://www.theatlantic.com/national/archive/2011/11/chart-one-year-of-prison-costs-more-than-one-year-at-princeton/247629/.

29. Tracey Kyckelhahn, "State Corrections Expenditures, FY 1982–2010," (Washington, DC: U.S. Bureau of Justice Statistics, December 2012, revised April 30, 2014): 6, http://www.bjs.gov/content/pub/pdf/scefy8210.pdf.

30. "Prison Costs; Opportunities Exist to Lower the Cost of Building Federal Prisons," (Washington, DC: General Accounting Office, October 1991): 5, http://www.gao.gov/assets/160/151231.pdf.

31. "State-by-State and National Crime Estimates by Year(s)," (Washington, DC: Federal Bureau of Investigation), accessed June 20, 2015, http://www.ucrdatatool.gov/Search/Crime/State/RunCrimeStatebyState.cfm.

32. "Income and Poverty in the United States: 2013—Tables & Figures," (Washington, DC: U.S. Census Bureau), accessed June 30, 2015, http://www.census.gov/hhes/www/poverty/data/incpovhlth/2013/tables.html.

33. Economic Mobility Project, "Economic Mobility of the States" (Washington, DC: Pew Charitable Trusts), accessed February 5, 2015, http://www.pewstates.org/research/data-visualizations/economic-mobility-of-the-states-85899381539.

34. "Migration/Geographic Mobility, State-to-State Migration Flows, 2013," (Washington, DC: U.S. Census Bureau), accessed June 30, 2015, https://www.census.gov/hhes/migration/files/acs/st-to-st/State_to_State_Migrations_Table_2013.xls.

35. "Education: Educational Attainment, Educational Attainment by State, 2009," (Washington, DC: U.S. Census Bureau), accessed June 30, 2015, http://www.census.gov/compendia/statab/2012/tables/12s0233.xls.

36. Patrick Griffin, Sean Addie, Benjamin Adams, and Kathy Firestine, "Trying Juveniles as Adults: An Analysis of State Transfer Laws and Reporting," (Washington, DC: U.S. Office of Juvenile Justice and Delinquency Prevention, September 2011), https://www.ncjrs.gov/pdffiles1/ojjdp/232434.pdf.

37. "Death Penalty," Gallup, accessed June 4, 2014, http://www.gallup.com/poll/1606/death-penalty.aspx.

38. Julian B. Rotter, *Social Learning and Clinical Psychology*, (Englewood Cliffs, NJ: Prentice Hall, 1954).

39. Julian B. Rotter, "Generalized Expectancies for Interval versus External Control of Reinforcement," *Psychological Monographs* 80 (1966): 1–28.

40. Caroline Wolf Harlow, "Education and Correctional Populations," (Washington, DC: U.S. Bureau of Justice Statistics, January 2003), http://www.bjs.gov/content/pub/pdf/ecp.pdf.

41. "UNICOR Fact or Fiction," (Washington, DC: Federal Bureau of Prisons), accessed June 30, 2015, http://www.unicor.gov/about/faqs/fact_fiction/.

42. "O'Brien First Senate Democrat to Oppose College in Prison," New York State of Politics, March 11, 2014, http://www.nystateofpolitics.com/2014/03/obrien-first-senate-democrat-to-oppose-college-in-prison/.

43. "Gov. Cuomo Drops the Ball," *New York Times*, April 8, 2014, http://www.nytimes.com /2014/04/09/opinion/gov-cuomo-drops-the-ball.html?_r=0.

44. Scott Baldauf, "Prison Education Rankles Critics," *Christian Science Monitor*, October 13, 1992, http://www.csmonitor.com/1992/1013/13121.html.

45. "Overview of the After Incarceration Support Systems Program (AISS)," (Springfield, MA: Hampden County Sheriff's Department), accessed June 27, 2015, http://www.hcsdmass.org/aiss.htm.

46. Howard Zehr, "Restorative Justice and Peacebuilding," *Zehr Institute for Restorative Justice* (blog), Eastern Mennonite University, April 20, 2009, http://emu.edu/now/restorative-justice/2009/04/20/restorative-justice-and-peacebuilding/.

47. Howard Zehr with Ali Gohar, *The Little Book of Restorative Justice*, (New York: UNICEF, 2003), http://www.unicef.org/tdad/littlebookrjpakaf.pdf.

48. M. Watt Espy and John Ortiz Smykla, *Executions in the United States, 1608–2002: The Espy File*, 4th ICPSR ed. (Ann Arbor, MI: Inter-university Consortium for Political and Social Research, 2004), http://doi.org/10.3886/ICPSR08451.v4.

49. Lawrence Friedman, "The Law of God and Men" in *Crime and Punishment in American History* (New York: Basic Books, 1993): 31–60.

50. G. de Beaumont and A. de Tocqueville, *On the Penitentiary System in the United States and Its Application in France*, (Philadelphia: Carey, Lea and Blanchard, 1833): 22, 51.

51. Ibid., 13, footnote 2.

52. Charles Dickens, *American Notes for General Circulation*, Volume I, 2nd ed. (London: Chapman and Hall, 1842): 238–239.

53. An Act to Amend the Vagrant Laws of this State, Mississippi Laws Chapter 6, section 2 (1865) found in Report of the Joint Select Committee to Inquire into the Condition of Affairs in the Late Insurrectionary States, Made to the Two Houses of Congress February 19, 1872: Testimony, Mississippi (Washington, DC: U.S. Government Printing Office, 1872), 886, https://books.google.com/books?id=tnQUAAAAYAAJ&pg=PA883&dq=%22an+act+to+amend +the+vagrant+laws+of+the+state%22&hl=en&sa=X&ei=o1O4VLffBtHksATYtYHQDw&ved=0C DgQ6AEwBA#v=onepage&q=%22an%20act%20to%20amend%20the%20vagrant%20laws%20of %20the%20state%22&f=false.

54. Ida B. Wells, Frederick Douglass, Irvine Garland Penn, and Ferdinand L. Barnett, *The Reason Why the Colored American Is Not in the World's Columbian Exposition: The Afro-American's Contribution to Columbian Literature*, ed. Robert W. Rydell (1893; Urbana; Chicago: University of Illinois Press, 1999): 26.

55. George W. Cable, *The Silent South Together with the Freedman's Case in Equity and the Convict Lease System* (New York: Charles Scribner's Sons, 1885): 124.

56. Hastings H. Hart, "Prison Conditions in the South," Proceedings of the Annual Congress of the American Prison Association (Indianapolis: Wm. M. Burford, Printer): 186–212, 200; Matthew J. Mancini uses the last words of this quotation as the title of his book on the convict lease system, *One Dies, Get Another* (Columbia: University of South Carolina Press, 1996).

57. Michelle Alexander, *The New Jim Crow: Mass Incarceration in the Age of Colorblindness*, revised ed. (New York: Free Press, 2012): 20.

58. "Timeline 1877–1895," (Tallahassee: Florida Department of Corrections), accessed June 27, 2015, http://www.dc.state.fl.us/oth/timeline/1877-1895.html.

59. Blake McKelvey, *American Prisons: A History of Good Intentions*, (Montclair, NJ: Patterson Smith, 1977): 202–203.

60. Sasha Abramsky, *American Furies: Crime, Punishment, and Vengeance in the Age of Mass Imprisonment* (Boston: Beacon Press, 2007): Kindle ed., chap. 2.

61. E.C. Wines and Timothy Dwight, *Report on the Prisons and Reformatories of the United States and Canada*, (Albany: Van Benthuysen & Sons, 1867): 287.

62. "Declaration of Principles," American Correctional Association, accessed June 27, 2015, http://www.aca.org/ACA_PROD_IMIS/docs/1870Declaration_of_Principles.pdf.

63. Zebulon Reed Brockway, *Fifty Years of Prison Service: An Autobiography* (New York: Charities Publication Committee, 1912).

64. Quoted in "Is Smelzer a Grabber?" *Elmira Telegram*, May 19, 1895, http://fulton-history.com/Newspaper4/Elmira%20NY%20Morning%20Telegram/Elmira%20NY%20Morning%20Telegram%201895%20Grayscale/Elmira%20NY%20Morning%20Telegram%201895%20Grayscale%20-%200343.pdf.

65. Brockway, 356–357.

66. Andrew Alexander Bruce, Albert James Harno, John Landesco, and Ernest Watson Burgess, *The Workings of the Indeterminate-Sentence Law and the Parole System in Illinois* (n.p, 1928): 48.

67. Joseph F. Fishman, *Crucibles of Crime: The Shocking Story of the American Jail*, (New York: Cosmopolis Press, 1923): 13–14.

68. Fishman, 37.

69. Sarah Lawrence and Jeremy Travis, *The New Landscape of Imprisonment: Mapping America's Prison Expansion*, (Washington, DC: Urban Institute, 2004): 8–9.

70. Nathan James, "The Federal Prison Population Buildup: Overview, Policy Changes, Issues, and Options," (Washington, DC: Congressional Research Service, 2014): 2; General Accounting Office, "Federal Prison Expansion: Overcrowding Reduced but Inmate Population Growth May Raise Issue Again," (Washington DC: General Accounting Office, 1993), http://www.gpo.gov/fdsys/pkg/GAOREPORTS-GGD-94-48/html/GAOREPORTS-GGD-94-48.htm.

Chapter 4

Is There a Better Way in Norway? The U.K.?

This chapter offers a comparative look at the differences between American correctional statistics and those of other nations. These statistical differences are the result of differences between American correctional policy and the correctional policies of other nations. As you will see, there are some stark contrasts.

United States as Outlier

In 2005, the U.S. Supreme Court was asked to consider in *Roper v. Simmons* the constitutionality of the use of the death penalty for defendants who were juveniles at the time of their criminal acts. In a five-to-four vote, the Court held that executing a person who was under the age of 18 at the time of the crime was unconstitutional, violating the Constitution's prohibition of cruel and unusual punishment. Writing for the narrow majority, Justice Anthony Kennedy noted that:

> only seven countries other than the United States have executed juvenile offenders since 1990: Iran, Pakistan, Saudi Arabia, Yemen, Nigeria, the Democratic Republic of Congo, and China. Since then each of these countries has either abolished capital punishment for juveniles or made public disavowal of the practice. In sum, it is fair to say that *the United States now stands alone in a world that has turned its face against the juvenile death penalty.*[1] (emphasis added)

There were two dissenting opinions. Justice Antonin Scalia, joined by Chief Justice William Rehnquist and Justice Clarence Thomas, criticized the majority for making

> itself sole arbiter of our nation's moral standards—and in the course of discharging that awesome responsibility purports to take guidance

from the views of *foreign courts and legislatures*. Because I do not believe that the meaning of our Eighth Amendment, any more than the meaning of other provisions of our Constitution, should be determined by the subjective views of five Members of this Court and *like-minded foreigners*, I dissent.[2] (emphasis added)

Scalia stated further that, "[t]hough the views of our own citizens are essentially irrelevant to the Court's decision today, the views of other countries and the so-called international community take center stage."[3]

Justice Sandra O'Connor wrote her own dissenting opinion, in which she stated:

Without question, there has been a global trend in recent years towards abolishing capital punishment for under-18 offenders. Very few, if any, countries other than the United States now permit this practice in law or in fact.... [However, b]ecause I do not believe that a genuine national consensus against the juvenile death penalty has yet developed, and because I do not believe the Court's moral proportionality argument justifies a categorical, age-based constitutional rule, I can assign no such confirmatory role to the international consensus described by the Court.... *Nevertheless, I disagree with Justice Scalia's contention ... that foreign and international law have no place in our Eighth Amendment jurisprudence. Over the course of nearly half a century, the Court has consistently referred to foreign and international law as relevant to its assessment of evolving standards of decency.*[4] (emphasis added)

Justice Kennedy's decision met with high-pitched criticism in the U.S. House Majority Leader Tom DeLay exclaimed on Fox News Radio, "We've got Justice Kennedy writing decisions based upon international law, not the Constitution of the United States. That's just outrageous, and not only that, he said in session that he does his own research on the internet. That is just incredibly outrageous."[5] Noted conservative commentator Phyllis Schlafly told a gathering of conservative leaders in Washington that Kennedy's opinion "is a good ground of impeachment."[6] Michael P. Farris, chair of the Home School Legal Defense Association, told the same gathering that Kennedy "should be the poster boy for impeachment" and that "If our congressmen and senators do not have the courage to impeach and remove from office Justice Kennedy, they ought to be impeached as well."[7]

Elsewhere, an article published in the *Irish Times* in the wake of the *Roper* decision commented that the willingness of American judges and other policy makers to observe international sentiments on how we treat offenders is "Ultimately ... a debate about whether America's strength lies in its historical independence from the whims of global society or from its leadership role therein."[8] The British magazine *The Economist* said of the *Roper* decision, "America may be happy to differ sharply from the world's other democracies on some moral and ethical issues, and this often irritates its closest friends. But this week's death-penalty ruling seems to show that even a superpower can sometimes be swayed, even if just a bit."[9]

Commenting on the domestic outcry that *Roper* evoked, Professor Michael E. Tigar of American University's Washington College of Law said in an address that federal courts "have a responsibility, in cases that come before them, to see that the United States is a law-abiding and respected member of the international community."[10]

At about the same time that the U.S. was debating whether juvenile offenders could be executed, France modified its juvenile laws, determining that a juvenile tried as an adult can receive no more than half of the sentence that would be incurred by an adult for the same offense.[11] In Japan, juveniles who commit crimes that could draw a life sentence if they were adults face a maximum term of fifteen years, and a maximum of ten years for lesser offenses (although there is current discussion to extend the maximum sentences to twenty and fifteen years, respectively).[12]

This book is not about the death penalty; the focus here is on incarceration, not execution. However, the fact that members of the U.S. Supreme Court have acknowledged that the American notion of what constitutes cruel and unusual punishment is discordant with the rest of the civilized world is remarkable. A majority of Americans consistently tell polling firms that they support the death penalty. Yet the U.S. is the only nation in the Americas that has the death penalty, and is among only twenty-two of the world's nearly 200 nations that used the death penalty in 2014.[13] Neither of our immediate neighbors, Canada and Mexico, will extradite a fugitive back to the U.S. if that fugitive is facing the death penalty. (Canadian officials refused to extradite Catherine Evelyn Smith to California to face homicide charges for the 1982 drug-related death of entertainer John Belushi until California assured that Smith would not face the death penalty.) A condition of membership in the European Union is prohibition of the death penalty; Turkey, seeking admittance to the EU, abolished its death penalty in 2004. Today, Belarus is the only European nation (of forty-seven) that still executes criminals.[14] Americans' embrace of the death penalty is merely one element of the peculiarly punitive nature of the American experience.

Americans Like to Punish

Alexis de Tocqueville and Gustave de Beaumont's work *On the Penitentiary System* was discussed in Chapter 3. Better known is Tocqueville's subsequent solo work, *Democracy in America*, first published in the U.S. in 1835. In it, Tocqueville wrote:

> [I]n no country does crime more rarely elude punishment. The reason is, that every one conceives himself to be interested in furnishing evidence of the act committed, and in stopping the delinquent. During my stay in the United States I witnessed the spontaneous formation of committees for the pursuit and prosecution of a man who had committed a great crime in a certain county. In Europe a criminal is an unhappy being who is struggling for his life against the ministers of justice, whilst the population is merely a spectator of the conflict; in America he is looked upon as an enemy of the human race, and the whole of mankind is against him.[15]

Tocqueville touched on a phenomenon that criminologists have labeled punitivity. Punitivity (it's not a common word) has four aspects. Legal punitivity looks at the sentencing range established by the statutes that have been passed by legislative bodies. Juridical punitivity is concerned with the sentences that are actually given to offenders in court. Operational punitivity is based on the actions of criminal justice agencies such as the police, corrections, probation, and parole. Finally, local punitivity is based upon the actions of local institutions, including employers, local government leaders, the media, and educational institutions; local punitivity is a measurement of how the attitudes a community has toward crime are shaped by those institutions while concurrently shaping those institutions.[16] It is this local punitivity that Tocqueville found characteristic of Americans.

Greta Olson, an Americanist teaching at the University of Giessen in Germany, sums it up nicely, "Punitivity may encompass policing policies that find more types of behavior to be criminal, harsher sentencing, worse conditions in prison, and greater stigmatization of criminals.... [A]ll of these aspects of punitivity apply to the American case."[17] Indeed, there seem to be significant factions within the U.S. that point to our high incarceration rate with pride, as it indicates an emphasis on the rule of law.

Punitivity Is Partly Politics

Comparative penologists Michael Cavadino, Iain Crow, and James Dignan have identified three general types of penal strategies in the world:

> Strategy A is an extremely harsh and punitive approach influenced by "law and order" ideology or "populist punitiveness" which involved punishing offenders as severely as possible. Strategy B represents the application of modern managerialism to punishment to attempt to make the criminal justice system as effective, efficient, and economical as possible. Strategy C seeks to protect and uphold the human rights of individuals, including offenders, victims, and potential victims of crime.[18]

Without question, the U.S. has firmly adopted Strategy A from this typology.

James Q. Whitman, a comparative law scholar at Yale, has written extensively about the differences between the American criminal justice system and the criminal justice systems of Western European nations. One key difference Whitman points to is how heavily politicized criminal justice policy is in the U.S.[19] As is discussed in the next chapter, it may be politically impossible to be too tough on crime in the U.S. This exacerbates the "populist punitiveness" that Cavadino, Crow, and Dignan identify as part of penal Strategy A, a term coined by Cambridge University penologist Sir Anthony Bottoms in 1995.[20] Numerous (it seems like nearly all) candidates for state legislatures and Congress, as well as candidates for governor and president, have tapped into the American public's antipathy for criminals for political gain.

This extends to all three branches of government. Thirty-nine states hold elections for the judges of general jurisdiction trial courts. Seventeen states hold elections for intermediate appellate court judges and another fourteen hold retention elections after intermediate appellate courts judges are initially appointed. Twenty-one states hold elections for judges of states' highest court (usually, but not always, called the state's Supreme Court) and another seventeen states have retention elections for those judges.[21]

On one hand, this is the way of democracy—*we the people* get to select or retain our judges. On the other hand, judicial elections are "down ballot" elections about which relatively few voters are fully informed. Judges and those who want to become judges know that appearing soft on crime can hurt them at election time. The worst nightmare of any trial court judge who is facing an election is a convicted defendant engaging in a high profile crime after serving the sentence handed down by that judge. Thus, it is understandable that when in doubt, trial judges often err in favor of longer sentences for defendants. For appellate judges, the fear is reversing the conviction of a defendant for what laypeople perceive as "mere technicalities" and thus being seen as soft on crime. (Both authors are lawyers who tell you that the law is *all about* technicalities.)

The framers of the U.S. Constitution were apprehensive about the effect of politics on the federal judiciary. While Article I set out rules for the election of members of Congress (modified by the Seventeenth Amendment, which decreed popular election of U.S. Senators) and Article II establishes the rules for the election of the President, Article III gives federal judges lifetime appointments. Article III also states that judges' compensation "shall not be diminished during their continuance in office," which prevents Congress from punishing judges through salary cuts. The goal is judicial independence, allowing federal judges to make decisions that are legally correct even when politically unpopular. (This chapter begins with a discussion of calls to impeach U.S. Supreme Justice Anthony Kennedy in the wake of *Roper v. Simmons*.)

Nevertheless, appointed judges often work in an intensely politicized environment. For example, in June 2015, there were fifty-nine vacant federal judgeships, some of which had been vacant for several years, particularly in states represented by two Republican U.S. Senators.[22] With a Democratic president in office and a Republican controlled U.S. Senate, which must approve presidential appointments, judicial appointments have been one of the more notable examples of gridlock in Washington. When the Democrats controlled the Senate earlier in Barack Obama's presidency, Republicans successfully used filibusters and other delaying tactics to prevent the approval of many Obama nominees.[23] Even in Massachusetts, commonly thought of as a liberal state, candidates for the Governor's Council, an elected body that must approve gubernatorial appointments, commonly vow to squelch the appointment of any judicial nominee who is supposedly soft on crime. (Despite Massachusetts's liberal reputation, gay and lesbian judicial nominees have also had to face additional scrutiny from the Massachusetts Governor's Council because of their sexuality.[24])

Because judicial positions in the U.S. are highly politicized, judges are under pressure to side (consciously or subconsciously) with the prosecution in a criminal case, as the public typically sees the prosecution as the right side in that case. Since American legislators who fund the criminal justice process must also appear to be tough on crime, they fund prosecutorial functions at a much higher rate than public defense functions relative to some other nations. The Justice Policy Institute found that:

> The United States spends .0002 percent of its per capita GDP on public defense per person. Comparatively, the United Kingdom budgets

.20 percent per person of its per capita GDP to defend people who cannot afford private counsel. Furthermore, the United States distributes resources in favor of prosecution, budgeting over twice the amount of money for prosecution as it spends on public defense. By contrast, the United Kingdom allocates approximately four times as much funding for public defense as it does for prosecution, while Finland spends more money on both sides but allocates more towards public defense than prosecution. Fewer resources for public defense likely affect quality of [counsel] and means more people may be found guilty and sent to prison.[25]

Remember also that many American prosecutors, including state attorneys general, state's attorneys, and district attorneys must seek voter approval to hold their offices, and a common campaign tactic is to characterize one's opponents for those offices as soft on crime.

By contrast, many European judges and prosecutors typically must engage in specialized training, often for a number of years, and then pass a qualifying exam, and may have to serve a probationary period before receiving permanent appointments. The appointments are made through a process this is roughly analogous to the U.S. civil service system, which arose from American efforts to replace politics and cronyism with hiring based on merit. As political scientist Mary L. Volcansek states in a *Fordham Law Review* essay on the appointment of European judges, "The virtues of the civil service model lie in its focus on training judges, protecting them from fickle political winds, and promoting the meritorious from within the judiciary."[26]

Punitivity Is Partly Sociological

Moving beyond politics, some scholars have strived to develop sociological theories to help explain why some nations have more punitive policies and practices than other nations. For example, sociologist Norbert Elias's civilization theory, discussed in his landmark 1939 book *The Civilizing Process*, suggests that as nations became more modernized and civilized, and attain better living conditions, people begin to internalize a sense of social control and are more likely to become tolerant of minor deviance. As a result, external (governmental) sanctions become less necessary, and civilized nations are likely to decriminalize some activities, reduce prison sentences, and emphasize alternatives to incarceration. If, as many Americans would like to believe, the U.S. is the most civilized and modern nation in the world, then according to Elias, the U.S would be among the world's least punitive nations. This is hardly the case.

Another sociological theory seems to align itself better with the American experience. British criminologists Leslie T. Wilkins and Ken Pease have theorized that there is a relationship between high incarceration rates and a high degree of income inequality.[27] (This theory presents itself in the title of Jeremy Reiman's oft-cited book *The Rich Get Richer and the Poor Get Prison.*) Quantitative work by German criminologists David J. Krus and Lenore S. Hoehl, using data from thirty nations, including the U.S., supports Wilkins and Pease.[28] The U.S. has the world's highest incarceration rate and high income inequality. Using the Gini index, which would score complete income equality at zero and complete income inequality at 100, the U.S. has a Gini co-efficient of 45.0. Among the 34 nations of the Organization for Economic Co-operation and Development (OECD), the U.S. has the fourth-highest inequality in distribution of family income, behind only Chile, Mexico, and Turkey.[29]

No single factor or theory explains American punitivity by itself. Nevertheless, the fact remains that the U.S. has the highest incarceration rate in the world, and that the U.S. tends to punish criminal offenders more severely than do many of the other developed nations of the world. We move next to comparative data, with some caveats.

Comparing Apples and Oranges: Definitional Problems

Definitional Problem #1: Defining Crime and Measuring Its Occurrence

Wide variances in the collection and interpretation of crime data make comparison among nations problematic. There are a little less than 200 sovereign nations in the world, each with its own criminal justice system. Each nation determines which commissions (doing something wrong, like robbing a liquor store) and omissions (not doing something that is legally required, like filing a tax return) constitute criminal behavior. Each nation develops methods of enforcing its criminal laws by creating law enforcement agencies, prosecutorial authorities, courts, correctional agencies, and alternatives to incarceration. These methods are often vastly different, and so are the methods of punishing people who break the law.

Cultural factors also influence whether crimes are reported. For example, rape and other types of sexual assault are highly stigmatized in many nations, including the U.S., and have been historically underreported. A high number of reported rapes in a particular nation might not necessarily reflect a high incidence of rape, but may be the consequence of a less-stigmatized cultural attitude toward sex crimes (or sex generally) or the result of victims trusting that nation's criminal justice system enough to come forward. Domestic violence is also underreported in many nations due to cultural attitudes about family relationships. Reliance on extrajudicial measures such as personal vengeance and group vigilantism instead of dependence on governmental criminal justice agencies is also common, particularly in underdeveloped nations.

Even if crimes are reported, there is still the issue of government officials recording those reports and compiling data based on those reports. The United Nations describes the problem:

> Lack of resources may often be considered the main obstacle to the collection and analysis of statistics. However, experts often suggest that lack of training, lack of commitment from the government, lack of proper legislation, fear of misuse of the data, or insufficient information on the good use that can be made of statistics may equally represent serious obstacles.[30]

With these limitations in mind, here is a selection of nations' crime rates and incarceration rates, according to the United Nations Office on Drugs and Crime and International Centre for Prison Studies.[31]

Figure 4.1. Crimes Reported and Incarceration Rates

Nation	Crimes Reported per 100,000 People	Incarceration Rate per 100,000 People
United States	3,730	698
Russian Federation	2,013	469
Israel	7,859	240
Portugal	3,779	137
China	287	119
Canada	8,304	118
Italy	940	86
Germany	7,651	76
Japan	1,609	49
India	445	33

Note that the U.S. and Portugal have roughly the same reported crime rate, yet the U.S.'s incarceration rate is five times higher. Are U.S. prisons that much less effective than Portugal's? If Portugal locked up as many criminals as the U.S. does per capita, would its crime rate plummet? Perhaps neither question is the correct one. As comparative criminologist Jerome L. Neapolitan tells us, "Past research has found little to no association between the amount or types of crimes in nations and either rates of imprisonment or use of capital punishment."[32] In other words, high incarceration rates cannot be attributed be to a high crime rate, nor does a low crime rate translate to a low incarceration rate. Now focus on the Germany, Israel, and Canada. Each has a reported crime rate that is much higher than that of the U.S., yet their incarceration rates are significantly lower. Then, what exactly do we mean by incarceration rates?

Definitional Problem # 2: Incarceration Rates

We will look at two different efforts to quantify the world's prison population, beginning with London's International Centre for Prison Studies (ICPS). This group, associated with the University of London, estimates that the world's prison population was between 10 and 11 million people in 2013.[33] The range in this estimate arises from the problem in determining if a person is being detained as a criminal. For example, political prisoners are often held on false claims of mental illness in some countries (where the view seems to be that if you publicly criticize a brutal authoritarian government, you must be crazy). In addition, millions of people are held for long periods before trial and many detainees have not even been formally charged, as not all nations have the requirement of the U.S. Constitution's Sixth Amendment that people "be informed of the nature and cause of the accusation," nor the Sixth Amendment's right to a speedy trial. Many nations also lack transparency on incarceration because of its political sensitivity. For example, researchers typically view official Chinese data on crime and punishment with skepticism.

That said, the ICPS estimates that the twenty highest incarceration rates in nations with over 100,000 inhabitants are as follows:[34]

Figure 4.2. World Incarceration Rates (per 100,000 people)

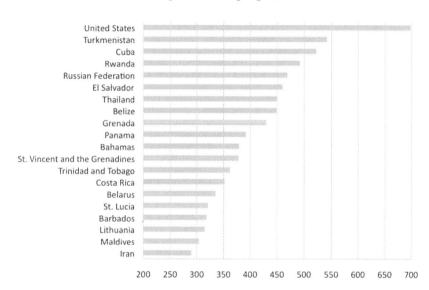

At first glance, this may seem to be a disparate collection of nations. However, notice that many of the nations listed are former island colonies (e.g., Grenada and Barbados) or former continental colonies that have attained independence since World War II (e.g., Rwanda and Belize). Russia and other former members of the U.S.S.R. (e.g., Turkmenistan and Belarus) are also on the list. These characteristics are shared among many of the nations that follow in the top fifty.

How can these common characteristics be explained? One is simply mathematical, as countries with small populations can have relatively few people incarcerated and yet generate a high incarceration rate. For example, Grenada, a former British colony in the Caribbean, had only 456 people incarcerated in 2013, but with only 110,000 inhabitants, the result is an incarceration rate that ranks seventh in the world among nations with at least 100,000 inhabitants. To compare, the U.S. has over two million people incarcerated and about 319 million inhabitants.

The fact that nations that formerly constituted the U.S.S.R. are among those with the highest incarceration rates likely reflects the historical, cultural, and political factors during previous decades of communist rule that contribute to those rates, in addition to political unrest in many of those nations since the breakup of the U.S.S.R. As we discussed above, cultural and political factors also contribute to the U.S.'s incarceration rate. That the U.S., the nation that has long celebrated itself as the apogee of human liberty, has a higher incarceration rate than the remnants of the "Evil Empire" of the repressive former Soviet Union should not go unnoticed.

Now we will look at data collected by the United Nations Office on Drugs and Crime (UNODC) on "persons held." The UNODC tells us that:

> "Prisons, Penal Institutions or Correctional Institutions" means all public and privately financed institutions where persons are deprived of their liberty. The institutions may include, but are not limited to, penal, correctional, and psychiatric facilities under the prison administration. "Persons Held" should exclude non-criminal prisoners held for administrative purposes, including persons held pending investigation into their immigration status and foreign citizens without a legal right to stay held prior to removal.[35]

Using this terminology, the UNODC tells us that the ten highest incarceration rates in 2010 in nations with over 100,000 inhabitants are as follows:[36]

Figure 4.3. UNODC Incarceration Rates

Nation	Incarceration Rate per 100,000 People
St. Vincent and the Grenadines	3235.1
United States	730.3
Bahamas	692.4
Russian Federation	573.1
Georgia	544.2
St. Kitts and Nevis	538.1
Chile	351.5
Botswana	349.0
Panama	345.5
Ukraine	338.9

You will notice that there are some considerable differences between the International Centre for Prison Studies' numbers and those of the UNODC, especially in the case of St. Vincent and the Grenadines. That small archipelago has only 103,000 inhabitants, which can cause great swings in statistical data. However, the U.S.'s incarceration rate is essentially the same in each ranking (thanks to relative transparency in U.S. government) and is still consistently much higher than most of the rest of the top ten.

Let us take a brief look at the region of the world that tends to have the lowest incarceration rates, Western Europe, more specifically Scandinavian nations, using the International Centre for Prison Studies' data.[37]

Figure 4.4. Scandinavian Incarceration Rates

Nation	Incarceration Rate per 100,000 People
Norway	71
Denmark	62
Sweden	60
Finland	57
Iceland	45

Clearly Scandinavian attitudes about crime and criminals are vastly different from those of the U.S.

If you are curious, yes, the U.S. also leads the world in number of females incarcerated per 100,000 people. Here are the world's top five nations for female incarceration, according to the U.N.:[38]

Figure 4.5. Female Incarceration Rates

Nation	Female Incarceration Rate per 100,000 People
United States	164.8
Botswana	124.1
Bahamas	108.5
Russian Federation	102.3
Chile	79.7

Although U.S. incarceration rates typically dwarf those of Western Europe, the European prison population has increased during this young century. According to the European Union:

> Between 2001 and 2010, the prison population of the 27 EU Member States increased from 582,000 to 635,000.* Over that period, 18 of the 27 EU Member States and Norway reported increasing numbers of prisoners, a trend observed in most countries worldwide. The current EU prison population represents an average of 135 prisoners per 100,000 population, with national figures ranging from 60–70 per 100,000 population in Denmark, the Netherlands, Slovenia, Sweden and Norway to more than 200 per 100,000 in the Czech Republic, Estonia, Latvia, Lithuania and Poland.[39]

Nevertheless, with a total population of about 503 million, the European Union has less than a third of the number of prisoners in the U.S., which has a population of about 319 million.

Within the U.S., we see significant differences in incarceration rates among the states. While Maine has an incarceration rate of 148 inmates per 100,000 people, Louisiana incarcerates 847 people per 100,000; one of every eight-six adult Louisianans is incarcerated. Including those detained while awaiting trial, the number of people detained in Louisiana jumps to nearly 1,600 per 100,000. As Cindy Chang of the *New Orleans Times-Picayune* tells us, "Louisiana is the world's prison capital. The state imprisons more of its people, per head, than any of its U.S. counterparts. First among Americans means first in the world. Louisiana's incarceration rate is nearly five times Iran's, 13 times China's and 20 times Germany's."[40] Louisiana is also the geographic center of the nation's imprisoned, with the five leading states in rates of incarcerated people adjoining each other. (See Figure 4.6.[41])

Are Americans that much worse than the inhabitants of other nations? Are Louisianans really that much more evil than Danes? Are the people who live in the south-central region of the U.S. particularly bad? Or are other nations merely more clever about their responses to criminal behavior? We devote the rest of this chapter to specific examples of how other nations react to crime.

---

* Croatia became the twenty-eighth member of the European Union in 2013. According to the International Centre for Prison Studies, Croatia has an incarceration rate of 108 per 100,000.

Figure 4.6. U.S. States with Highest Incarceration Rates

State	Incarceration Rate per 100,000 People Prisons	Incarceration Rate per 100,000 People Prisons & Jails
Louisiana	847	1,555
Mississippi	692	1,080
Oklahoma	659	926
Alabama	647	968
Texas	602	884

Looking Elsewhere

As we shift to look at some correctional policies and practices in other nations, we focus on some so-called Western-style democracies. This is not meant as a critique of the policies and practices of nations that do not fit within that definition, but rather is intended to focus on nations where cultural transference with the U.S. is more likely. ("Culture transference" in this case meaning that the U.S. is more likely to adopt some of the policies and practices used in other nations.) According to the scale developed by the Center for Systemic Peace, nations with the highest levels of democracy share several characteristics. They:

- Institute procedures for open, competitive, and deliberate political participation;
- Choose and replace chief executives in open, competitive elections; and,
- Impose substantial checks and balances on the power of the chief executive.[42]

By these standards, the U.S. clearly rises to the highest levels of democracy. (Here is a paradox that we hope makes readers uncomfortable: American punitivity has a lot more in common with some third-world dictatorships than it does with most Western-style democracies.)

Norway: 21 Years for Mass Murder

Anders Breivik killed seventy-seven people on July 22, 2011. Breivik first bombed a government building in Oslo, killing eight people, then moved on to the nearby island of Utøya, where he shot and killed sixty-nine people (most of whom were teenagers) attending a summer youth camp. He said he was trying to avoid a takeover of Norway by Muslims. Breivik was tried and convicted in 2012. He received a sentence of "preventative detention," which can be extended indefinitely, but officially is limited to no more than twenty-one years, which is the maximum civilian sentence in Norway for most crimes.

While outsiders were astonished at the light sentence, *Time* magazine published a story entitled, "Why Norway Is Satisfied with Breivik's Sentence," quoting one survivor of the shootings at the Utøya youth camp, "That's how it should work. That's staying true to our principles and the best evidence that he hasn't changed society."[43] Realistically, Norwegian legal experts believe that Breivik will be confined for a far longer period, as additional five-year terms can be added upon the determination that Breivik remains dangerous.

As horrible as the *Breivik* case is, it introduces us to a correctional practice that is the opposite of the U.S.'s. While the American model is to provide a long sentence and give the offender hope (often, false hope) that there will be a chance to carve some time off that sentence through good time or parole, Norway begins with a lesser sentence and later re-evaluates whether that sentence should be extended. As we discuss in Chapter 5, the recent trend in U.S. legislation has been to impose mandatory minimum sentences, charge with overlapping, often poorly described crimes, and assess longer sentencing ranges. All of these make incarceration a highly likely outcome of a criminal prosecution, often without a judge, jury, or a parole board being able to use discretion when evaluating the crime and the criminal.

The United Kingdom: Cautioning

Criminal justice policy in many nations, including the U.S., has long been conflicted between a focus on decreasing the supply of drugs and decreasing demand. Western European laws are said to be tough on drugs, soft on users. Trafficking drugs is treated harshly, but personal possession of drugs presumed to be for one's own (ab)use is often treated as a public health issue rather than a crime. For example, British police employ the practice of "cautioning." Formal cautioning can include confiscation of drugs, and a formal warning of prosecution for a repeated offense; informal cautioning can include simply encouraging the drug user to seek treatment.

Cautioning applies to other minor offenses. In some cases, restorative justice is prescribed; someone caught damaging someone else's property may have to repair the damage. Another policing alternative is the penalty notice, which assesses a civil fine rather than issuing a criminal citation for situations such as shoplifting, simple possession of marijuana, or being drunk and disorderly.[44] Police in England and Wales issue over 200,000 cautions annually.[45]

Spain: Family Solutions

Spain's Centro Penitenciario Madrid VI, also known as the Cárcel de Aranjuez, about an hour's drive south of Madrid, has thirty-six family units. Couples who have been convicted and incarcerated can remain together. Children can stay with their parent(s) until their third birthday. Approximately sixty children are housed in Aranjuez, where they attend nursery schools staffed with early childhood specialists.[46] Article 38 of Spain's Prison Act gives female prisoners the right to keep their children with them until the child turns three, and provides generous visitation rights for children up to the age of ten.[47] As the Spanish explain it, "It is a pioneering experience in Europe, which aims to create an environment for children to develop emotionally and educationally for the time they have to stay in the center, while favoring the social reintegration of mothers."[48]

Denmark: Least Possible Intervention

Denmark also allows female prisoners to have their children live with them until the age of three, if it is believed to be in the child's best interests. Male and female inmates are placed in the same facilities, and may visit each other's cells. At the prison in Ringe, couples who are both serving prison sentences can live together. Inmates in most Danish prisons prepare their own meals with food purchased at the prison store. The Danish government refers to these practices as normalisation. One of the central tenets of the Danish correctional system is to use the least possible intervention:

> To make use of maximum resources of powers is not necessarily the most effective method. On the contrary, the aim should be to develop problem-solving methods which make use of the least possible intervention in the lives of the inmates or clients whilst, at the same time, ensuring that the difficulties which have to be faced are effectively dealt with.[49]

Recidivism, the Ultimate Prison Metric

The best way to evaluate the efficacy of incarceration across borders is to compare recidivism rates. Simply put, the more successful the period of incarceration, the lower the recidivism rate. A problem here is that nations define recidivism differently and measure it over different periods.

Although these varying definitions complicate comparing U.S. recidivism rates with those of other nations, bear in mind that the U.S. maintains a much higher incarceration rate than any of the nations listed above. The U.S. is much more likely to send people to prison than these nations; another way to look at it is that these others nations are fussier than the U.S. is about which offenders they choose to incarcerate. Thus, for these other nations, their recidivism figures are for prisoners who are among the "worst of the worst."

Incarceration as Deterrent to Crime

One argument made by supporters of high incarceration rates and long sentences goes, "Yes, incarceration rates and average sentence lengths have increased in the U.S. in the past few decades, but the result is that most types of crime have steadily gone down during that period." We addressed this argument in Chapter 1. As we said there, this argument supposes that there is a causal relationship between increased incarceration and a decrease in crime. However, a European Union report found that, "sentencing policies in Europe as a whole are considerably less punitive than in the USA ... and yet crime is falling just as steeply in Europe as it is in the USA. *No relationship between the severity of sentencing of countries and trends in national levels of crime is therefore in evidence*"[51] (emphasis added). To explore this, let us look at some other countries with lower incarceration rates and shorter average sentence lengths and compare their crime rates to those of the U.S.

The Dutch Way

Imagine that a group of American policymakers found that seventy percent of former prisoners commit another crime within seven years from their release. What would the American response be? If you've been paying attention thus far, you would guess that the decision would be to extend the sentences for the crimes in question, and you would probably be correct. When the Dutch determined that seventy percent of their ex-prisoners were recidivating within seven years of release, they chose a different route; they

Figure 4.7. Definitions of Recidivism[50]

Five Ways of Measuring Recidivism			
Nation	**Period**	**Definition of Recidivism**	**Recidivism Rate**
United States U.S. Bureau of Justice Statistics (2002)	1994–1997	Criminal acts that resulted in the rearrest, reconviction, or return to prison with or without a new sentence during a three-year period following the prisoner's release.	Of the 272,111 persons released from prisons in fifteen states in 1994, an estimated 67.5% were rearrested for a felony or serious misdemeanor within three years, 46.9% were reconvicted, and 25.4% resentenced to prison for a new crime.
United States Pew Center on the States (2011)	2004–2007	The act of reengaging in criminal offending despite having been punished. The prison recidivism rate … is the proportion of persons released from prison who are rearrested, reconvicted or returned to custody within a specific time period. Typically, recidivism studies follow released offenders for three years following their release from prison or placement on probation.	Alaska had the highest recidivism rate, with 50.4% of offenders reincarcerated within three years; Wyoming had the lowest rate, 24.8%; overall, the states average a 43.3% rate.
Netherlands (2011)	2008–2010	Those who came into contact with the judicial system within two years of leaving a penitentiary.	48.5%
England and Wales (2013)	2010–2011	Those who were cautioned, convicted without incarceration or released from custody and committed another offense within a one-year follow-up period and received a court conviction, caution, reprimand or warning in the one-year follow-up.	25.5%
Scandinavian Nations (2010)	2005–2007	Those released from prison who received new sentences to be served in the correctional services within two years.	Denmark 29% Finland 36% Iceland 27% Norway 20% Sweden 43%

chose to incarcerate fewer offenders. We restate for emphasis—when the Dutch found that incarceration did not work as well as they had hoped, they did not increase incarceration, they instead sought alternatives to incarceration. Because of the Dutch government's policy shift, the use of community service placements climbed considerably, from 27,115 in 2002 to 40,610 in 2007.[52] In 2007, community service accounted for thirty percent of all judicial sentences, forty-four percent were other alternatives to incarceration such as electronic monitoring and fines, and only twenty percent resulted in incarceration. Meanwhile, crime in the Netherlands has declined, just as it has in the U.S.[53]

Norway, Again

As we discussed above, the maximum sentence for most crimes in Norway, even mass murder, is twenty-one years. Also noted was Norway's recidivism rate of twenty percent, less than a third of the U.S. rate. Norway's correctional system seems to be much more efficient than that of the U.S. So what are its prisons like?

The newest Norwegian prison, Halden Fengsel, received a lot of press when it opened in 2010. Prisoners live in individual cells with small refrigerators, televisions, private bathrooms, and windows without bars. Each section of cells shares a kitchen. The facility includes jogging trails, a sound studio, and a freestanding house where prisoners can occasionally stay with their families for a couple of nights. There are walls around the prison, but they have large murals painted on them. Prison director Are Hoidal said, "In the Norwegian prison system, there's a focus on human rights and respect. We don't see any of this as unusual. When they arrive many of them are in bad shape and we want to build them up, give them confidence through education and work and have them leave as better people."[54] Hoidal's statement reflects some of the basic principles of the Norwegian Directorate for Correctional Services:

- The punishment is the restriction of liberty; no other rights have been removed by the sentencing court. Therefore the sentenced offender has all the same rights as all other[s] who live in Norway.
- No-one shall serve their sentence under stricter circumstances than necessary for the security in the community. Therefore offenders shall be placed in the lowest possible security regime.
- During the serving of a sentence, life inside will resemble life outside as much as possible.[55]

It is safe to guess that successful reintegration of prisoners back into free society is facilitated by these principles.

The effort to avoid disrupting prisoners' lives is not confined to Norway. In German and Dutch prisons, prisoners wear their own clothes, decorate their cells (to which they have their own keys) and keep many personal possessions. Within these prisons, most prisoners have freedom of movement and have access to kitchens where they can prepare their own meals and arrange their own leisure activities.[56] Contrast this to many American prisons, in which an inmate may be in a single or double cell for more than twenty hours a day, with out-of-cell activities limited to meals, showers, and brief recreation time.

As Watson discovered, the artificiality of the American prison environment is such that even seemingly normal activities like eating and recreation do not encourage the inmate to develop or maintain normal social skills of everyday life, although these skills are essential for reintegration into free society and having healthy relationships with family, friends, and coworkers. This loss of social skills and the resulting inability to relate to people other than prison staff and fellow inmates increases the chance for alienation from family and outside friends, and makes it difficult to establish well-functioning relationships in the workplace.

As we discussed in Chapter 2, Watson witnessed a salient example of this as he rode a van from the halfway house in San Antonio to the Goodwill store to use their computer to look for jobs. Three other men in the van with Watson had been released from prison after serving seven to nine years each. Watson could tell they were apprehensive of being in the real world as they huddled together and looked around fearfully. Once they arrived at the Goodwill store, they continued to look nervous and unsure as they attempted to use the computer, a device they had been not been given any preparation to use. It was obvious that they were unprepared for life in the real world and were a long way from being well-adjusted and productive citizens.

The typical American correctional experience is both artificial and alienating, in stark contrast to the Norwegian model:

> Crucial services for reintegration are delivered to the prison by local and municipal service providers. Prisons do not have their own staff delivering medical, educational, employment, clerical or library services. These are imported from the community. The advantages are:

> • A better continuity in the deliverance of services—the offender will already have established contact during his time in prison;

- Involvement from the community with the prison system—more and better cross-connections and an improvement of the image of prison and prisoners;
- The services in questions are financed by other bodies as they are part of the rights of any inhabitant of Norway.[57]

Germany: Location, Location, Location

The subtitle refers to the three most important elements of real estate. Location is also important in corrections. Almost all German prisons are located in cities or suburban areas. This facilitates family visits, the delivery of educational and behavioral services, and work and community service opportunities. Contrast this to the trend in the U.S. to build correctional facilities where land is widely available and relatively inexpensive, far away from populated areas. (While in law school, Paxson remembers visiting a Texas juvenile detention facility that was located far from any major city but squarely in a former Texas Speaker of the House's legislative district.) German prisons also allow private visits by spouses and children every two months, unless a prisoner has committed a serious violation of prison rules.

England and Wales: Independent Monitoring Boards

The British Prisons Act of 1952 and the Immigration and Asylum Act of 1999 require that all English and Welsh prisons and immigration detention centers, as well as some short-term holding facilities, have independent monitoring boards. Unpaid board members volunteer several days each month visiting their facility. They undertake additional training as well as continued development training. As the Ministry of Justice tells us,

> Members have unrestricted access to their local prison or immigration detention centre at any time and can talk to any prisoner or detainee they wish to, out of sight and hearing of a members of staff if necessary. A typical monitoring visit, for example, might include time spent in the kitchens, workshops, accommodation blocks, recreation areas, healthcare centre and chaplaincy.
>
> Board members also play an important role in dealing with problems inside the establishment. If a prisoner or detainee has an issue that he or she has been unable to resolve through the usual internal channels, he or she can put in a confidential request to see a member of the IMB. Problems might include concerns over lost property, visits from

family or friends, special religious or cultural requirements, or even serious allegations such as bullying.[58]

The boards submit annual reports to the Secretary of State, and those reports are available online: http://www.imb.org.uk/reports/. The reports contain observations and suggestions for improvement, and at times offer stern criticism. These suggestions and criticisms concern the safety and welfare of both prisoners and corrections officers.

France: Corrections Judges

France has had in place an office of *juges de l'application des peines,* translated literally as judges of the enforcement of sentences, since the 1950s. These corrections judges make initial determinations of length of sentences, grant (or deny) parole, determine the conditions of community releases, and monitor prison conditions. At least once a month, they visit the facilities within their jurisdiction, where they meet with both prisoners and prison administrators. Italy has a somewhat similar office, the Magistracy for the Enforcement of Sentences. As a former prison inmate, Watkins strongly believes that American judges should directly experience prison conditions themselves, which we touch on in Chapter 7.

Scotland: Short-Term Sentences versus Community Corrections

While it makes sense that those who commit lesser crimes receive lesser sentences, those who serve relatively short prison sentences in Great Britain have been found to be more likely to reoffend. This may seem somewhat paradoxical, but it may be as simple as this: those who receive short prison sentences receive little or no rehabilitative treatment while incarcerated. The typical American response to this problem would likely be issuing longer sentences, hoping that the rehabilitation process has more time to "take."

Scotland, however, has addressed the problem by diverting many of the offenders who would receive short prison sentence into community correction programs, based on data that suggest that community sentences are more effective in reducing recidivism than short-term (less than 12 months) prison sentences. A 2011 study says that, "this may be due to the fact that offenders on community sentences have more opportunities to access rehabilitation services compared to offenders on short-term prison sentences that have limited access to rehabilitation programmes in the short period of time they are in prison."[59] Just as the Dutch have done, when the Scots realized that incarceration was not working, they sought alternatives.

The U.S. vs. Other Western Democracies: Lock 'em Up versus Let 'em Out

The Scottish focus on community corrections is merely one example of a distinct difference in correctional practices between the U.S. and many European nations. A 2013 study for the VERA Institute of Justice, a nonpartisan center for justice policy and practice, found that seventy percent of U.S. criminal convictions resulted in incarceration, while only six percent of German cases and ten percent of Dutch cases did so.[60] The United Nations Survey of Crime Trends and Operation of Criminal Justice Systems released in 2011 found that among those adults sentenced between 1995 and 2000, 69.9% of American sentences resulted in imprisonment, compared to only 33.8% of those in Canada and 7.5% of those in Germany.[61] (Note that while we have stressed that different definitions and methods lead to different results in data collection, the VERA and UN studies yield a nearly identical figure for the percentage of sentences leading to incarceration in the U.S.) In essence, the default criminal punishment in the U.S. is often incarceration, while alternatives to incarceration, including fines, suspended sentences, and community corrections, are the norm in Germany and the Netherlands.

Not only are Americans more likely to be sentenced to incarceration than those in other nations studied; they are also typically serving longer sentences. The VERA study found that while more than ninety percent of German prison sentences were for two years or less and ninety-five percent of Dutch prison sentences were for two years or less, the average American prison sentence is approximately three years.[62] The UN found that the average sentence for robbery, which in Australia was seventy-two months, averaged ninety-one months in the U.S. An assault conviction would yield an average of sixty months in the U.S., but only 15.2 months in England and Wales. A fraud conviction would bring a defendant an average sentence of 8.1 months in Finland and forty-four months in the U.S. The average sentence for drug offenses is 34.4 months in England and Wales, compared to fifty-seven months in the U.S.[63]

Tocqueville Revisited

In June 2013, Alan Vinegrad, a former U.S. Attorney for the Eastern District of New York and a partner in the New York law firm of Covington & Burling, and Jason Levine, an associate at the firm, published an article in the *New York Law Journal* entitled "Tocqueville in Reverse: Looking to Europe in Reassessing U.S. Prisons," which highlights recent efforts by some American corrections officials to study European correctional initiatives.[64] One effort is the European-American Prison Project, in which directors of corrections departments, state legislators, judges, district attorneys, and other criminal justice stakeholders from Colorado, Georgia, and Pennsylvania collaborated with officials from Germany and the Netherlands.

The American officials visited their European counterparts in early 2013 to learn firsthand about best practices, which included alternative sanctions such as day fines, restitution, and community service orders. Do these alternatives to incarceration work? They seem to work for the Germans and the Dutch, with incarceration rates approximately one tenth those of the U.S. As Vinegrad and Levine point out, "Whereas less than 3 percent of federal prison sentences imposed in the United States are for one year or less, more than 40 percent of prison sentences imposed in the Netherlands and Germany are for a similarly short duration."[65]

The community-based correctional practices commonly used in European nations often meet with resistance in the U.S. American conventional wisdom seems to be that community-based corrections such as probation and parole are, as is the common expression, merely a slap on the wrist. When Paxson asks his students if they would rather serve the remaining term of a sentence in prison or be released under the supervision of a parole officer for the same period, his students almost uniformly say that they would prefer to be released early. However, many prisoners chose instead to "wrap up," finishing their sentences and avoiding supervised parole. Despite what countless Americans believe, many American criminals know that community supervision can be challenging, as the temptations and frictions of life outside of prison are again present, albeit with correctional officials still keeping watch.

Conclusion

As noted earlier in this chapter, nations deal with crime and criminals in different ways, based on cultural, economic, and political ideologies. Even something as basic as defining what types of behavior constitute crime is not as simple as it would seem. For example, as you read this, people in some nations are imprisoned, and some will be executed, for political behavior that falls well within the zone of First Amendment protection in the U.S. In addition, Americans enjoy having relatively transparent governmental processes, with prison data carefully compiled and broadly distributed, which is not the case in many other nations. These differences make a comparative approach to corrections tricky. That said, the U.S. remains among the "punishingest" nation in the world, and certainly the most punitive among Western-style democracies.

Not that this seems to bother most Americans. Americans strongly adhere to a conception of American exceptionalism that makes many of us unwilling to consider adopting the attitudes and practices of other nations, even if evidence-based practices elsewhere prove to be clearly more effective than American practices. The movement of the U.S. correctional system away from rehabilitation and toward mass incarceration in the last quarter of the twentieth century has placed the nation among the outliers of incarceration practices among developed ("first world") nations. Although the last few years have seen American politicians and the American public begin to display some reticence about mass incarceration, the U.S. will continue to have one of the highest incarceration rates in the world. The death penalty will also remain in effect in the U.S. At any time that there is highly publicized criticism of American correctional practices by a foreign political figure or foreign journalist, many Americans will respond with an ardent defense of those practices.

We note, however, that in a reversal of the process by which Europeans such as Alexis de Tocqueville and Charles Dickens sailed to the U.S. to observe its relatively progressive correctional practices in the nineteenth century, American correctional officials and public policy makers are today traveling to other Western democracies to see what works there. If the key motivation for this is an effort to save taxpayer dollars by adopting more efficient and effective correctional practices, rather than the noble pursuit of humanitarian goals, so be it.

American tax dollars can be saved by using effective diversions from incarceration, making a committed effort to rehabilitate those under the supervision of correctional agencies, and employing methods of incarceration that are less disruptive to convicted criminals and their families (which includes reduced sentences and more opportunities for supervised early release), which are some of the practices that other nations successfully employ. Many of those nations have recidivism rates that are lower than that of the U.S. and employ correctional methods that are ultimately less expensive to taxpayers than incarceration. We conclude this book with reference to some of these foreign practices in our suggestions in Chapter 7.

Notes

1. Roper v. Simmons, 543 U.S. 551, 577 (2005).

2. Ibid., 608.

3. Ibid., 622.

4. Ibid., 604.

5. "DeLay Rips Justice Kennedy," Fox News Radio, April 20, 2005, http://www.foxnews.com/story/2005/04/20/delay-rips-justice-kennedy.html.

6. Dana Milbank, "And the Verdict on Justice Kennedy Is: Guilty," *Washington Post*, April 9, 2005, http://www.washingtonpost.com/wp-dyn/articles/A38308-2005Apr8.html.

7. Ibid.

8. Sarah H. Cleveland, "Highest Court in US Divided over Its Place in the World," *The Irish Times*, March 29, 2005, http://www.irishtimes.com/opinion/highest-court-in-us-divided-over-its-place-in-the-world-1.427300.

9. "An End to Killing Kids," *The Economist*, March 2, 2005, http://www.economist.com/node/3714479.

10. Michael E. Tigar, "Universal Rights and Wrongs: *Roper v. Simmons*, Torture and Judge Posner," *Monthly Review*, May 21, 2006, http://monthlyreview.org/commentary/universal-rights-and-wrongs/.

11. Anne Wyvekens, "The French Juvenile Justice System," *International Handbook of Juvenile Justice,* ed. Josine Junger-Tas and Scott H. Decker, (New York: Springer, 2008): 173–186.

12. Tomohiro Osaki, "Should Young Criminals Face Harsher Penalties?" *The Japan Times*, February 24, 2014, http://www.japantimes.co.jp/news/2014/02/24/reference/should-young-criminals-face-harsher-penalties/#.VXHeI89Viko.

13. Amnesty International, "Death Sentences and Executions," (London: Amnesty International Publications, 2015): 5.

14. "Death Sentences and Executions 2014," Amnesty International, March 31, 2015, http://www.amnestyusa.org/research/reports/death-sentences-and-executions-2014?page=2.

15. Alexis de Tocqueville, *Democracy in America*, 3rd American ed. (New York: George Adlard, 1839): 89–90.

16. Helmut Kury and Theodore N. Ferdinand, "Punitivity: An Introduction" in *International Perspectives on Punitivity*, (Crime and Crime Policy Vol. 4), ed. Kury and Ferdinand (Bochum, Germany: Universitätsverlag Brockmeyer, 2008) 1–12, 2.

17. Greta Olson, "Issues in American Punitivity," *Pólemos* 2/2010 (2010): 45–66, 47.

18. Michael Cavadino and James Dignan, *Penal Systems; A Comparative Approach*, (London: Sage, 2006): xii–xiii.

19. James Q. Whitman, "What Happened to Tocqueville's America?" *Social Research* 74, no. 3 (Fall 2007): 251–268, 258–259.

20. Anthony Bottoms, "The Politics of Sentencing Reform," in *The Philosophy and Politics of Punishing and Sentencing*, ed. C. M .V. Clarkson and R. Morgan (Oxford, UK: Oxford University Press, 1995): 17–49.

21. "Fact Sheet on Judicial Selection Methods in the States," American Bar Association, February 6, 2002, http://www.americanbar.org/content/dam/aba/migrated/leadership/fact_sheet.pdf.

22. "Current Judicial Vacancies," (Washington, DC: U.S. Courts, updated June 18, 2015), http://www.uscourts.gov/judges-judgeships/judicial-vacancies/current-judicial-vacancies.

23. "The State of the Judiciary; Judicial Selection at the Beginning of President Obama's Second Term," Alliance for Justice, March 5, 2013, 4, http://www.afj.org/judicial-selection/state-of-the-judiciary-march-2013.pdf.

24. See for example, Matt Murphy, "Governor's Councilor Charles Cipollini Skeptical about SJC Nominee Judge Barbara Lenk, Chosen by Gov. Patrick," Mass Live, April 6, 2011, http://www.masslive.com/news/index.ssf/2011/04/governors_councilor_charles_ci.html.

25. Amanda Petteruti and Jason Fenster, "Finding Direction: Expanding Criminal Justice Options by Considering Policies of Other Nations," (Washington, DC: Justice Policy Institute, 2011).

26. Mary L. Volcansek, *Appointing Judges the European Way*, Fordham Urb. L.J. 34 (January 2007): 363–385, 375.

27. Leslie T. Wilkins and Ken Pease, "Public Demand for Punishment," *The International Journal of Sociology and Social Policy* 7, no. 3 (1987): 16–29.

28. David J. Krus and Lenore S. Hoehl, "Issues Associated with International Incarceration Rates," *Psychological Reports* 75, no. 3 (1994): 1491–1496.

29. "Crisis Squeezes Income and Puts Pressure on Inequality and Poverty," Organization for Economic Co-operation and Development, May 2013, http://www.oecd.org/els/soc/OECD2013-Inequality-and-Poverty-8p.pdf.

30. Anna Alvazzi del Frate, "Chapter 8 — Crime and Criminal Justice Statistics Challenges," *International Statistics on Crime and Justice,* ed. Stefan Harrendorf, Markku Heiskanen, and Steven Malby (Helsinki: European Institute for Crime Prevention and Control/United Nations Office on Drugs and Crime, 2010): 167.

31. Stefan Harrendorf, Markku Heiskanen, and Steven Malby, ed., *International Statistics on Crime and Justice*, (Helsinki: European Institute for Crime Prevention and Control/United Nations Office on Drugs and Crime, 2010): 96–97; "World Prison Brief," (London: International Centre for Prison Studies), accessed June 21, 2015, http://www.prisonstudies.org/highest-to-lowest/prison_population_rate?field_region_taxonomy_tid=All.

32. Jerome L. Neapolitan, "An Examination of Cross-National Variation in Punitiveness," *International Journal of Offender Therapy and Comparative Criminology* 45, no. 6 (2001): 691–710, 691.

33. Roy Walmsley, "World Prison Population List," 10th ed., (London: International Centre for Prison Studies, 2013).

34. Ibid.

35. "Total Persons Held in Prisons, Penal Institutions or Correctional Institutions," United Nations Office on Drugs and Crime, accessed February 13, 2014, http://www.unodc.org/documents/data-and-analysis/statistics/crime/CTS12_Persons_detained.xls.

36. Walmsley.

37. Ibid.

38. United Nations Office on Drugs and Crime.

39. "Prisons and Drugs in Europe: The Problem and Responses," (Lisbon: European Monitoring Centre for Drugs and Drug Addiction, European Union, last modified November 2012): 8, http://www.emcdda.europa.eu/publications/selected-issues/prison.

40. Cindy Chang, "Louisiana Is the World's Prison Capital," *New Orleans Times-Picayune*, last modified May 29, 2012, http://www.nola.com/crime/index.ssf/2012/05/louisiana_is_the_worlds_prison.html.

41. E. Ann Carson, "Prisoners in 2013," (Washington, DC: U.S. Bureau of Justice Statistics, 2014): 7, http://www.bjs.gov/content/pub/pdf/p13.pdf.; "Prison Population," (Wash-

ington, DC: Sentencing Project), accessed June 27, 2015, http://www.sentencingproject.org/map/map.cfm#map.

42. Monty G. Marshall and Benjamin R. Cole, "Global Report 2011; Conflict, Governance, and State Fragility," (Vienna, VA: Center for Systemic Peace, 2011).

43. Mark Lewis, "Why Norway Is Satisfied with Breivik's Sentence," *Time*, last modified August 27, 2012, http://world.time.com/2012/08/27/why-norway-is-satisfied-with-breiviks-sentence.

44. "Police Cautions, Warnings and Penalty Notices," Gov.UK, last modified April 10, 2015, https://www.gov.uk/caution-warning-penalty.

45. "Metropolitan Police Issue Cautions for Crimes Including Rape, Figures Reveal," *The Guardian*, last modified May 13, 2013, http://www.guardian.co.uk/uk/2013/may/13/metropolitan-police-cautions-rape.

46. "Unidades de madres," Secretería General de Instituciones Penitenciarias (Spain), last modified October 5, 2012, http://www.institucionpenitenciaria.es/web/portal/centros-Penitenciarios/unidadesMadres.html; Angela Turrin, "Volunteerism and Community Service: Aranjuez Prison," (Madrid: U.S. Embassy in Spain), last modified June 18, 2011, http://madrid.usembassy.gov/news/volunteerism/0618aranjuezprison.html.

47. "Título II. Del Régimen Penitenciario," Secretería General de Instituciones Penitenciarias (Spain), accessed June 19, 2015, http://www.institucionpenitenciaria.es/web/portal/documentos/normativa/LeyOrganica/lo1-1979.t2.html#c3.

48. "Unidades de madres."

49. "A Programme of Principles for Prison and Probation Work in Denmark," Ministry of Justice (Denmark), 14, July 2011, http://www.unodc.org/documents/justice-and-prison-reform/EGM-Uploads/DENMARK-GOV-13-En.pdf.

50. Patrick A. Langan and David J. Levin, "Recidivism of Prisoners Released in 1994," (Washington, DC: U.S. Bureau of Justice Statistics), last modified June 2002, http://www.bjs.gov/content/pub/pdf/rpr94.pdf; *State of Recidivism: The Revolving Door of America's Prisons,* Pew Center on the States, (Washington, DC: The Pew Charitable Trusts, April 2011): 7; "Recidivism Report 2002–2008," Ministry of Security and Justice (United Kingdom), 2011, http://english.wodc.nl/onderzoeksdatabase/actualisering-recidivemeting-sancties-2011.aspx; "Proven Re-offending Statistics Quarterly Bulletin" Ministry of Security and Justice (United Kingdom), last modified April 25, 2013, https://www.gov.uk/government/uploads/system/uploads/attachment_data/file/192631/proven-reoffending-jul-10-jun-11.pdf; "Relapse Study in the Correctional Services of the Nordic Countries," Council of Europe Penal Statistics, 2010, http://www3.unil.ch/wpmu/space/publications/recidivism-studies/.

51. Jan van Dijk, Robert Manchin, John van Kesteren, Sami Nevala, and Gergely Hideg, "The Burden of Crime in the EU: A Comparative Analysis of the European Survey of Crime and Safety," (Brussels: Gallup Europe): 23, http://vorige.nrc.nl/redactie/binnenland/Misdaad.pdf.

52. Gert Van Langendonck, "Less Is More in Debate about Prison Population," NRC.NL, last modified June 3, 2009, http://vorige.nrc.nl/article2259194.ece.

53. Ibid.

54. "World's Poshest Prison? Cells with En-suite Bathrooms and No Window Bars (Plus £1m Banksy-Style Art)," *Mail* Online, last modified May 12, 2010, http://www.dailymail.co.uk/news/article-1277158/Halden-Prison-Inside-Norways-posh-new-jail.html.

55. "Norwegian Directorate for Correctional Services," Kriminalomsorgen (Norway), accessed July 29, 2013, http://www.kriminalomsorgen.no/english.293899.no.html.

56. Ram Subramanian and Alison Shames, "Sentencing and Prison Practices in Germany and the Netherlands: Implications for the U.S.," (New York: VERA Institute, Center on Sentencing and Corrections, 2013): 13.

57. "Norwegian Directorate for Correctional Services."

58. "About the Independent Monitoring Board," United Kingdom Ministry of Justice, last modified July 3, 2013, https://www.justice.gov.uk/about/imb.

59. Maria Sapouna, Catherine Bisset, and Anne-Marie Conlong, "What Works to Reduce Reoffending: A Summary of the Evidence," Justice Analytical Services, Scottish Government, October 2011: 7.

60. Subramanian and Shames, 9.

61. Kauko Aromaa and Markku Heiskanen, eds., "Crime and Criminal Justice Systems in Europe and North America 1995–2004," (Helsinki: The European Institute for Crime and Prevention Control, 2008).

62. Subramanian and Shames, 9–10.

63. Petteruti and Fenster, 22.

64. Alan Vinegrad and Jason Levine, "Tocqueville in Reverse: Looking to Europe in Reassessing U.S. Prisons," *New York Law Journal* 249, no. 116 (June 18, 2013): 1–3.

65. Ibid., 2.

Chapter 5

Politics and Prisons

Without the mass incarceration that we currently practice,
millions fewer people would be living in poverty.
Hillary Clinton, April 29, 2015[1]

We don't have mass incarcerations in America. Individuals are brought
before tribunals, and they have counsel. They're given certain rights.
Are we not going to lock people up who commit crimes?
Mitt Romney, May 4, 2015[2]

The Role of Fear

Politicians do not lose votes by being too tough on crime (here, visualize the politician punching the palm of one hand with the fist of the other as s/he explains his/her approach to punishing criminals). A 2004 Gallup poll found that nearly two-thirds of Americans believed that the criminal justice system is not tough enough on crime.[3] More recently, a Gallup poll in 2011 revealed that forty-two percent of Americans reported having only "some" confidence in the U.S.'s criminal justice system, while twenty-seven percent said that they had very little confidence.[4] For voters, perception is typically reality. Thus, despite the fact that most violent and property crime rates have decreased since the 1990s, a majority of Americans polled by the Gallup organization annually since 2003 have said that they believed the crime rate was increasing each year, with sixty-three percent of those polled in 2014 saying so.[5]

As we mentioned in Chapter 1, this misinformation may be partly the product of what the late communications scholar George Gerbner labeled Mean World Syndrome, a skewed perception of the prevalence of violence among those who have been repeatedly exposed to violent imagery on television and in other media.[6] Violent television shows, violent movies, and violent video games are staples of our popular culture, and local television stations frequently subscribe to the belief that "if it bleeds, it leads" on news broadcasts, emphasizing violent crime when it does occur in our communities.

Why the prevalence of violence in our entertainment and news media? Because it's graphic, lending itself to visual depictions and it's quick, catering to short attention spans. When Paxson asks his students what the difference is between the popular video game "Grand Theft Auto V" and earlier versions of the game, they respond that the more recent version is better. By better, they mean more violent. In addition, as the popularity of the work of Alfred Hitchcock, Stephen King, and many others has proven, people like to be scared. In King's essay, "Why We Crave Horror Movies," he writes that when we choose to watch horror movies, "we are daring the nightmare."[7]

When voters express the mistaken belief that crime rates are going up, politicians do not attempt to dispel that misinformation but use it instead for political advantage. They know that people want to be afraid. Like it or not, fearmongering gets votes. As former prosecutor Erik Luna writes:

> Lawmakers have every reason to add new crimes and punishments, which make great campaign fodder, but no countervailing political interest in cutting the penal code. The benefits of overcriminalization are concentrated on the political class, providing nice sound bites and resume filler at reelection time, while the costs are either very diffuse ... or borne by discrete and insular minorities without sway in the political process, such as members of lower socioeconomic classes or those accused of crime.[8]

The U.S. Bureau of Prisons' budget in fiscal year 2014 was about seven billion dollars.[9] As the late U.S. Senator Everett Dirksen of Illinois is crediting with saying, "A billion here, a billion there, and pretty soon you're talking about real money." Still, with an overall federal budget of 3.5 trillion dollars that year, federal corrections spending amounted to a mere two-tenths of one percent of federal expenditures.[10] This (relative) pittance makes it politically expedient for members of Congress to create new criminal laws without being held accountable for the cost of incarcerating those who violate those laws.

Overlapping Laws

As we discussed in Chapter 1, there is a common misperception that federal offenses are somehow more serious, or worse, than state offenses. This simply isn't true. Most violent crimes are prosecuted by the states, and the majority of state prisoners (53.8%) are serving time for violent offenses. By contrast, the majority (56%) of federal prisoners are serving time for drug offenses, many of them nonviolent.[11] (Remember, Al Capone served time in federal prison for tax evasion, not murder.)

As the United States system of government was originally conceived, most policing was to be done at the state and local levels. Historically, the federal government's law enforcement efforts have stemmed from the commerce clause in Article I of the U.S. Constitution, which gives Congress the power to regulate interstate and foreign commerce. (The courts have extended this power to regulation of local activities that significantly affect interstate commerce.) Accordingly, federal law enforcement agencies have been established to regulate specific types of legal and illegal commerce, including the Bureau of Alcohol, Tobacco, and Firearms, the Drug Enforcement Administration, and Immigration and Customs Enforcement. The Secret Service, now known for protecting the president as an agency within the Department of Homeland Security, originated within the Treasury Department, reflecting its earlier responsibility for suppressing counterfeiting.

The Federal Bureau of Investigation, which evolved from a group of special federal agents within the Justice Department in 1908, was originally quite controversial, widely perceived as eroding the sovereignty of state and local government. However, the failed experiment of Prohibition (1919–1933) led to the ascendancy of organized crime in the U.S. and consequently, the growth of the FBI. The escalation of organized crime also caused criminal law to become the subject of presidential politics for the first time in 1928.[12] Since then, the federal government has becoming increasingly active in arresting, prosecuting, and incarcerating people for crimes, many of which were formerly only state offenses.

In the American Bar Association's Criminal Justice magazine, former federal prosecutor Ronald F. Wright tells readers:

> Because of remarkable growth in the reach of the federal criminal code over many generations, a huge potential overlap now exists between federal and state criminal justice.... This overlap has grown relentlessly for generations. As the American Bar Association's Task Force on the Federalization of Criminal Law concluded in 1998, both the number of federal criminal statutes and the volume of federal criminal cases have increased over the years.[13]

The task force that Wright references stated that "it is clear that the amount of individual citizen behavior now potentially subject to federal criminal control has increased in astonishing proportions in the last few decades."[14] Since that 1998 report, numerous legal scholars and state as well as federal officials have criticized the still-increasing federalization of criminal law.

Not that Congress is solely to blame; the American public is also complicit. A political saying often attributed to Ronald Reagan is, "If you're explaining, you're losing." When voters clamor for new laws, legislators enact new laws, regardless of whether new laws are needed. There may well be existing laws that adequately address the problem. Yet the public seems to believe that if a particular crime is receiving lots of media attention, a new law will deter people from engaging in that crime. Thus, when the young son of famed aviator Charles Lindbergh was kidnapped in 1932, citizens called for a new federal kidnapping law, although states already had existing kidnapping statutes. Congress complied and promptly passed the Federal Kidnapping Act, popularly known at the time as the Lindbergh Law.[15]

More recently, when the rising use of anti-theft devices in automobiles in the early 1990s led to an increase in thieves stealing cars at gunpoint, voters demanded new laws against carjacking. There was no need for such laws, as carjacking falls within the definition of the long-established crime of robbery. Regardless, state legislators responding to the public's outcry and passed a slew of anti-carjacking statutes. Congress also passed a federal statute signed into law by President George H.W. Bush in 1992.[16]

As this book was being written, there was a push for new laws against "revenge porn." This offense occurs when people post pornographic images of their ex-lovers online without consent. Although existing harassment and invasion of privacy laws already address the problem in most states, several states have passed new revenge porn laws and other states are in the process of doing so. Continuing the trend of federal criminalization, U.S. Representative Jackie Speier of California has proposed a federal revenge porn law.[17]

Federal and state overlap operates in both directions. With smoke still rising from where the World Trade Center fell, New York passed a state anti-terrorism act in 2001. As the introduction to the law explains:

> The devastating consequences of the recent barbaric attack on the World Trade Center and the Pentagon underscore the compelling need for legislation that is specifically designed to combat the evils of terrorism.... Although certain federal laws seek to curb the incidence of terrorism, there are no corresponding state laws that facilitate the prosecution and punishment of terrorists in state courts.[18]

Unfortunately, we think it is likely that the attacks would still have occurred even if the state of New York had enacted this law prior to 9/11. The reason that the state of New York didn't have an antiterrorism law before then was because it didn't need one — federal laws were already in place.

Overcriminalization

In 2015, the Brennan Center for Justice at New York University School of Law published a collection of essays, *Solutions: American Leaders Speak Out on Criminal Justice*, from political and policy leaders from across the political spectrum, including otherwise ideologically disparate presidential candidates Hillary Clinton and Mike Huckabee, and U.S. Senators Ted Cruz and Corey Booker. Senator Cruz of Texas identifies three problems contributing to mass incarceration: "overcriminalization, harsh mandatory minimums, and the demise of jury trials."[19] We look at each of these phenomena in this chapter. Cruz points out that between 2000 and 2007, Congress created 450 new crimes, at a rate of more than one per week. Because of federal overcriminalization, as the title of Boston criminal defense attorney Harvey Silverglate's book tells us, many of us may be unwittingly committing *Three Felonies a Day*.[20] In his introduction, Silverglate warns:

> [I]t is only a slight exaggeration to say that the average busy professional in this country wakes up, goes to work, comes home, takes care of personal and family obligations, and then goes to sleep, unaware that he or she likely committed several federal crimes that day. Why? The answer lies in the very nature of federal criminal laws, which have become not only exceedingly numerous ... and broad, but also ... impossibly vague.[21]

How many federal criminal laws are there? That's a hard question to answer; the American Bar Association's Task Force on the Federalization of Criminal Law found that, "So large is the present body of federal criminal law that there is no conveniently accessible, complete list of federal crimes."[22] According to the *Wall Street Journal*, "Counting them is impossible. The Justice Department spent two years trying in the 1980s, but produced only an estimate: 3,000 federal criminal offenses.... A Justice spokeswoman said there was no quantifiable number. Criminal statutes are sprinkled throughout some 27,000 pages of the federal code."[23] Senator Cruz offers a solution; "Congress should begin by requiring that all criminal offenses are put into one title of the Code, Title 18, or if that proves too difficult, Congress can enact a law that prohibits criminal liability on the basis of any statute that is not codified or otherwise cross-referenced in Title 18."[24]

In 2015, what is believed to be the first time the term "overcriminalization" has appeared in a U.S. Supreme Court opinion occurred in *Yates v. U.S.* Justice Elena Kagan's dissenting opinion complained of "overcriminalization and excessive punishment in the U.S. Code."[25] Yates, a commercial fisher, was charged under 18 U.S.C. §1519, part of the Sarbanes-Oxley Act of 2002. That act, passed soon after the collapse of Enron (more on that below) was aimed at preventing the cover-up of improprieties in corporate record keeping, and has been called the "anti-shredding law." In *Yates*, federal prosecutors attempted to apply the act to throwing undersized fish off a boat.

As it turned out, the entire case turned on the definition of the term "tangible object," used in §1519. The plurality opinion written by Justice Ruth Bader Ginsburg said that a tangible object in the context of the statute applied to files, not fish. Kagan's dissent argued that tangible objects include fish and should apply to Yates—but that was precisely the problem with the statute in question. Kagan wrote that "§1519 is a bad law—too broad and undifferentiated, with too-high maximum penalties, which give prosecutors too much leverage and sentencers too much discretion. And I'd go further: In those ways, §1519 is unfortunately not an outlier, but an emblem of a deeper pathology in the federal criminal code."[26]

Just as Congress has demonstrated a propensity to overcriminalize, so have the states. For example, a study by University of North Carolina government professor Jeff Welty found that between 2008 and 2013, the North Carolina "General Assembly enacted 101 new felonies, an average of 16.8 per year. It also enacted 105 new misdemeanors, an average of 17.5 per year. Across both types of crimes, the total was 206 new offenses, a rate of 34.3 per year."[27] For that same period, a study for the Manhattan Institute found that Michigan "added more than 45 crimes annually, 44 percent of which were felonies."[28]

Overcriminalization: Drug-Free Schools

It is good politics to impose especially harsh penalties on those who sell drugs within a school zone. Decent members of society certainly do not tolerate drug dealers who prey on children, and laws that attempt to create drug-free schools exist in all fifty states and the District of Columbia.[29] These statutes provide additional punishment, treating the drug offense as an aggravated offense. But how is a school zone defined? Assume a state enacts a law making it an aggravated offense to sell drugs within 1,000 feet of a school, the most common distance used in this type of law. Some statutes also include public swimming pools, playgrounds, movie theaters, parks, video arcades, churches, and libraries. In a densely populated urban area, this may include nearly the entire community.

Suppose the men's room of a bar lies within 1,000 feet of a school. Should the low-level drug dealer who sells a small amount of drugs in that men's room at 12:15 AM, when the school is closed, be subject to the law? In a few states, drug-free school laws include simple possession of an illegal drug. Thus, a motorist with a personal stash of drugs in his or her pocket who drives past a school when it is out for the summer could also be prosecuted for a school zone violation. You might be telling yourself about these two examples, "Hey, that's not what the legislature was talking about." You're probably right. Nevertheless, some states' school zone statutes come with mandatory minimums sentences, which we discuss in more detail below. If the prosecutor decides to add a school zone violation to the charges and the defendant is found guilty, neither the judge nor the jury can prevent the mandatory minimum from being imposed.

Recently, some states have begun modifying their school zone statutes in order to better serve the goal of protecting children by using more careful statutory language and providing more judicial discretion. A common reform is to shrink the protected area within the statute from within 1,000 feet of a school to 300 feet, and to exempt private residences located within the zone. Another modification is to limit the hours when the school zone law applies to exclude the nighttime. In addition, some states allow the trial judge to recognize certain defenses, such as no minors being in the area at the time the defendant was apprehended.[30] These reforms, however, remain exceptions to the nation's school zone drug laws.

Overcriminalization: Habitual Offender Statutes

Habitual offender statutes, popularly known as "three strikes and you're out" laws, were discussed in Chapter 1 as one of the causes of mass incarceration in the U.S. Originally targeting violent offenders such as murderers, rapists, and child molesters, legislators found it politically advantageous to extend recidivist statutes to nonviolent offenses. Thus, Leandro Andrade, convicted under California's habitual offender statute after stealing nine children's videos worth about $150 in two visits to a Kmart, and with previous convictions for nonviolent offenses, received two consecutive terms of twenty-five years to life. In California, a person convicted of second-degree murder receives a sentence of fifteen years to life.[31] You may be once again telling yourself, "Hey, that's not what the legislature was talking about." Perhaps you're right, but the state of California defended this application of its habitual offender statute in each of Andrade's appeals as his case made its way up to the U.S. Supreme Court, which affirmed his conviction.[32] Andrade's predicament is not unique. A study by the University of San Francisco School of Law notes that "fifty-four percent of third strike commitments under California's three strikes law were for drug, property, and other non-violent crimes. Less than half

(46%) of third strike commitments in California were for crimes involving actual physical violence."[33] At the time, California was believed to have the nation's toughest (and least equitable) three-strikes law.

At least sixteen states have amended their three-strikes legislation to allow for greater flexibility in sentencing, allowing increased judicial discretion and replacing mandatory sentences with sentencing ranges, according to a Harvard Law School report published in 2012.[34] That same year, California voters passed Proposition 36, scaling back the state's three-strikes law to apply only to violent felons. Although Proposition 36 received the support of more than two-thirds of voters, the California District Attorneys Association, the Police Chiefs Association, and the California State Sheriffs' Association opposed the measure.[35]

Ironically, in the same year that the Californians voted to scale back their three-strikes laws, the Massachusetts Legislature considered implementing its first habitual offender law. Former Massachusetts Commissioner of Correction Kathleen Dennehy cautioned, "We need smarter choices for safe communities. We need to consider all the facts before we advance yet another tough-on-crime piece of legislation. We need a rigorous assessment of the costs and impacts associated with this."[36] The Harvard Law School report on three-strikes legislation estimated the new law could cost Massachusetts taxpayers up to $125 million annually.[37] Nonetheless, the bill passed easily with bipartisan support and was signed into law by liberal Democratic Governor Deval Patrick. Three-strikes laws remain on the books in a majority of the states.

Permanently incarcerating those criminals who are indeed the "worst of the worst" makes sense. There is no question that we need to keep the most dangerous predators out of our communities. However, we advocate for carefully considered and drafted laws that limit the application of habitual offender laws to those who are indeed the worst of the worst, and we advocate for laws that allow judges and juries to consider the specific circumstances of each case.

Lack of Intent

Consider the following three scenarios:

- Accidentally running over and killing somebody while driving stone cold sober.
- Accidentally running over and killing somebody while driving drunk.
- Purposely running over and killing somebody.

The result (the harm) is the same in each situation: the victim is dead. Nevertheless, when deciding the charges and the punishment, we look at the state of mind of the offender. An intentional crime is typically punished more severely than an accidental crime. Some crimes require that the prosecutor prove that the defendant intended the harm that resulted—this is specific intent. Specific intent crimes tend to be the worst crimes, such as murder. The need to prove specific intent places a great burden on the prosecutor. There is less of a burden on the prosecutor for general intent crimes, which require that the prosecutor prove that the defendant intended only the act. For example, in many states, if the defendant punched somebody, the prosecutor would have to prove only that the defendant intended the contact, not that the defendant intended a particular harm to the victim from that contact.

Lesser crimes may require that the prosecutor prove that the defendant was reckless, meaning that the defendant knew of the risk but failed to guard against it. Still lesser crimes require establishing that the defendant, acting as a reasonable person, should have known of the risk but failed to guard against it. In all of these situations, the prosecutor has the burden of proving *mens rea*, or a guilty mind.

However, there are also strict liability offenses. These crimes require no discussion of the defendant's state of mind, only that the defendant committed

Figure 5.1. *Mens Rea*

Burden on Prosecutor to Prove *Mens Rea* Increases				
Strict Liability	Negligence	Recklessness	General Intent	Specific Intent
•The prosecutor does not have to prove a state of mind in order to gain a conviction. •Example: running a red light	•Unintentional/accidental: The prosecutor must prove that the defendant should have been aware of the risk of harm but failed to guard against it. •Example: negligent operation of a motor vehicle for driving too fast during a snow storm	•Unintentional/accidental: The prosecutor must prove that the defendant was aware of the risk of harm but failed to guard against it. •Example: involuntary manslaughter because the emergency exits in a public building were intentionally locked	•The prosecutor must prove that the defendant intended the act. •Example: simple assault, because the defendant punched the victim	•The prosecutor must prove that the defendant intended the result (the harm). •Example: murder, because defendant repeatedly shot the victim intending the victim to die
Severity of Crime Increases				

a prohibited act. For example, not knowing the traffic light was red isn't a good defense to running a red light. If the driver ran the red light, the driver receives a ticket, and arguing to the cop or a judge that the driver didn't know the light was red will make no difference. Strict liability offenses tend to be the least serious offenses.

Here's where it gets tricky. If a criminal statute prohibits certain behavior but does not specify which state of mind needs to be proven for that crime, the courts will often interpret the crime as a strict liability offense. In the 1952 case of *Morissette v. United States*, the U.S. Supreme Court distinguished traditional crimes based on the Anglo-American common law principle that a defendant must be proven blameworthy from modern laws that seek to punish those who commit what the court characterized as "public welfare offenses." The court explained:

> Many of these offenses are not in the nature of positive aggressions or invasions, with which the common law so often dealt, but are in the nature of neglect where the law requires care, or inaction where it imposes a duty. Many violations of such regulations result in no direct or immediate injury to person or property, but merely create the danger or probability of it which the law seeks to minimize. While such offenses do not threaten the security of the state in the manner of treason, they may be regarded as offenses against its authority, for their occurrence impairs the efficiency of controls deemed essential to the social order as presently constituted. In this respect, whatever the intent of the violator, the injury is the same, and the consequences are injurious or not according to fortuity. *Hence, legislation applicable to such offenses, as a matter of policy, does not specify intent as a necessary element.* The accused, if he does not will the violation, usually is in a position to prevent it with no more care than society might reasonably expect and no more exertion than it might reasonably exact from one who assumed his responsibilities. Also, penalties commonly are relatively small, and conviction does no grave damage to an offender's reputation. *Under such considerations, courts have turned to construing statutes and regulations which make no mention of intent as dispensing with it and holding that the guilty act alone makes out the crime.*[38] (emphasis added)

These public welfare offenses for which defendants are strictly liable include violations of food and drug laws, public health laws, building codes, and as we'll see, some environmental laws.

In December 1996, former Indy racecar driver Bobby Unser and a friend got lost in a blizzard while snowmobiling near Unser's ranch on the New Mexico and Colorado border and unknowingly crossed into protected wilderness area within the Rio Grande National Forest. They spent two nights there in subzero temperatures. Later, Unser sought help from the U.S. Forest Service to find one of the abandoned snowmobiles, only to be charged with violating a federal law prohibiting operation of a motor vehicle within a wilderness area.[39] Unser was convicted at trial and fined seventy-five dollars. He appealed to the Tenth U.S. Circuit Court of Appeals. Noting that the statute at hand did not include a *mens rea* requirement, the Tenth Circuit wrote that, "Our task is to determine, as best we can, the intent of Congress in empowering the Secretary of Agriculture to adopt regulations applicable to National Forest lands and enforceable by criminal penalties. Then, having found that intent, we must determine whether the intent is compatible with due process. *Unfortunately, we find little direct guidance in the language Congress used*"[40] (emphasis added).

Nevertheless, relying on *Morissette*, the Tenth Circuit upheld Unser's conviction, explaining, "This 1996 offense occurred in a time frame when heavier sentences of imprisonment and fines are more common. In light of these circumstances and the lack of besmirching an offender's reputation by a felony conviction, we are persuaded that the public welfare offense in question here was properly held by the district judge not to have a required *mens rea* element."[41]

Note that the Tenth Circuit stated that Congress did not specify *mens rea* in the Wilderness Act, but the appellate court affirmed Unser's conviction anyway. In a rare alliance, the Heritage Foundation and the National Association of Criminal Defense Lawyers jointly issued a special report in 2010 entitled *Without Intent: How Congress Is Eroding the Criminal Intent Requirement in Federal Law*. The report offers five recommendations to Congress:

- Enact default rules of interpretation ensuring that guilty-mind requirements are adequate to protect against unjust conviction.
- Codify the rule of lenity, which grants defendants the benefit of the doubt when Congress fails to legislate clearly.
- Require adequate judiciary committee oversight of every bill proposing criminal offenses or penalties.
- Provide detailed written justification for and analysis of all new federal criminalization.
- Redouble efforts to draft every federal criminal offense clearly and precisely.[42]

These recommendations arose from analysis of 446 new non-violent criminal offenses proposed in the 109th session of Congress, which met in 2005 and 2006. According to the study, "Over 57 percent of the offenses introduced, and 64 percent of those enacted into law, contained inadequate *mens rea* requirements, putting the innocent at risk of criminal punishment."[43] By inadequate, the study meant those proposed offenses that had either no *mens rea* requirement (25.3 percent) or that had a weak *mens rea* requirement (31.8 percent).[44]

For those proposed offenses that had no *mens rea* requirement, "The defendant's knowledge, intent, misperceptions, mistakes, or accidents are essentially irrelevant to his innocence or guilt."[45] This is strict liability—you did it, you're guilty, period. For proposed offenses categorized as having weak *mens rea* requirements, these include offenses that require the defendant to knowingly engage in an activity without necessarily knowing, or having reason to know, that the activity is itself illegal.[46]

After the publication of *Without Intent* in 2010, Unser was asked to address the Subcommittee on Crime, Terrorism, and Homeland Security. In his prepared statement, Unser said, "Laws should not be written so that the government can prosecute us for things we have no idea are illegal or wrong. There was nothing I could have done on that day to keep from becoming a criminal short of staying at home in my house. Lord knows there are probably laws that the government could use to make me a criminal in my own home as well."[47]

Unser's statement also touches on a basic theme of this book: the issues we address don't skew to one side of the political spectrum. As Unser told Congress,

> I also understand that one of the things this hearing is about is a report by two organizations on opposite ends of the spectrum, the National Association of Criminal Defense Lawyers (NACDL) and the Heritage Foundation. I've followed politics and government for a long time. I never thought I'd see two organizations like that, along with the American Bar Association, the National Federation of Independent Business, and the ACLU (American Civil Liberties Union), all supporting the same thing. That's not a lineup probably anyone thought they would see.
>
> This isn't a Republican problem or a Democrat problem. It's not about liberals or conservatives or progressives or whatever. It's not about who's rich or who's poor, or who's black, brown, or white. These bad laws can trap any American. Anyone can be the victim of over-criminalization, and bad laws and bad prosecutions ruin our criminal justice system.[48]

Void for Vagueness

When does the pastime of "hanging out" become the crime of loitering? When does "chilling" become the crime of being an idle person? Nuisance crimes, while minor, are often hard to describe in words that can be easily understood and fairly applied. The ability to distinguish between enjoying our leisure and engaging in criminal activity has proven so difficult that the courts have overturned many loitering and vagrancy statutes as violations of the U.S. Constitution's Fifth and Fourteenth Amendment protections of due process.

Due process essentially means fairness, and criminal laws that do not provide an adequate description of the activity they prohibit will be ruled a violation of our due process rights. Accordingly, such laws will be declared void due to their vagueness. Paxson asks his students to define what is meant by playing one's music "too loud" or staying out "too late" at night. He has discovered that among some college students, there is no such thing as music being "too loud" and staying out "too late" can mean returning home several days later.

In 1931, the Ninth Circuit U.S. Court of Appeals voided a Hawaiian law that punished those who "habitually loaf, loiter, and/or idle upon any public street or highway or in any public place." As the court pointed out, idling was good business for Hawaii and other places that are popular with tourists. "In short, the multitudes who seek rest, recreation, and pleasure at summer and winter resorts and at sea shores are at best little more than idlers or loiterers."[49] In 1972, the U.S. Supreme Court ruled that a Florida vagrancy statute was unconstitutional because it failed "to give a person of ordinary intelligence fair notice that his contemplated conduct is forbidden by the statute," and because it encouraged "arbitrary and erratic arrests and convictions."[50]

Former Enron officer Jeffrey Skilling found himself charged under a federal indictment for a variety of crimes, including conspiracy to commit "honest-services" wire fraud, a violation of 18 U.S.C. § 1346 (1988) described as a "scheme or artifice to deprive another of the intangible right of honest services." Skilling was convicted of this and other crimes related to his efforts to deceive investors about Enron's financial performance shortly before the company collapsed in late 2001. His appeals brought the case to the U.S. Supreme Court. The court's decision, written by Justice Ruth Bader Ginsburg, held that the statute itself was not vague as it applied to bribes and kickback schemes. However, the court found that the federal prosecutor's attempt to use it against Skilling, whose crimes included neither bribes nor kickbacks, would require an interpretation of the statute that was vague.

Justice Antonin Scalia agreed with Skilling's argument that the statute failed to provide fair notice of what constituted criminal activity and thus it encouraged arbitrary enforcement. Scalia was one of three justices who concurred with the decision written by Justice Ginsburg that Skilling had not violated the statute, but disagreed with Ginsburg's assessment that the statute clearly applied to bribes and kickback schemes. As Scalia plainly put it, §1346 "fails to define the conduct it prohibits."[51] In an earlier case, Scalia said of the law, "it would seemingly cover a salaried employee's phoning in sick to go to a ball game."[52] As some commentators have pointed out, being a bad employee doesn't necessarily constitute a crime. But a broad interpretation of § 1346 could indeed treat a slacker as a criminal.

Sentencing Concerns

In the late twentieth century, legislatures passed numerous laws that affected sentencing in criminal trials. Many of these changes were seen at the time as reforming the sentencing process. As Ashley Nellis of the Sentencing Project explains, "Mounting public dissatisfaction with the justice system, particularly in the late 1980s and 1990s, was part of a larger movement toward more legislative control of the criminal justice process at the expense of the discretion of judges and parole boards."[53] In many states, judges are appointed by governors rather than directly elected by the people; this is also true of state parole boards. Elected legislators, mindful of voters' mistrust of the criminal justice process, enacted legislation that was portrayed as creating better accountability to voters, and even more significantly, to victims of crime.

"Truth-in-sentencing" legislation focused on more accurately aligning the sentences enumerated in criminal statutes and the sentences actually served. For example, the old "Concord sentence" in Massachusetts allowed a judge to sentence a convicted defendant to serve a purported term of years at the state prison in Concord, when in reality, the defendant would only have to serve a tenth of that sentence. (The pretense of a Concord sentence is particularly apparent when considering that some female defendants received Concord sentences although the Concord prison houses only male prisoners.) Truth-in-sentencing legislation in Massachusetts accordingly did away with the Concord sentence.

Other legislation in the states generated changes in how "good time" is calculated and how it affects time actually served. Accumulating good time allows prisoners to reduce their sentence as an incentive for good behavior while incarcerated. In its most basic form, good time means that a prisoner has not been cited for infractions of prison rules over a specified period. Prisoners can also be rewarded good time for participation in educational, vocational, or behavioral programming. For example, Watson received one year off his sentence, plus additional days of good time, for participating in the Residential Drug Abuse Treatment Program (RDAP) while incarcerated at the Federal Prison

Camp in Beaumont, Texas, thanks to subsection (e) in the federal sentencing law, 18 U.S.C. § 3621. The trend in the late twentieth century was to reduce or eliminate good time in order to facilitate truth in sentencing. Unfortunately, this took away an incentive that prison administrators found helpful in maintaining prisoners' behavior.

Mandatory Minimums

Another common sentencing change in the late twentieth century was the enactment of mandatory minimum sentences for a wide variety of offenses, both violent and nonviolent. When legislation establishes a mandatory minimum sentence, the trial judge's sentencing role is diminished or even eliminated, with the judge required to provide the sentence that the legislature has prescribed, regardless of any mitigating factors. One of the more infamous examples occurred in 2004 in the case of *U.S. v. Angelos*. The defendant sold eight one-ounce bags of marijuana to a government informant. The informant said that he observed that Angelos was in possession of a gun during two of the drug sales; there was no claim that Angelos threatened anyone with the gun. The facts of the case triggered a combination of federal laws that resulted in Angelos being subject to a mandatory minimum sentence of fifty-five years. It was Angelos's first criminal conviction.

As U.S. District Court Judge Paul Cassell told Angelos at sentencing, "While the sentence appears to be cruel, unjust and irrational, in our system of separated powers Congress makes the final decisions as to appropriate criminal penalties."[54] Cassell pointed out that Angelos was subject to a prison term "which more than doubles the sentence of, for example, an aircraft hijacker (293 months), a terrorist who detonates a bomb in a public place (235 months), a racist who attacks a minority with the intent to kill and inflicts permanent or life threatening injuries (210 months), a second-degree murderer, or a rapist."[55] Despite calls for a presidential commutation of his sentence, Angelos remains imprisoned.

Angelos's case highlights the role of mandatory minimum sentences in the government's War on Drugs. Mandatory minimums for simple (personal) possession and possession with intent to distribute (small-time drug dealing) have proved to have a particularly significant impact on females. Between 1986 and 1996, the number of women incarcerated in state facilities for drug offenses increased 888 percent.[56] More recently, the Bureau of Justice Statistics (BJS) tells us that the female prisoner population increased an average 2.2% between 2000 and 2009; the male prisoner population averaged a 1.7% increase during the same period.[57]

Two-thirds of female offenders are mothers of minor children.[58] Many of these mothers are single parents. It is certainly appropriate to question the suitability of children living with a drug-dealing parent. The point here is that mandatory minimum sentencing statutes don't give judges the authority to consider whether the children are better off living with their mother, placed in a foster home, or placed in the home of another friend or relative. The first option simply is not available to judges. This means that incarcerated mothers and their children are often required to spend years of separation. Women at the Massachusetts Correctional Institute (MCI) in Framingham, Massachusetts' state prison for female offenders, are only allowed to make collect calls. Because state agencies are not allowed to accept collect calls, mothers at MCI Framingham are unable to talk by telephone to children in foster homes because foster homes are officially categorized as state agencies.[59]

As we discussed in Chapter 3, scholars have explored how former slave states met the labor needs of former slave owners through the convict lease system in the nineteenth century. Egregious laws, such as laws that made vagrancy a crime punishable by imprisonment, were passed in part to round up and imprison former slaves. While incarcerated, these prisoners would then be leased by local sheriffs to plantation owners, many of whom had previously owned the prisoners as slaves. The situation isn't much better today.

Let's look at Louisiana, a state where convict leasing had been widespread. Today, Louisiana has the highest incarceration rate in the United States, which itself has the highest incarceration rate among the nations of the world. With its prison population of 39,328 in a state with 4.65 million people, Louisiana's incarceration rate in 2013 was 840 per 100,000. Louisiana's embrace of mandatory minimum sentences for a wide variety of crimes helps explains this. In 2014, while many states were discussing scaling back mandatory minimum sentences, Louisiana Governor Bobby Jindal, preparing to run as a Republican candidate for the 2016 presidential election, signed into law a bill that raised the mandatory minimum for even first-time convictions for selling heroin from five years to ten, and increased the maximum penalty for repeat offenders from fifty years to ninety-nine.[60]

Additionally, all life sentences in Louisiana are life without parole. Not only does Louisiana have the highest incarceration rate in the U.S., it has the highest percentage of state prisoners serving life sentences without parole—almost eleven percent.[61] Nonviolent offenders are serving many of these life sentences. As a Republican-appointed federal judge has said, sentences for non-violent crimes that extend past the age of 60 are "pointless."[62]

Chief Justice Ralph Gants of the Massachusetts Supreme Judicial Court has been stridently advocating for the elimination of mandatory minimums for drug offenses. Gants, speaking at a legal symposium in October 2014, said, "We need our sentences not merely to punish and deter, but also to provide offenders with the supervision and the tools they will need to maximize the chance of success upon release and minimize the likelihood of recidivism."[63] Noting that 674 people died of opiod overdoses in 2013, compared to 338 in 2000, Gants said, "To those who favor the status quo in the so-called War on Drugs, I ask: How well is the status quo working?"[64]

Legislative support for increased incarceration and mandatory minimums is not just about maintaining a politically popular stance; there are also financial motives. The Justice Policy Institute found that the three main private prison companies (Corrections Corporation of America, the GEO Group, and Cornell Companies, which has since merged with GEO) contributed $835,514 to federal candidates between 2000 and 2010 and about $6.1 million to state politicians between 2003 and 2010.[65] They also spend millions on lobbying efforts at the federal and state level. CCA spent over $900,000 on federal lobbying and GEO spent between $120,000 to $199,992 in Florida alone during a three-month span in 2011.[66] Obviously, laws that require a mandatory sentence provide financial benefits to firms that profit from the incarceration of prisoners. We look at the various entities that benefit financially from mass incarceration in the next chapter.

There have been some encouraging developments recently. New legislation at the federal and state level allows judges to render sentences that are less than the mandatory minimums. These departures, as they are known, are based on criteria listed in the reform legislation. In a 2013 report, the organization Families Against Mandatory Minimums praised a federal statute, 18 U.S.C. § 3553(f), which allows departures in sentencing for drug offenses. Five criteria must be met to grant the defendant a departure from the mandatory minimum sentence; he must prove to the sentencing judge, by a preponderance of the evidence (i.e., that it is more likely than not), that:

> [h]is past criminal record must be minimal; he must not have been a leader, organizer, or supervisor in the commission of the offense; he must not have used violence in the commission or the offense, and the offense must not have resulted in serious injury; and prior to sentencing, he must tell the government all that he knows of the offense and any related misconduct.[67]

The Families Against Mandatory Minimums report also identified eight states that have implemented "safety valve" legislation that allows sentencing judges to make departures from mandatory minimums based on specified conditions.[68] Oklahoma has since followed suit. In 2015, Republican governor Mary Fallin signed into law Oklahoma's Judicial Safety Valve Act, which allows judges to depart from mandatory minimum sentences if imposing the mandatory minimum would "result in substantial injustice to the defendant" or "is not necessary to the protection of the public." At the time, Oklahoma had more than 100 offenses with mandatory minimums attached.[69]

Republican U.S. Senator Rand Paul and Democrat U.S. Senator Patrick Leahy introduced a federal safety valve bill in 2013, which failed to pass, and reintroduced it in 2015.[70] In an address at the Georgetown University Law Center in January 2013, Leahy said,

> We also have to examine issues related to our high rate of imprisonment ... and mandatory minimum sentences, to make sure that we have approaches that effectively reduce crime and target violent offenders. I say this as a former prosecutor and I say this as a chairman of the Senate Judiciary Committee: I think our reliance on mandatory minimums at the state and federal level has been a great mistake. I'm not convinced it has lowered crime, but I [know] that we have imprisoned people who should not be there, and we have wasted money that is better spent on other things. I think at the federal level and at the state level, get rid of these mandatory minimum sentences. Let judges act as judges and make up their own mind [about] what should be done. The idea that we protect society by one-size-fits-all, or the idea that we can do this kind of symbolism to make us safer—it just does not work in the real world.[71]

There remain over 100 federal offenses that carry mandatory minimum sentences; these range from killing the president of the United States (life) to failure to report seaboard saloon purchases to customers (three months).[72]

We are pleased to see that those calling for sentencing reforms come from various points along the political spectrum. From the left, the National Lawyers Guild has said, "Judges must be allowed to fulfill their proper role of imposing sentences that fit the crime while still protecting public safety. That will require the repeal of mandatory minimum sentencing laws altogether."[73] These words were echoed from the right by billionaire Tea Party patron Charles G. Koch in an article for the online journal *Politico* in January 2015, calling for legislatures to "end unduly harsh sentences and resulting disparities by eliminating mandatory minimum sentences that dictate punishment unrelated to the nature or harm of the underlying crime and facts. We must honor the ideal of the punishment fitting the crime by allowing judges to exercise discretion."[74]

Parole

During the "nothing works" era of the late twentieth century, abolishing parole was politically popular, and nearly a third of the states did so. Congress eliminated parole for new federal prisoners in 1984. One of the easiest to anticipate consequences of abolishing parole was a surge in the nation's prison population, as the outflow of prisoners from prison decreased while the inflow increased. This proved to be one of the many factors that contributed to mass incarceration in the U.S. Some states, including Connecticut, Colorado, and Florida, have since reinstituted parole with the primary goal of relieving prison overcrowding.[75]

Another consequence of abolishment was less apparent, although there were warnings by corrections officials: getting rid of parole meant that prisoners were released back into free society without correctional supervision. This presents another problem with mandatory minimum sentences. When an act of the legislature requires a judge to impose a mandatory sentence and binds the corrections system to house a prisoner for that mandatory sentence, what happens when that mandatory sentence ends? Too often, an offender is released back into free society—where he or she got into trouble the last time—without supervision. As Massachusetts and some other states have seen, there needs to be a point during an offender's sentence at which he or she can be considered for parole. Here is a recent example from Massachusetts:

Figure 5.2. Sentencing Reform

M.G.L. 94C section 32(b) Distribution of Class A drug (i.e. heroin) second offense

Old law: five year mandatory minimum incarceration

New law as of 2012: eligible for parole after 3 1/2 years' incarceration

If deemed ineligible for parole, the offender remains incarcerated. If the offender receives parole, he or she is released back into society while remaining under correctional supervision, which typically will include drug testing.

Some critics of parole have pointed to the high recidivism rates of parolees. However, many of these parolees return to prison due to technical violations of their parole rather than criminal violations. For example, a condition of parole may be not to patronize bars and other places where alcohol is served.

Another condition may be not to associate with other known criminals. Neither of these acts by themselves is a crime, but either can constitute a technical violation for which an attentive parole officer may choose to return the parolee to prison.

While many critics argue that parole is a slap on the wrist, many prisoners dread it. As we discussed in the last chapter, given a choice between early release on parole and remaining incarcerated until their prison sentence is completed, many prisoners choose to remain in prison. This choice—"wrapping up" one's sentence—is made because prisoners do not want to be released under parole supervision.

The Sixth Amendment's Right to Trial by Jury: What Happened?

Despite what many would believe from watching courtroom dramas, most criminal prosecutions don't go to trial. As the U.S. Supreme Court acknowledged in its 2012 decision of *Missouri v. Frye*, "Ninety-seven percent of federal convictions and ninety-four percent of state convictions are the result of guilty pleas."[76] Former federal prosecutors Mary Patrice Brown and Stevan E. Bunnell have stated, "Plea bargaining is a defining, if not the defining, feature of the federal criminal justice system."[77]

In the discussion of Watson's guilty plea in Chapter 2, we commented that many Americans have a distorted view of plea bargaining, believing that defendants usually prevail in the process. (One tough-on-crime book typical of the 1990s described plea bargaining as the defendant's "arrogant manipulation of a paper-tiger court system."[78]) In reality, the prosecution has much more bargaining power than does the defense, and many plea bargains are adhesion contracts, with the prosecutor dictating the terms and the defendant forced to adhere to those terms.

When a defendant agrees to a plea bargain, s/he is waiving Fifth Amendment protection against forced self-incrimination, and most of the Sixth Amendment, which articulates protections such as the right to a jury trial and the right to confront adverse witnesses, among other provisions. In *Brady v. U.S.*, the U.S. Supreme Court unanimously upheld plea bargaining:

> [W]e cannot hold that it is unconstitutional for the State to extend a benefit to a defendant who in turn extends a substantial benefit to the State and who demonstrates by his plea that he is ready and willing to admit his crime and to enter the correctional system in a frame of

mind that affords hope for success in rehabilitation over a shorter period of time than might otherwise be necessary.[79]

There are two types of plea bargaining. Charge bargaining occurs when the
prosecutor offers to drop some charges or bring lesser charges in exchange for
the defendant's guilty plea. In sentencing bargaining, the prosecutor offers to
recommend a sentence less than the maximum for the offenses to which the
defendant offers to plead guilty. Note, however, that a prosecutor can only recommend a sentence to the judge. The length of the sentence remains the judge's
decision to make. Paxson has seen judges refuse to accept guilty pleas because
they disagreed with the recommended sentences.

Many judges, lawyers, and others who study the courts argue that plea bargaining is of absolute necessity in face of an already overburdened judicial system. (There is a similar aversion to going to trial in civil matters; when you
see advertisements for personal injury lawyers, they usually tell you that they
will get you the best possible *settlement*.)

Others are concerned that plea bargaining rarely results in justice. In a note
in the *Review of Law and Social Justice*, Tina Wan writes:

> The prosecutor's unlimited discretion to pick and choose which charges
> to bring against defendants and ability to create significant sentenc-
> ing differentials between similar defendants can lead to the practice
> of overcharging and the use of threats to seek the harshest sentence to
> keep defendants from going to trial. Innocent, risk-averse defendants
> may not be willing to risk going to trial to receive an exceedingly se-
> vere sentence, and instead, will choose to plead guilty to ensure a more
> lenient sentence.[80]

As U.S. Senator Ted Cruz has stated, "In this plea-bargaining system, prosecutors
have extraordinary power, nudging both judges and juries out of the truth-
seeking process. The prosecutor is now the proverbial judge, jury, and execu-
tioner.... Given the risks involved in turning down a plea offer, it is not unheard
of for people to plead guilty to crimes they never committed."[81]

In a 2014 essay in the *New York Review of Books*, Senior U.S. District Judge
Jed S. Rakoff points to studies that estimate that between two to eight percent
of those who plead guilty are actually innocent.[82] Rakoff continues:

> The size of that range suggests the imperfection of the data; but let
> us suppose that it is even lower, say, no more than 1 percent. When
> you recall that, of the 2.2 million Americans in prison, over 2 million
> are there because of plea bargains, we are then talking about an esti-

mated 20,000 persons, or more, who are in prison for crimes to which they pleaded guilty but did not in fact commit.[83]

Watson faced the possibility of serving more than twenty years in prison, had he chosen to go to trial. Instead, he pleaded guilty in return for a sentence of fifty-seven months. With the advantage of hindsight, Watson knows that he made the right decision. Unfortunately, Watson is hardly alone among defendants who are innocent yet plead guilty.

Plea-bargained cases are typically preferable to judges than cases that go to trial. This is especially the case in those states in which judges are elected; as discussed in the previous chapter, thirty-nine states hold elections for the judges of general jurisdiction trial courts.[84] As the son of a Texas trial court judge who had to stand for reelection every four years, Paxson knows how important it is for trial judges to have a "rocket docket." When running for reelection, judges like to boast about the number of cases that proceeded through his or her court each year. The common belief is, the more cases handled, the more hardworking the judge will appear to voters. Therefore, while judges are required to enter into a colloquy with each defendant offering to plead guilty to make certain that the defendant is doing so knowingly and intelligently, and is not under duress, judges often have a bias toward accepting guilty pleas, even when the defendant's status is not quite clear.

In *North Carolina v. Alford*, the U.S. Supreme Court considered whether it was permissible to allow a defendant to plead guilty to a lesser charge in order to avoid facing the possibility of the death penalty, although the defendant denied his actual guilt. The court ruled:

> An individual accused of crime may voluntarily, knowingly, and understandingly consent to the imposition of a prison sentence even if he is unwilling or unable to admit his participation in the acts constituting the crime ... when ... a defendant intelligently concludes that his interests require entry of a guilty plea and the record before the judge contains strong evidence of actual guilt.[85]

This case introduced what is now known as an "*Alford* plea," available today in federal and most state courts. Similar to a plea of *nolo contendere* (no contest), an *Alford* plea allows a trial judge to accept the defendant's offer to plead guilty even though the defendant does not admit actual guilt. Unlike a plea of *no contendere*, which does not require supporting evidence, there is a safeguard in the *Alford* plea, as the judge must find strong evidence of guilt. Nevertheless, there remains pressure on judges to accept guilty pleas for efficiency's sake.

University of Chicago law professor Albert W. Alschuler has pronounced, "Alford pleas are awful. There could hardly be a clearer violation of due process than sending someone to prison who has neither been found guilty nor admitted his guilt. If anything short of torture can shock your conscience, Alford pleas should."[86] Alschuler goes on to describe a criminal justice system in which it is in everybody's best interest for a defendant to enter a guilty plea; everybody except the defendant, that is. The trial judge clears another case from the docket. The prosecutor has a conviction. As for the defense attorney, Alschuler says,

> A lawyer's duty in a plea bargaining system is often to confront her client forcefully with the strength of the evidence against him.... These lawyers regard themselves, not as saving their clients' souls, but as encouraging them to make sound tactical decisions. They may be influenced by the fact that a guilty plea can save the lawyers themselves days of work. From a defense attorney's perspective, a guilty plea can be a quick buck.[87]

Some commentators argue that plea bargaining allows for laziness on the part of various members in the criminal justice system, include police, judges, prosecutors, and defense attorneys, all of whom can avoid the effort and scrutiny of the trial process through plea bargaining. Others argue that it is unfair to victims to allow defendants to plead guilty to lesser crimes and thus avoid their proper punishment. Still others claim that plea bargaining harms defendants by forcing them to admit to crimes that they may have not committed in order to avoid an uncertain outcome at trial.

Grand Juries

Parts of the U.S. Constitution arose as a reaction against the perceived inequities of British rule. These include the First Amendment's separation of church and state and the Fourth Amendment's requirement that search warrants provide particular descriptions of the persons, places, and things to be searched. Other parts of the Constitution embody principles inherited from the British. The grand jury system existed for centuries in Britain before its inclusion in the Fifth Amendment of the U.S. Constitution in 1791. The original purpose of grand juries was to provide scrutiny by citizens over cases in which the government had charged someone with, in the language of the Fifth Amendment, an "infamous" crime, before those cases went to trial. The belief was that grand juries would protect defendants from malicious prosecutions based on little evidence. Today, an infamous crime is generally any serious felony.

Many of the provisions of the U.S. Constitution have been incorporated to the states via the Fourteenth Amendment's state due process clause. These include freedom of speech, the right to a search warrant, and the right to bear arms. However, when the U.S. Supreme Court was asked to incorporate the right to a grand jury to the states in 1884, the court declined to do so.[88] Only about half of the states and the federal government provide grand juries today.

The standard for a grand jury indictment is probable cause to believe that the defendant committed the crime, a much lesser standard of certainty than at trial, which is proof of guilt beyond a reasonable doubt. (Probable cause is also the standard required for a police officer to make an arrest.) Unlike juries at criminal trials, a grand jury does not have to be unanimous. Some states, such as Massachusetts, and the federal government use twenty-three member grand juries, of which only a majority of grand jurors (twelve or more) have to agree to indict. Some states have smaller grand juries, of which typically a supermajority (e.g., nine out of twelve) of members must agree to indict, issuing a "true bill." If a grand jury declines to indict ("no bill"), the prosecutor may still convene another grand jury to consider the case. This is not a double jeopardy violation, which prohibits two trials for the same offense, as a grand jury hearing is not a trial.

Unlike trials, which the Sixth Amendment requires to be public, grand jury hearings are highly secretive. This secrecy protects witnesses but it also leaves many people concerned about what exactly happens in private proceedings. Hearsay evidence, illegally obtained evidence, and even rumors may be discussed in grand jury proceedings. Over time, the grand jury process has largely skewed in favor of the prosecution, so much so that it is common practice for defense attorneys to waive the defendants' right to a grand jury hearing. This is because unlike a trial, which is an adversarial proceeding where both the prosecution and defense can present evidence and challenge the evidence of the other side, in a grand jury proceeding, only the prosecution gets to present its case to the grand jury. The defense is not present.

In an article in the *Cornell Law Review*, Andrew D. Leipold writes, "although the nominal purpose of the grand jury is to protect those accused of crimes, few defendants take comfort from its presence; indeed, the staunchest defenders of the institution are prosecutors."[89] Many defense attorneys believe that grand jury proceedings merely provide prosecutors with a forum for testing their cases before going to trial.

Solomon Wachtler, former Chief Justice of the New York Court of Appeals, is quoted by author Tom Wolfe as saying "a grand jury would 'indict a ham sandwich,' if that's what you wanted."[90] By "you," Wachtler is referring to the prosecutor. Leipold's analysis of grand juries uses less figurative language, but reaches the same conclusion. "As long as the grand jury proceeding is nonadversarial, and as long as the jurors are asked to make a legal determination based on a single set of facts, there will be no reason to believe that prosecutors will refrain from submitting cases because they fear a no bill."[91]

In the wake of the 2014 deaths of Michael Brown in Ferguson, Missouri, and Eric Garner on Staten Island, grand juries were asked to consider homicide charges against the police officers involved. In both cases, the grand jury refused to indict the officers. Many observers believe this was the result of prosecutors submitting the cases to grand juries to appease the public, and then intentionally presenting a confusing case to the grand jury (in Missouri) or a weak case (in Staten Island). We weren't there, so we won't judge. However, prosecutors must work alongside the police and must have the trust and confidence of police officers. This creates a conflict of interest in cases where police officers are potential defendants and prosecutors meet with grand jurors to consider those cases in private.

Some of those who are critical of the current grand jury system argue for an adversarial process before a judge in which both the prosecution and defense put forward arguments about why a criminal case should or should not advance to trial. In some states, there are pretrial proceedings known as probable cause hearings or preliminary hearings that serve this purpose. However, in some of those states that do provide for these hearings, the prosecutor can still submit a case to a grand jury afterward, even if the defense waives its right to a grand jury. While there have been calls for improving the current grand jury system or getting rid of it altogether, there has been little serious discussion of it among legislatures and courts. As Leipold's *Cornell Law Review* article summarizes the issue:

> [T]he dramatic changes needed to fix the problems with grand juries will come at a high cost, and the decision whether to pay those costs raises questions that are more political and philosophical than legal. Perhaps the best explanation for the continued existence of the grand jury is that those in a position to improve the screening process are content with the appearance of protection for the accused, even if there is a large gap between appearance and reality.[92]

Currently, and for the foreseeable future, the grand jury system protects neither us nor our sandwiches from malicious prosecution.

Conclusion

There is no question that being tough on crime is good politics. There is a widely held misperception among the public that crime continues to increase in the U.S. As a result, voters complain about crime to their legislators and legislators respond by giving voters they want: more criminal laws. This had led to the overcriminalization of American society, with significant overlap in federal and state law. Exacerbating the problem is the fact that many criminal laws are enacted in such haste that they lack precise definitions of what constitutes criminal behavior and the requisite criminal state of mind. Because there so many crimes today, often only vaguely described and with disproportionally high sentences, many defendants are often willing to forego their opportunity to have their case heard by a judge or jury and settle instead for a plea bargain.

There is also a common belief among Americans that rational choice theory explains most criminal activity—that criminals choose to be criminals. As a result, in the late twentieth century, politicians began steadily increasing punitive measures for criminal offenders while reducing or eliminating efforts at rehabilitation. Many Americans believed that mandatory minimums and the elimination of parole would help deter criminal offenders from engaging in crimes. The dramatic increase in mandatory minimums meant that judges are often unable to make the punishment fit the crime and the offender. Elimination of parole not only aggravated prison overcrowding, it prevented correctional officials from helping offenders reintegrate back into free society. Finally, the grand jury process, originally conceived as a means of shielding Americans from malicious prosecutions, is seen as having been largely coopted by the prosecution.

We end this chapter with guarded optimism. As we've noted above, there is bipartisan support for reforming many of the concerns we discuss here. The current distrust of government emanating from both the right and left flanks of the political spectrum may force legislators and other policy makers to address these concerns.

Notes

1. Hillary Clinton, Keynote Address, David N. Dinkins Leadership and Public Policy Forum, Columbia University, New York, April 29, 2015.

2. Mitt Romney, interview by Brian Kilmeade, *Fox and Friends*, *Fox News*, May 4, 2015.

3. Heather Mason Kiefer, "Public on Justice System: Fair, but Still Too Soft," Gallup, February 3, 2004, http://www.gallup.com/poll/10474/public-justice-system-fair-still-too-soft.aspx.

4. Lydia Saad, "Americans Express Mixed Confidence in Criminal Justice System," Gallup, July 11, 2011, http://www.gallup.com/poll/148433/Americans-Express-Mixed-Confidence-Criminal-Justice-System.aspx?utm_source=&utm_medium=&utm_campaign=tiles.

5. Justin McCarthy, "Most Americans Still See Crime Up Over Last Year," Gallup, November 21, 2014, http://www.gallup.com/poll/179546/americans-crime-last-year.aspx.

6. George Gerbner, Larry Gross, Michael Morgan, and Nancy Signorielli, "The 'Mainstreaming' of America: Violence Profile No. 11," *Journal of Communication* 30, no. 3 (1980): 10–29.

7. Stephen King, "Why We Crave Horror Movies," in *The Simon and Schuster Short Prose Reader*, ed. Robert W. Funk, Susan X. Day, Elizabeth McMahan, and Linda S. Coleman, 4th ed. (Upper Saddle River, NJ: Pearson Prentice Hall, 2006): 280.

8. Erik Luna, "Overextending the Criminal Law," in *Go Directly to Jail: The Criminalization of Almost Everything*, ed. Gene Healey (Washington, DC: Cato Institute, 2004): Kindle ed., chap. 1.

9. "U.S. Federal Bureau of Prisons, FY 2013 Budget Request at a Glance, Federal Prison System (BOP)," (Washington, DC: Federal Bureau of Prisons), February 2, 2014, http://www.justice.gov/sites/default/files/jmd/legacy/2014/02/02/fy13-bop-bud-summary.pdf.

10. "Joint Statement of Treasury Secretary Jacob J. Lew and Office of Management and Budget Director Shaun Donovan on Budget Results for Fiscal Year 2014," (Washington, DC: U.S. Treasury Department, October 15, 2014), http://www.treasury.gov/press-center/press-releases/Pages/jl2664.aspx.

11. E. Ann Carson, "Prisoners in 2013," (Washington DC: U.S. Bureau of Justice Statistics, September 30, 2014), http://www.bjs.gov/content/pub/pdf/p13.pdf.

12. James D. Calder, *The Origins and Development of Federal Crime Control Policy: Herbert Hoover's Initiatives*, (Westport, CT: Praeger, 1993): 25.

13. Ronald F. Wright, *Federal or State? Sorting as a Sentencing Choice*, 21 CRIMINAL JUSTICE 16, 17 (Summer 2006).

14. James A. Strazzella, *The Federalization of Criminal Law*, TASK FORCE OF FED. OF CRIM. LAW REP. A.B.A. CRIM JUST. SEC., 10 (1998).

15. Federal Kidnapping Act 18 U.S.C. § 1201 (1932).

16. Anti-Car Theft Act of 1992, 18 U.S.C. § 2119 (1992).

17. Steven Nelson, "Federal 'Revenge Porn' Bill Will Seek to Shrivel Booming Internet Fad," *U.S. News and World Report*, March 26, 2014, http://www.usnews.com/news/articles/2014/03/26/federal-revenge-porn-bill-will-seek-to-shrivel-booming-internet-fad.

18. NY Penal Law § 490.00, accessed June 2, 2015, http://public.leginfo.state.ny.us.

19. Ted Cruz, "Reduce Federal Crimes and Give Judges Flexibility," in *Solutions: American Leaders Speak out on Criminal Justice*, ed. Inimai Chettiar and Michael Waldman, (New York: Brennan Center for Justice at New York University Law School, April 27, 2015): 31, https://www.brennancenter.org/analysis/reduce-federal-crimes-and-give-judges-flexibility.

20. Harvey Silvergate, *Three Felonies a Day: How the Feds Target the Innocent*, (New York: Encounter Books, 2009): Kindle ed.

21. Ibid., Introduction.

22. James A. Strazzella, *The Federalization of Criminal Law*, TASK FORCE OF FED. OF CRIM. LAW REP. A.B.A. CRIM JUST. SEC. 9 (1998).

23. Gary Fields and John R. Emshwiller, "As Criminal Laws Proliferate, More Are Ensnared," *Wall Street Journal*, July 23, 2011, http://www.wsj.com/articles/SB10001424052748703749504576172714184601654.

24. Cruz, 33.

25. Yates v. United States, 574 U.S. __ , __ (2015) (Kagan, J., dissenting).

26. Ibid.

27. Jeff Welty, *Overcriminalization in North Carolina*, 92 N.C. L. REV. 1935, 1942 (2014).

28. James R. Copland, Isaac Gorodetski, and Michael J. Reitz, "Overcriminalizing the Wolverine State: A Primer and Possible Reforms for Michigan," Manhattan Institute for Policy Research, Issue Brief no. 31, October 2014, http://www.manhattan-institute.org/html/ib_31.htm#.VWeVWs9Vikp.

29. Nicole D. Porter and Tyler Clemens, "Drug Free Zone Laws: An Overview of State Policies," (Washington, DC: The Sentencing Project, December 2013), http://sentencing-project.org/doc/publications/sen_Drug-Free%20Zone%20Laws.pdf.

30. Porter and Clemens.

31. California Penal Code 190(a).

32. Lockyer v. Andrade, 538 U.S. 63 (2003).

33. Connie de la Vega, Amanda Solter, So-Ryun Kwon, and Dana Marie Isaac, "Cruel and Unusual: U.S. Sentencing Practices in a Global Context," University of San Francisco School of Law (May 2012): 33, http://www.usfca.edu/law/clgj/criminalsentencing_pr/ citing Aaron Rappaport and Kara Dansky, *State of Emergency: California's Correctional Crisis,* 22 FED. SENT'G REP. 133 (2010).

34. Charles Hamilton Institute for Race & Justice, "Three Strikes: The Wrong Way to Justice," (Cambridge, MA: Harvard Law School, June 26, 2012), http://www.charleshamiltonhouston.org/wp-content/uploads/2013/11/CHHIRJ-3-Strikes-Report-Merged.pdf.

35. Tracey Kaplan, "Proposition 36: Voters Overwhelmingly Ease Three Strikes Law," *San Jose Mercury News*, November 6, 2012, http://www.mercurynews.com/ci_21943951/prop-36-huge-lead-early-returns.

36. Deborah Becker, " 'Three Strikes' Bill Strikes Nerve among Many in Mass.," WBUR, January 25, 2012, http://www.wbur.org/2012/01/25/three-strikes-bill.

37. Charles Hamilton Institute for Race & Justice.

38. Morissette v. United States, 342 U.S. 247, 254–255 (1952).

39. 16 U.S.C. § 551 (1964).

40. United States v. Unser, 165 F.3rd 755, 761 (10th Cir. 1999) cert. denied, 120 S. Ct. 40 (1999).

41. Ibid., 764.

42. Brian W. Walsh and Tiffany M. Joslyn, *Without Intent: How Congress Is Eroding the Criminal Intent Requirement in Federal Law,* (Washington, DC: The Heritage Foundation and National Association of Criminal Defense Lawyers, 2010): ix.

43. Ibid., x.

44. Ibid., 12.

45. Ibid., 14.

46. Ibid., 15–16.

47. *Reining in Overcriminalization: Assessing the Problems, Proposing Solutions, Making an American Racing Legend Prove He Did Not Commit a "Crime": Testimony Before the Subcommittee on Crime, Terrorism, and Homeland Security of the H. Committee on the Judiciary,* 111th Cong. 2010 (statement of Robert "Bobby" Unser): 10.

48. Ibid., 3.

49. Territory of Hawaii v. Anduha, 48 F.2d 171, 173 (9th Cir. 1931).

50. Papachristou v. City of Jacksonville, 405 U.S. 156, 161 (1972).

51. Skilling v. United States, 561 U.S. __ (2010) (Scalia, J., concurring).

52. Sorich v. United States, 555 U.S. 1204 (2009) (mem.) (Scalia, J., dissenting).

53. Ashley Nellis, *Throwing Away the Key: The Expansion of Life without Parole Sentences in the United States,* 23 FED. SENT'G REP. 1, 28 (2010).

54. United States v. Angelos, 345 F. Supp. 2d 1227, 1230 (D. Utah 2004).

55. Ibid., 1244–1245.

56. The Sentencing Project, "Women in the Criminal Justice System; Briefing Sheets," May 2007, citing Marc Mauer, Cathy Potler, and Richard Wolf, "Gender and Justice: Women, Drugs, and Sentencing Policy," (Washington, DC: The Sentencing Project, November 1999): 7, http://www.sentencingproject.org/doc/publications/womenincj_total.pdf.

57. Paul Guerino, Paige M. Harrison, and William J. Sabol, "Prisoners in 2010," (Washington, DC: U.S. Bureau of Justice Statistics, December 2011, revised February 9, 2012), http://bjs.ojp.usdoj.gov/index.cfm?ty=pbdetail&iid=2230.

58. The Sentencing Project, "Women in the Criminal Justice System; Briefing Sheets," May 2007, citing Christopher J. Mumola, "Incarcerated Parents and Their Children," (Washington, DC: U.S. Bureau of Justice Statistics, August 2000), http://www.sentencingproject.org/doc/publications/womenincj_total.pdf.

59. Faiza Elmasry "Women's Life Behind Bars: Punishment or Reform?" Voice of America, July 5, 2006, http://www.wunrn.com/news/2006/07_03_06/070906_usa_women.htm.

60. Emily Lane, "Bobby Jindal Signs into Law Bill Increasing Heroin Penalties for Dealers to 99 Years," *Times-Picayune,* last modified May 31, 2014, http://www.nola.com/politics/index.ssf/2014/05/bobby_jindal_heroin_penalties.html.

61. Nellis, 31.

62. David M. Zlotnick, *The Future of Federal Sentencing Policy: Learning Lessons from Republican Judicial Appointments in the Guidelines Era,* 79 U. COLO. L. REV. 1, 37 (2008).

63. Milton J. Valencia, "SJC Chief Seeks Reform in Drug Cases," *Boston Globe,* October 16, 2014, https://www.bostonglobe.com/metro/2014/10/16/sjc-chief-justice-ralph-gants-criticizes-mandatory-minimum-sentences-for-drug-offenses/JGBiWv402c4r90il606CsI/story.html.

64. Ibid.

65. Paul Ashton and Amanda Petteruti, "Gaming the System: How the Political Strategies of Private Prison Companies Promote Ineffective Incarceration Policies," (Washington, DC: Justice Policy Institute, June, 2011): 15–16, http://www.justicepolicy.org/uploads/justicepolicy/documents/gaming_the_system.pdf.

66. Ibid., 22.

67. Chris Doyle, "Federal Mandatory Minimum Sentences: The Safety Valve and Substantial Assistance Exceptions," (Washington, DC: Congressional Research Service, October 21, 2103): Summary.

68. "Turning Off the Spigot: How Sentencing Safety Valves Can Help States Protect Public Safety and Save Money," (Washington, DC: Families Against Mandatory Minimums, 2013): 13–18.

69. Rick Green, "Oklahoma Governor Signs Bill to Give Judges More Discretion in Sentencing," *The Oklahoman,* May 4, 2015, http://newsok.com/oklahoma-governor-signs-bill-to-give-judges-more-discretion-in-sentencing/article/5416267.

70. Scott Shackford, "Oklahoma Governor Signs Mandatory Minimum Sentencing Reform Bill," Reason.com, May 5, 2015, http://reason.com/blog/2015/05/05/oklahoma-governor-signs-mandatory-minimu.

71. "Sen. Leahy Calls for Repealing Mandatory Minimums," Families Against Mandatory Minimums, January 16, 2013, http://famm.org/sen-leahy-calls-for-repealing-mandatory-minimums/.

72. "Federal Mandatory Minimums," Families Against Mandatory Minimums, February 25, 2013, http://famm.org/Repository/Files/Chart%20All%20Fed%20MMs%202.25.13.pdf.

73. Barb Dougan, "Drug Sentencing Reforms," National Lawyers Guild Massachusetts Chapter, December 2012, http://www.nlgmass.org/2012/12/drug-sentencing-reforms/.

74. Charles G. Koch and Mark V. Holden, "The Overcriminalization of America," *Politico*, January 7, 2015, http://www.politico.com/magazine/story/2015/01/overcriminalization-of-america-113991_Page2.html#ixzz3bqiVFq7v.

75. Debra Baker, *What Role for Parole?* 85 ABA JOURNAL 14 (May 1999).

76. Missouri v. Frye, 566 U.S. __. __ (2012).

77. Mary Patrice Brown and Stevan E. Bunnell, *Negotiating Justice: Prosecutorial Perspectives on Federal Plea Bargaining in the District of Columbia*, 43 Am. Crim. L. Rev. 1063, 1072 (2006).

78. Robert James Bidinotto, "Subverting Justice," in Robert James Bidinotto, ed., *Criminal Justice? The Legal System Versus Individual Responsibility*, 2nd ed. (Irvington-on-Hudson, NY: The Foundation for Economic Education, 1996): 77.

79. Brady v. U.S., 397 U.S. 742, 753 (1970).

80. Tina Wan, Note, *The Unnecessary Evil Of Plea Bargaining: An Unconstitutional Conditions Problem and a Not-So-Least Restrictive Alternative*, 17 S. CAL. REV. L. & SOC. JUST. 1, 40 (2007).

81. Cruz, 34.

82. Jed S. Rakoff, "Why Innocent People Plead Guilty," *New York Time Review of Books*, November 20, 2014, http://www.nybooks.com/articles/archives/2014/nov/20/why-innocent-people-plead-guilty/.

83. Ibid.

84. "Fact Sheet on Judicial Selection Methods in the States," American Bar Association, February 6, 2002, http://www.americanbar.org/content/dam/aba/migrated/leadership/fact_sheet.pdf.

85. North Carolina v. Alford, 400 U.S. 25, 37-38 (1970).

86. Albert W. Alschuler, *Straining at Gnats and Swallowing Camels: The Selective Morality of Professor Bibas,* 88 CORNELL LAW REVIEW, 1412, 1412 (2003).

87. Ibid., 1422–1423.

88. Hurtado v. California, 110 U.S. 516 (1884).

89. Andrew D. Leipold, *Why Grand Juries Do Not (and Cannot) Protect the Accused*, 80 CORNELL L. REV. 260, 261 (1995).

90. Tom Wolfe, *The Bonfire of the Vanities*, (New York: Bantam Books, 1988): 629.

91. Leipold, 311.

92. Ibid., 323–324.

Chapter 6

As Prosecutors Say, "Follow the Money": Prisons and Profits

When the legendary bank robber Willie Sutton was asked why he robbed banks, he allegedly replied, "Because that's where the money is." Today we could pose a similar question to those in the corrections industry about why they chose their line of work and receive the same answer. There are more ways to make money from crime than just being a criminal; in fact, the money criminals make from their crimes is often far less than what those in the corrections industry earn; and, of course, the corrections industry makes significant amounts of money from crimes that are not for monetary gain, such as personal drug use. Cashing in on others' crimes is a multibillion-dollar business that private corporations and government agencies perpetuate.

There are two main types of players in the prison industrial complex. First, those who are directly involved in the corrections industry, including private prison operators, their investors and employees, as well as those who work in government-run public prisons and the bureaucracies that manage them. Second, those who are not directly involved in corrections, but hold a stake in keeping certain activities illegal. These include pharmaceutical companies, liquor producers, and vendors who supply goods and services to prisons. We now look at how the efforts of these groups contribute to the U.S. having the world's highest incarceration rate. We start with the first group, those who are directly involved in the criminal justice business.

Private Prisons and Incarcerating for Profit

Private prisons for adults were virtually non-existent until the early 1980s, but the number of prisoners in private prisons increased by approximately 1600% between 1990 and 2009. Today, for-profit com-

panies are responsible for approximately 6% of state prisoners, 16% of federal prisoners, and, according to one report, nearly half of all immigrants detained by the federal government. In 2010, the two largest private prison companies alone received nearly $3 billion dollars in revenue, and their top executives, according to one source, each received annual compensation packages worth well over $3 million.
American Civil Liberties Union, 2011[1]

As was discussed in Chapter 1, when Ronald Reagan beat Jimmy Carter in the U.S. presidential election in 1980, there were 474,368 inmates in American prisons and jails. By 1990, there were 1,148,702 inmates, an increase of nearly 250 percent in ten years. Ten years later, the Bureau of Justice Statistics estimated that there were nearly two million inmates in the U.S. [2]

Anticipating new opportunities to profit from imprisonment, Corrections Corporation of America (CCA) arose in 1983. The company won its first federal contract later that year, to operate a detention facility in Texas for suspected illegal immigrants on behalf of the Immigration and Naturalization Service (now the Bureau of Immigration and Customs Enforcement, or ICE). The following year, CCA contracted to run a juvenile detention facility in Tennessee, and opened another immigration facility in Houston, the first detention center in the world designed and constructed by a private corrections company.[3] Private prison companies have had particular success in contracting for immigration detention facilities; today, nearly half of all immigration detainees in the U.S. are held in privately operated facilities.[4]

CCA is the nation's largest owner and operator of privatized correctional and detention facilities and one of the largest prison operators in the United States, behind only the federal government and three states. In 2015, CCA operated sixty-four facilities, including fifty-two company-owned or controlled facilities, with a design capacity of more than 84,500 beds in nineteen states and the District of Columbia.[5] CCA went public in 1986, originally listing its stock on the NASDAQ exchange, and switching to the New York Stock Exchange in 1994. Its net income for 2014 was $225 million based on revenues of $1.646 billion.[6] In June 2015, its market capitalization was nearly $4 billion, with over 117 million outstanding shares of stock.[7]

CCA is not alone in the private corrections industry. The GEO Group, established in 1984 as a subsidiary of the former Wackenhut private security firm, today manages or owns 106 correctional, detention, and residential treatment facilities with approximately 85,500 beds, primarily in the U.S., but also operating in Australia, South Africa, and the United Kingdom. GEO had a net income of $122.8 million and revenues of $1.69 billion in 2014.[8] With more than seventy-four million outstanding shares of stock trading on the New York Stock Exchange, GEO had a market capitalization of $2.6 billion in June 2015.[9]

GEO gained some unwanted attention in February 2013, when it pledged $6 million to be paid over twelve years to Florida Atlantic University (FAU) in exchange for the naming rights to the school's new football stadium. Within hours of the announcement of the pledge, online petitions assailing the offer appeared. FAU's team name is the Owls, and critics quickly labeled the stadium "Owlcatraz." On April 1, 2013, a coalition of dozens of groups delivered a letter to FAU's president. The letter criticized the GEO Group for what the coalition said was a long history of abuses in its facilities and of the deaths of people in its custody, along with citations for violations from state and federal regulators and a series of lawsuits.[10] GEO withdrew its pledge later that day.

The third largest private prison company in the U.S. is Management & Training Corporation, headquartered outside of Salt Lake City. Like its two larger competitors, the privately held firm, which already had federal contracts to operate Job Corps facilities, entered the private prison sector during Ronald Reagan's presidency, beginning with a community correction center in California. It currently operates twenty-five correctional facilities in eight states with over 5,300 employees and over 29,000 inmates.[11]

Private prison companies rely on three core strategies for growth. First, they contribute generously to the campaigns of candidates identified as sympathetic. The Justice Policy Institute found that the three largest private prison companies gave over $800,000 to federal candidates between 2000 and 2011. They gave over $6 million to state politicians during that period, including $2.2 million during the 2010 election cycle. GEO spent nearly $1.5 million on campaign contributions in Florida alone between 2003 and 2010.[12] GEO reported political contributions of $1.724 million to state and federal political candidates in 2014.[13] CCA reported political contributions of $875,000 in 2013.[14]

Second, private prison companies lobby heavily, both directly and through advocacy groups that advance their agenda. They lobby at the federal level supporting or opposing specific bills before Congress or promoting congressional appropriations to federal agencies that contract with those companies. The three largest private prison companies spent $3.5 million for federal lobbying in 2005, although they have spent considerably less since, with a little over $1.5 million expended in 2010. At the state level, CCA employed 179 lobbyists in thirty-two states between 2003 and 2010; GEO used 63 lobbyists in sixteen states during this period.[15] GEO reported that it spent $2.5 million on direct lobbying in 2014; CCA spent $2.7 million in 2013.[16]

Third, private prison companies obtain influence in government by cross hiring. Many current private prison officials were formerly government prison officials and many current governmental prison officials were once private prison officials. For example, U.S. Bureau of Prisons director Harley G. Lappin, shortly after being arrested for drunk driving in 2011, quit his government position and joined CCA as its Chief Corrections Officer. Joe Williams, a former warden for GEO, later served as New Mexico's Secretary of Corrections between 2003 and 2010. During that period, he received criticism for not fining CCA and GEO millions of dollars for contract violations. Williams then returned to GEO as its Director of U.S. Operations in 2011.[17]

Failure Is the Best Option: Recidivism Drives Private Prison Profits

As noted earlier, the stock of CCA and GEO trade publicly on the New York Stock Exchange. The officers and directors of corporations must answer to their shareholders, who want the value (price per share) of their stock to grow or want income (quarterly dividends) or some combination of growth and income. Few investors are satisfied when a corporation's revenues are steady or flat.

However, for-profit prison companies have a business model that seems unsustainable. To illustrate, we will compare private prisons to fast food chains. Fast food corporations grow revenues and profits in two ways; first, by increasing sales to current customers and attracting new customers to existing restaurants, and second, by increasing the number of restaurants they operate. A fast food restaurant doesn't want to sell you one hamburger. It wants to sell you hundreds of hamburgers over your lifetime. How does a private prison generate repeat business? By failing to rehabilitate its prisoners, who reoffend after release.

Ironically, the most daunting problem in American corrections—its high recidivism rate—becomes the foundation of private prison firms' business model. Just as fast food places rely on repeat business, so do private prisons. Thus, according to one study conducted in Oklahoma, "private prison inmates had a greater hazard of recidivism in all eight [regression] models tested, six of which were statistically significant."[18] The authors of the study conclude that, "there was no empirical support for claims of superior service from private corrections."[19] Another study from Minnesota found, "offenders who had been incarcerated in a private prison had a greater hazard of recidivism in all 20 [regression] models, and the recidivism risk was significantly greater in 8 of the models."[20] In the review of literature in his 2014 study of race and private prisons, Oregon State University sociologist Brian Burkhardt summed up the problem with for-profit prisons:

Recent empirical analysis has found that, relative to their public counterparts, private prisons have more inmate misconduct ... offer fewer
inmate work assignments ... generate more inmate grievances ... offer
less training for employees ... have higher staff turnover ... and have
worse public safety outcomes.

Although evidence is somewhat mixed ... the most recent and most
sophisticated analyses show that inmates who spend more time in private prisons (versus public ones) re-offend at higher rates ... or about
equally ... depending on the sample analyzed.[21]

It is certainly ironic that private prisons can profit from their failure. It is also
tragic.

The fast food company wants to sell more hamburgers to more people next
year than this year, attempting to generate more profit and satisfy shareholders.
Just as fast food executives evaluate each restaurant for its profitability and
expect each restaurant to increase their sales, each private prison facility is
expected to earn increasing profits for the shareholders of the corporation
operating that prison. How does a for-profit prison increase its profitability?
Besides increasing the cost to the government per inmate, which of course
the government will resist, more profit per square foot can come from reducing operating costs by reducing personnel costs through paying lower
wages, as well as reducing the number of staff at each prison. However, in-
sufficiently staffed prisons are more dangerous and less effective, as is a lower-
paid, less-well trained staff.

Continuing with our fast food analogy, once a new restaurant is built, the
corporation must then fill it with customers. The most common way to drum
up new business for many companies is through advertising and other marketing
efforts as a means of pull marketing—getting the customer to come to them.
In the case of a new prison facility, the customer is the government, and the
prison corporation's primary challenge, since it does not have the power to
convict people and sentence them to prison, is getting the government to fill
it with inmates. In essence, the private prison companies use push marketing,
lobbying legislatures to create a political climate that best serves those firms
and helps populate its prisons. Remember, the three main private prison companies are competing with each other for a limited resource: people convicted
of a crime and being sent to prison. If there is a drop in crime, private prison
companies lose business. That brings up the next problem with the private
prison business model.

Recidivism Isn't Enough; They Need More Criminals

Since the U.S. has twenty-five percent of the world's prisoners and only five percent of the world's population, there is growing pressure on private prison corporations to find new sources of prisoners. Accomplishing this requires push marketing, by reaching out to state and federal legislators and lobbying them to create new crimes (in other words, "manufacturing criminals"), add harsher punishments to existing crimes, suppress correctional alternatives to incarceration, and making it harder for inmates to be released on parole. Legislators have typically responded by passing the laws lobbied for by private prison companies and their advocacy groups; we the taxpayers end up paying billions for those laws and the human costs of needlessly damaged or destroyed lives are ignored.

A classic example of the private prison industry lobbying to manufacture more criminals can be seen in the area of illegal immigration. Considering the nation's economic problems and heightened xenophobia in the wake of 9/11, it is not hard to understand why illegal immigration is such a controversial topic in the U.S. today. There are already numerous federal laws and federal law enforcement agencies that seek to prevent illegal immigration and to find and deport illegal immigrants. There are more than 20,000 Border Patrol agents on the Mexican border today, more than twice the number of agents in 2001.[22] In fiscal year 2014, U.S. Immigration and Customs Enforcement deported 315,943 individuals.[23]

Sharing a 372-mile-long border with Mexico, Arizona has problems with illegal immigrants traveling to or through the state. In April 2010, Governor Jan Brewer signed SB 1070, which made illegal immigration a state offense. Thirty of the thirty-six cosponsors of the bill received contributions from prison interests or private prison companies, including CCA, GEO, and Management & Training Corporation.[24]

Shortly after SB 1070 was signed into law, GEO held a conference call with investors. When asked about the new law by an investor, GEO chief executive officer George Zoley responded in jest, "What, they have some new legislation? I never heard about it. I think I'm increasingly convinced of their need for 5,000 new beds." GEO chief operating officer Wayne Calabrese added, "I can only believe the opportunities at the federal level are going to continue apace as a result of what's happening. Those people coming across the border and getting caught are going to have to be detained and that for me, at least I think, there's going to be enhanced opportunities for what we do."[25]

Preying on the Weak

In addition to housing illegal immigrants, private prison firms also operate juvenile facilities. It should not be surprising that for-profit firms have had considerable luck in obtaining contracts for detaining suspect illegal aliens and juveniles. Illegal aliens are, in most cases, quite poor. Neither illegal aliens nor juveniles can vote. Juvenile offenders often come from dysfunctional homes with relatively few resources and often lack effective adult advocates. Thus, it is disappointing yet hardly surprising to learn of negligence and abuse in for-profit facilities that hold suspected illegal aliens and juvenile offenders. One of the more troubling examples occurred in Mississippi. Based on complaints, in 2012 the U.S. Justice Department investigated the Walnut Grove Youth Correctional Facility (WGYCF), a facility operated by GEO. The investigation found:

- Deliberate indifference to staff sexual misconduct and inappropriate behavior with youth;
- Use of excessive use of force by WGYCF staff on youth;
- Inadequate protection of youth from youth-on-youth violence;
- Deliberate indifference to youth at risk of self-injurious and suicidal behaviors; and
- Deliberate indifference to the medical needs of youth.[26]

Later that year, U.S. District Judge Carlton W. Reeves wrote in his approval of a consent decree in a class-action suit against the Mississippi Department of Corrections that the "WGYCF has allowed a cesspool of unconstitutional and inhuman acts and conditions to germinate, the sum of which places the offenders at substantial ongoing risk."[27] Within a month of the consent decree, GEO announced that it was ceasing its operations in Mississippi, claiming that they had been "financially underperforming."[28] Mississippi quickly awarded a new contract for the three facilities formerly run by GEO to Management & Training Corporation.

For its part, CCA states publicly that it, "unequivocally has not at any time lobbied—nor have we had any outside consultants lobby—on immigration law."[29] Yet CCA has engaged in direct marketing of a sort in Arizona. On October 31, 2012, Vista Grande High School in Casa Grande was locked down for the first time in its four-year history. As the Casa Grande police proceeded from classroom to classroom with drug-sniffing dogs, they were accompanied by two other law enforcement agencies, along with four employees of CCA. Caroline Isaacs, program director of the Tucson office of the American Friends Service Committee, which advocates for criminal justice reform, said, "To invite for-profit prison guards to conduct law enforcement actions in a high school is perhaps the most direct expression of the 'schools-to-prison pipeline' I've ever seen." Alas, business for CCA was poor on this particular Wednesday; Vista Grande High, with over 1,700 students, yielded only three busts for marijuana possession, and two of those students possessed only the equivalent of one joint each.

CCA's efforts to generate business in high schools go far beyond the occasional drug raid. It has worked with state legislators to promote a "Drug-Free School Act" that provides for "increased apprehension" (i.e., increased arrest and incarceration) and other drug laws that prescribe mandatory prison sentences for violators. Under current Arizona drug laws, even the two students at Vista Grande High caught with small amounts of marijuana could face prison time. In addition, the drug laws that CCA promotes typically prohibit judges from placing those convicted on probation nor do they allow any other alternative to incarceration.

In the most egregious case of private prison companies profiting from the incarceration of children, Mark Ciavarella and Michael Conahan, judges in Wilkes-Barre, Pennsylvania, were convicted and sent to federal prison in 2011 for participating in a "kids for cash" scheme, pocketing over $2 million in the process. Ciavarella pleaded guilty to accepting bribes from the operators of two for-profit juvenile facilities, which benefited from Ciavarella's rulings that caused many juveniles to be detained for long periods. These included a thirteen-year-old incarcerated for throwing a piece of steak at his mother's boyfriend, a fifteen-year-old for throwing a sandal at her mother, an eleven-year-old for calling the police after his mother locked him out of the house, and a fourteen-year-old for writing a satirical Myspace profile.[30] Conahan held the administrative post of President Judge of Luzerne County, and used that position to have the funding of a publicly operated juvenile facility discontinued, and had juveniles sent instead to a for-profit facility.

Cherry Picking: Optimal Conditions Mean Maximum Profits

Private prisons have also been accused of cherry picking their inmates, by not bidding to house inmates who are elderly, are HIV positive, or who otherwise need ongoing medical or mental health treatment. A study by the Arizona Department of Corrections found that in fiscal year 2010:

> Five of eight private prisons serving Arizona did not accept inmates with "limited physical capacity and stamina" or severe physical illness or chronic conditions, according to the state's analysis, issued last

month. None took inmates with "high need" mental health conditions. Some inmates who became sick were "returned to state prisons due to an increase of their medical scores that exceeds contractual exclusions."[31]

Private prison firms also rarely bid for maximum-security facilities, due to the higher cost of single-bed cells and intensive staffing that these facilities require, as well as the higher salaries of the elite management teams needed to run these facilities safely.

Obviously, after carefully selecting the types of inmates that they will agree to house, it becomes much easier for for-profit prison companies to compare their costs favorably against the operating costs of government-run prisons. This is because the sickest, oldest, and most dangerous inmates remain under government supervision after the for-profit prisons have culled these inmates out of the populations that they supervise. Another consideration when comparing the operating costs of a government operated facility and a privately operated facility is that government facilities typically have employees with some seniority (and with seniority comes experience). Privately operated facilities are more likely to rely on newly hired personnel who are paid less because of their lack of seniority and experience.

In a new effort to expand its revenue stream by adding capacity, CCA sent a letter to forty-eight states at the beginning of 2012 to promote its CCA Corrections Investment Initiative. CCA told its readers that the company was earmarking $250 million to purchase and manage government-owned corrections facilities. At a time when many states were facing significant budget shortfalls due to tough economic times, CCA's offer was likely given serious consideration by many of its recipients. Here again, however, CCA was cherry picking, seeking only facilities that offered:

- A minimum rated occupancy of 1,000 beds;
- A structure age of no more than twenty-five years;
- A designation that the structure is suitable for immediate occupation or is already occupied by an inmate population; and
- An assurance by the agency partner that the agency has sufficient inmate population to maintain a minimum ninety percent occupancy rate over the term of the contract.[32]

Note the last provision. In the eyes of the for-profit CCA, the only good prison is a crowded prison.

Ironically, although private prison firms solicit government contracts by promising to reduce costs to the governmental entity, that has yet to be proven. As one meta-analysis (a study of studies) done by a team of researchers at the

University of Utah's Utah Criminal Justice Center determined, "Cost savings from privatizing prisons are not guaranteed and appear minimal."[33] Even if private prisons can demonstrate an obvious cost savings to the government, if recidivism among former inmates at private prisons is higher than among former inmates at public prisons, is that cost savings really worth it, or is it a false economy?

Prisons Are Also Revenue Streams for Government Entities

Cindy Chang of the *New Orleans Times-Picayune* points out in her discussion of Louisiana's incarceration rate, the highest in the U.S. that, "The hidden engine behind the state's well-oiled prison machine is cold, hard cash. A majority of Louisiana inmates are housed in for-profit facilities, which must be supplied with a constant influx of human beings or a $182 million industry will go bankrupt."[34] However, privately owned prisons are not the only explanation for Louisiana's incarceration rate, which is thirteen times that of China and twenty times that of Germany. Parish (akin to county) sheriffs in Louisiana receive $24.39 a day from the state for each prisoner, a revenue stream that encourages sheriffs to keep their cells full.

There are other examples of government built and operated facilities that seek a steady stream of prisoners. These intentionally oversized facilities were built with the idea that the excess capacity could be used to generate revenue by charging a daily rate for inmates from other jurisdictions. However, because tough economic times have caused many correctional agencies to trim their budgets, the demand for prison cells has dropped over the past few years, leaving many facilities underutilized and others empty.

In 2007, the Two Rivers Detention Facility in Hardin, Montana, was completed at a cost of $27 million. The facility can accommodate 464 inmates. However, the inmates never came. When discussions arose among federal authorities about the possible closing of the Guantanamo Bay detention facility in Cuba, the Two Rivers Authority unsuccessfully offered its complex as an alternative. The authority later attempted to enter into a contract to lease the facility to a company calling itself American Police Force, whose CEO turned out to be a convicted con man with a long list of aliases.[35] In 2013, the Two Rivers Authority announced that the facility was available to "Any person or parties interested in operating or leasing space in the Two Rivers Detention Facility," with a YouTube video of the facility provided on the Two Rivers Authority website.[36] After being vacant for seven years, Emerald Correction Management of

Louisiana began operating the facility in 2014 to house inmates for the U.S. Bureau of Indian Affairs.[37]

There are also relatively new but empty facilities in Texas, Colorado, New Mexico, Virginia, and elsewhere, typically financed by bonds on which taxpayers' money continues to make payments.[38] Beyond the cost of the facility itself, there are often substantial infrastructure costs, including roads, electricity, sewage, and water supply. Another complicating factor is that many speculative prisons are sited in rural areas. With a surplus of land and a shortage of jobs, many rural county and small municipal governments lobby for private prisons and offer generous tax incentives. When one of these facilities closes, it has a significant impact on the labor market and the local economy in general. It is also quite difficult to repurpose a correctional facility for other uses.

In some cases, a state or local government functions as a "middle man." One example is Essex County, New Jersey. Under an agreement with the U.S. Immigration and Customs Enforcement (ICE), Essex County receives $108 per night for people detained as illegal immigrants. Many of these immigrants are housed in a for-profit facility operated by Community Education Centers. The county pays the company $71 a night for each detainee, keeping $37. As Essex County Executive Joseph N. DiVincenzo, Jr. said, "The $250 million we expect to receive over the five-year contract [with ICE] will significantly help reduce the financial burden on our taxpayers."[39]

Prisons as Employers

"I don't know much about prisons, but I do know about jobs and I know that the people I represent need more and better jobs," said Maine state senator Douglas Thomas in April 2011. Thomas added, "I could pretend this bill is all about prisons, but it is really a jobs bill. It is time those of us in Augusta stopped pretending that everything is all right and started doing more to create a climate where the jobs we need can be created."[40] CCA was lobbying to build a $100 million for-profit prison in Milo, Maine, promising to offer 300 to 400 jobs with benefits, and Thomas was a sponsor of a bill that would allow CCA to build the facility. CCA shrewdly claimed that it was also considering locating the facility in New Hampshire, thereby generating competition between the politicians of two states and enhancing CCA's bargaining power.

The prospect of jobs appeals to New Hampshire's politicians as well. One example comes from Berlin, New Hampshire, a former mill town of 10,000 in northernmost Coos County, once dominated by the wood pulp and paper industries. In late 2011, Governor Jeanne Shaheen expressed optimism about the opening of a new federal prison that had been completed in Berlin in 2010 but had remained vacant due to federal budget cuts. The governor stated that the prison would provide a $40 million economic stimulus annually and added, "That's not just jobs, that also reflects money for businesses in the area whose goods and services will be purchased by the prison."[41] When the prison was finally set to open in late 2012, local officials heralded the expanding need for day care, dry cleaning, and dog walking services.[42] The City of Berlin created a website to tell those interested, "What you can do to be ready to do business with the Bureau of Prisons."[43]

A 2010 study by the Georgetown University Center on Education and the Workforce predicts that there will be 101 million jobs in the U.S. in 2018 that require some post-secondary education, but high school dropouts or those with only a high school diploma will hold only sixty-one million jobs.[44] In post-industrial America, many semi-skilled and unskilled workers are experiencing the erosion of wages or the outright loss of jobs. It is understandable that many of these workers are attracted to jobs as corrections officers, which usually require only a high school diploma or GED, and provide an annual salary of over $44,910.[45] An average of thirty-five jobs is created for every 100 prison beds added, and these jobs are perceived as relatively stable, even during economic downturns.[46] The U.S. Bureau of Labor Statistics anticipates that there will be nearly 500,000 correctional officers in 2020.[47]

There are also prison jobs that require advanced education or training. However, the stressful and depressing setting makes prison work unattractive to many professionals. Thus, the U.S. Bureau of Prisons (BOP) website states that the BOP is "*always* accepting applications" for positions such as chaplain, clinical psychologist, dental officer, medical officer, nurse practitioner, physician assistant, and registered nurse (emphasis added).[48]

Plenty of Prisoners Means Job Security

Those who already have jobs in corrections understandably want job stability. In contractual situations where seniority provides protection from layoffs, current correctional employees advocate for increased hiring, in order to provide a buffer of less-senior employees. To ensure demand for corrections officers and other correctional personnel, there must be a steady stream of prisoners and a propensity to incarcerate those prisoners for long periods. Thus, the Rhode Island Brotherhood of Correctional Officers began a campaign in December 2012 to keep violent criminals in prison longer through reduction of prisoner credit for "good time" and creating more barriers to parole.[49] As part of this campaign, the Rhode Island Brotherhood established a website, endtheviolenceri.com, the purpose of which is a "public safety campaign" to notify Rhode Islanders "when dangerous criminals are indefensibly let out early." The site seems to disavow any public benefit of prisons other than incapacitation (i.e., warehousing) stating, "We know that just because you behave in prison does not mean you are fit to be back in our communities, living amongst our families and our children."[50]

Similarly, the California Correctional Peace Officers Association's website features articles about crimes committed by convicted offenders who have been released on parole.[51] Unfortunately, it is not difficult to find stories about horrible crimes committed by individuals while on parole or after their period of parole has expired. As part of the general shift away from the rehabilitation model to the punishment model of corrections that took root in the 1970s, the legislatures in several states eliminated parole. However, some of these states have found that eliminating parole results in prison overcrowding, which forces the release of some prisoners who reenter society without supervision.[52]

The message emphasizing public safety over salary and job security is shared among those who negotiate contracts on behalf of law enforcement officers. As a California law firm that focuses on police contract negotiations formerly stated on its website:

> The public could [not] care less about your pay, medical coverage and pension plan. All they want to know is "what is in it for them." Any public positions or statements by the association should always keep that focus. The message should always be public safety first. You do not want wage increases for yourselves, but simply to attract better qualified candidates and to keep more experienced officers from leaving.[53]

"Three-strikes" laws, popular with voters in the 1990s, have also received support from corrections officers' unions. These laws typically provide for lengthy prison terms, up to life imprisonment, for those found guilty of committing a variety of crimes at least three times. The California Correctional Peace Officers Association (CCPOA) was the second-largest contributor to the campaign supporting Proposition 184, California's three-strikes law, in 1994. The CCPOA spent over $1 million to prevent the law from being made less harsh in 2004.[54]

In essence, if legislation gets people convicted more easily, lengthens sentences, ignores alternatives to incarceration, and limits the use of parole and probation, corrections officers unions support that legislation. We understand that people want jobs and job security. We also support the right of employ-

ees, including public employees, to unionize, and to hire lobbyists to advocate on their behalf. Paxson has been an officer in his college faculty union for
many years. He also likes being able to rely on a steady biweekly paycheck.
However, Paxson would not support legislation that forced people into college or that made it harder for them to graduate. Unfortunately, corrections
officers know that their job security depends on harsh laws and a high incarceration rate.

Although they would never say so publicly, many in the corrections field
want a high recidivism rate. The for-profit firms want revenue, and corrections employees want job security. We now look at others who profit from the
prison industrial complex.

Prisons and Jails as Profit Centers: Vendors

There are over two million people in U.S. correctional facilities. This is greater
than the population of Philadelphia; it is more than the entire population of
Nebraska. That's a lot of people, and people represent markets for many businesses. Fortunately, for the residents of Philadelphia and Nebraska, they have choices
in the marketplace. For those who are incarcerated, this is often not the case.

Two firms control approximately eighty percent of the prison telephone service market in the U.S., a $1.2 billion business.[55] Securus, based in Dallas, relies
on correctional facility telephone service for the bulk of its revenue, contracting
with approximately 2,200 facilities in forty-five states.[56] Mobile, Alabama, based
Global Tel*Link began as a provider of payphone services in the late 1980s, and
later focused on prison payphones, contracting with about 2,400 corrections facilities in fifty states and the District of Columbia.[57] Both firms often share a portion of their billings with corrections agencies, with $152 million in profit-sharing
in 2008 alone, and telephone contracts typically go to the firm offering the highest margin of profit-sharing.[58] As a result, telephone calls from an inmate can
include a setup charge of $3.95 plus an additional eighty-nine cents per minute.

For the past decade, the Federal Communications Commission (FCC),
which holds some regulatory authority over telecommunications firms, had
the so-called Wright petition before it. The petition takes its name from Martha
Wright-Reed, the grandmother of a man sentenced to prison for manslaughter. When her grandson was transferred to a facility operated by CCA, Wright
saw the cost of her calls increase dramatically. It should not be surprising that
some of the highest telephone charges for inmates occur in private, for-profit
prisons. However, government operated facilities also award contracts based
on profit-sharing provisions referred to as site commissions. The *Washington*

Post found that the state of Maryland received a commission of up to sixty per-cent from Securus, which charged eighty-five cents for local calls, while in-trastate calls cost $2.55 plus thirty cents per minute and interstate calls cost $2.70 plus thirty cents per minute.[59] In 2013, the FCC finally announced caps on interstate telephone calls from prison facilities, with collect calls capped at twenty-five cents a minute and debit card calls capped at twenty-one cents a minute. Local and intrastate telephone charges remain outside of the FCC's price caps; the agency is currently seeking comment on extending caps to these calls as well.[60] Nevertheless, Securus was still able to report a fifty-one percent gross profit margin in 2014.[61]

Renovo, a videoconferencing firm, has recently expanded into "corrections solutions," offering VisManager, its "visitation management solution." Renovo tells prospective clients, "While the demands of your staff and facility continue to grow, budgets continue to shrink. As a result, correctional facilities have sought out ways to generate revenue to offset costs. Services such as inmate phones, commissary, and inmate deposits have helped to defray costs; but until now, there has not been an effective system to generate revenue from inmate visitation."[62] To do so, Renovo promotes its ability to "[s]et up unique fee struc-tures."[63] Renovo's services apply to on-premise video visitation, internet video visitation, and face-to-face visitation. That's right—Renovo encourages cor-rections officials to charge for face-to-face visitation by loved ones, including charging a premium for "[v]isits in excess of your weekly visitation quota."[64]

Charging excessive rates for telephone calls and charging anything at all for family visitations means potentially limiting or eliminating communication and contact between inmates and their families. Furthermore, the U.S. Justice Department's National Institute of Corrections tells us that, "Maintaining fam-ily ties has been shown to reduce the strain of separation and *increase the like-lihood of successful community reintegration for offenders following release from incarceration*"[65] (emphasis added).

At least one vendor claims that it is attempting to help inmates maintain ties to their families. Western Union tells us that, "The Western Union brand has been a symbol of trust for over 150 years. In keeping with our history of helping family and friends stay connected with their loved ones, we have es-tablished strong relationships with correctional facilities around the nation, and over 60% of all inmates in the U.S. benefit from our services."[66]

Western Union charges a service fee of approximately $1 for every $10 trans-ferred. To a financially struggling family, particularly one whose primary wage earner may be incarcerated, Western Union offers reassurance, stating that, "You can keep your relationships strong by sending money with Western Union to any inmate's commissary account."[67] A competing firm, MoneyGram, also offers money transfer services for friends and family members of inmates, at a charge of $11.50 per $100 transfer. The firm tells visitors to its website that, "MoneyGram helps you stay connected to incarcerated loved ones."[68]

You can imagine that prison life can be monotonous. Many inmates struggled in school and are not comfortable readers. Therefore, books and periodicals are out of the question for many of them. Not surprisingly, television, radio, and recorded music and videos are quite popular in correctional facilities. However, televisions, radios, and audio and video players can serve as places for inmates to hide weapons and other contraband. The solution is simple: transparent devices. Thus, Swintec offers clear typewriters for sale, with both American English and Spanish keyboards, which use typewriter ribbons also housed in clear plastic casing. The Keefe Group, a subsidiary of the privately held Centric Group based in Missouri, offers its line of AMP'D clear televisions and a clear CD player with AM/FM radio, as well as clear plastic headphones, fans, and watches. (Ironically, they are somewhat stylish; these companies should also consider the non-correctional market.)

Keefe discovered during the early years of the mass-incarceration movement how profitable selling to prisoners could be. In 1975, it began offering food products in single-serve packets for sale to prisoners through prison commissaries. Using paper rather than plastic, metal, or glass packaging was Keefe's simple but effective way of maintaining safety in correctional settings. Since then, the company has developed a substantial line of name brand and private label (house brand) food items and toiletries. Keefe also offers its Securepak to families and friends of inmates. These "care packages" are assembled by Keefe based on the particular requirements and restrictions of corrections officials in various jurisdictions. They can include food items such as cookies and chips, toiletries such as shampoo and shaving cream, and electronic items.

Keefe has since expanded into prison telecommunications and other electronic services through its ICSolutions, offering inmate banking and telephone services, video visitation, as well as systems for monitoring communications between inmates and individuals outside of correctional facilities. Keefe's Access line of products includes an MP3 media library with over five million song titles available for inmates to download onto playing devices that come, "programmed with the inmate's DOC #, eliminating the necessity for engraving by the facility. The player also has built in features to prevent and deter theft, including a termination feature which disables the functionality of the player if reported lost or stolen."[69]

Keefe faces competition in the field of inmate banking and electronic media services. JPay, a Miami-based, privately held firm purchased by Securus in 2015, tells visitors to its website that they can "[s]end money to your loved one in state prison. Email your cousin in county jail. Chat with a friend using video visitation or give the gift of music with the JP4® player."[70] JPay's JP4, available for about $50, is prison approved, and can be loaded with music from JPay's library of over ten million songs at kiosks in common areas of correctional facilities. To gain access to correctional facilities for the kiosks, JPay, which charges more per song than do other music download services such as Apple's iTunes or Amazon's MP3 service, offers revenue sharing to correctional agencies. The result, just as with telephone services, is that inmates are paying more for music than are those of us outside of correctional facilities.

Government agencies that operate correctional facilities also enjoy revenue sharing from the Keefe Group. For example, in 2006 Keefe won a contract with Dallas County, Texas, to provide commissary services to the county's approximately 7,000 inmates. In exchange, Keefe promised a forty percent commission on sales to the county, or $2 million annually, whichever was greater.[71] Because Keefe gains an effective monopoly when it wins a commissary contract, it can charge whatever the market will bear, without fear of being undersold by competitors. In California, for example, transgender prisoners who remain in male prisons must wear bras, according to prison regulations. The sole source of those bras is Keefe's online catalog.[72]

Supporting Criminalization as a Business Strategy

Another factor contributing to the exponential growth of the prison industrial complex may appear tangential, at least initially. Numerous elements of the American economy want to maintain the current prohibition against many drugs in general, and marijuana in particular. For example, the California Beer and Beverage Distributors trade association contributed to campaigns against the legalization or decriminalization of marijuana in California, and opposed efforts to reduce the punishments for non-violent drug offenses.[73]

Pharmaceutical firms understandably feel threatened by the prospect of marijuana being legalized for medicinal use, allowing people to grow their own medicine, rather than paying for expensive medications protected by patents, and have supported efforts to keep marijuana illegal. The Partnership at Drugfree.org (formerly the Partnership for a Drug-Free America) the organization known for its attention-getting "this is your brain on drugs" advertising campaign, receives funding from a number of pharmaceutical companies.

Keeping marijuana illegal protects the jobs of law enforcement officials as well. This explains why various police groups paid a lobbyist $386,000 in 2010 to help defeat California's Proposition 19, which would have decriminalized use of marijuana by adults.[74]

ALEC

A key advocate for increased incarceration in the past has been the American Legislative Exchange Council (ALEC). Founded in 1973, ALEC describes itself as, "A nonpartisan membership association for conservative state lawmakers who share a common belief in limited government, free markets, federalism, and individual liberty."[75] While purporting to be an association for lawmakers, dues from its 2,000 legislative members provide less than ten percent of the organization's funding, with ALEC's real financial support coming from its 300 or so corporate members. Corporate members are guaranteed access to ALEC's task forces. These task forces draft model legislation that ALEC distributes to its legislative membership. Of key interest to private prison firms was the Public Safety and Elections task force. This group drafted ALEC's model drug legislation, which sought to increase time served for drug offenses, in part by imposing mandatory minimum sentences. The proposed legislation was titled the Minimum-Mandatory Sentencing Act. ALEC summarized how the proposed law would operate: "The severity of the penalties would be based solely on the type and amount of drug and whether it is a repeat offense. There would be no distinction between possession and manufacture, sale, or distribution."[76] That's right—an addict whose personal "stash" happened to be the same amount held by a drug dealer would receive the same punishment as if s/he were selling the drug. The agenda supporting this proposed legislation followed in the next paragraph of the proposed law:

> The Act would also require that an estimate be made of the cost of additional prison construction entailed by enforcement of the Act, and would authorize a referendum on a bond issue to cover that expected cost. The effective date of the sentencing component of the Act would be tied to approval of the bond issue.[77]

Here, ALEC placed more emphasis on the financial concerns of prison operators rather than it does on the rehabilitation of drug addicts. ALEC's model legislation for juvenile offenders, the Habitual Juvenile Offenders Act, would have categorized many juvenile offenders as young as fourteen years old as adults for purposes of punishment. This would have meant that more juvenile offenders would be incarcerated, and for longer periods. Similar to the ways tobacco companies historically tried to get teenagers hooked on nicotine, prison operators benefit from incarcerating as many youthful offenders as early as possible, since being sent to prison once greatly increases the chances of being re-incarcerated several times during one's lifetime.

Just as private prison companies perceive detention of juveniles and illegal aliens as their special niche, or "sweet spot," in the corrections market, so did ALEC. Arizona State Senator Russell Pearce, the key sponsor of the Arizona's SB 1070, the bill discussed earlier in this chapter that made illegal immigration a state crime, was also an ALEC member. The immigration bill enacted in Arizona became a key source of ALEC's model legislation for adoption in other states.

Although CCA disavowed any support of the Arizona illegal immigration statute, CCA has benefited from ALEC's efforts and has been a major corporate sponsor of ALEC; one of CCA's officers was a member of ALEC's Public Safety and Elections Task Force Executive Committee. The GEO Group has also contributed to ALEC. It might not surprise you to find that Walmart had been a major corporate sponsor of ALEC, which helps to explain why ALEC's proposed "Theft from Three Separate Mercantile Establishments Act" would have repeated shoplifting a felony, regardless of the value of the goods stolen.

In 2012, Walmart "suspended" its membership in ALEC, which it had joined in 1993.[78] The killing of Trayvon Martin by George Zimmerman in February 2012 brought attention to Florida's "Stand Your Ground" law, which the National Rifle Association had employed ALEC to guide through state legislatures. ALEC membership quickly became a public relations liability for a number of corporations and foundations. An exodus began in the spring of 2012, with more than 100 corporations and nineteen not-for-profit agencies, including Coca-Cola and the Gates Foundation, abandoning ALEC.[79] Chastened, ALEC announced in April 2012 that it was eliminating its Public Safety and Elections task force.[80] The liberal advocacy organization Common Cause responded, "In folding its Public Safety and Elections Task Force, ALEC is abandoning under pressure the most controversial part of its agenda; that's an important victory for the American public."[81]

Conclusion

There is no question that private companies typically provide products and services more efficiently and at better prices than governments. However, research has shown this not to be the case with prisons. Private prisons can cost taxpayers as much or more to operate, tend to have higher than normal rates of violence, and most importantly, appear to have higher rates of recidivism than do government-run prisons. Since the business model of private prisons depends on more and more people losing their freedom, there are also profound ethical issues with privatizing the prison industry. It is simply indefensible in a free society.

Most people who are incarcerated are there because they broke the law. Here and elsewhere in the book, we have called for a better examination of why some activities are against the law to begin with. We have also attempted to focus attention in this chapter on the economic agenda of those who benefit from the criminalization of certain activities, and on those who benefit from keeping prisons full.

It is understandable that government correctional agencies strive to recover some of the expense of incarcerating individuals by gaining revenue through commissions on commissary sales, banking services, and telecommunications. However, this can place even more financial burdens on the friends and families of prisoners. Most importantly, any action that limits prisoner access to family members, especially children, violates the basic criminological theory that remaining connected to family is a foundation of rehabilitation.

In the next and final chapter, we propose some solutions.

Notes

1. "Banking on Bondage: Private Prisons and Mass Incarceration," American Civil Liberties Union, November 2, 2011, http://www.aclu.org/prisoners-rights/banking-bondage-private-prisons-and-mass-incarceration.

2. Vincent Shiraldi and Jason Ziedenberg, "The Punishing Decade: Prison and Jail Estimates at the Millennium," (Washington, DC: Justice Policy Institute, May 1, 2000), http://www.justicepolicy.org/research/2064.

3. "About CCA," Corrections Corporation of America, accessed June 30, 2015, http://www.cca.com/about/cca-history/.

4. Chris Kirkham, "Private Prisons Profit from Immigration Crackdown, Federal and Local Law Enforcement Partnerships," Huffington Post, June 7, 2012, updated November 26, 2013, http://www.huffingtonpost.com/2012/06/07/private-prisons-immigration-federal-law-enforcement_n_1569219.html.

5. "Corporate Profile," Corrections Corporation of America, accessed June 28, 2015, http://ir.correctionscorp.com/phoenix.zhtml?c=117983&p=irol-homeProfile&t=&id=&.

6. "CCA Reports Fourth Quarter and Full Year 2014 Financial Results," Bloomberg Business, February 11, 2015, http://www.bloomberg.com/article/2015-02-11/aaDSo1hZTML0.html.

7. "Corrections Corp of America," Bloomberg Business, June 26, 2015, http://www.bloomberg.com/quote/CXW:US.

8. "The GEO Group Reports Fourth Quarter and Full-Year 2014 Results," Bloomberg Business, February 18, 2015, http://www.bloomberg.com/article/2015-02-18/aSqdI7O1y WFI.html.

9. "GEO Group," Bloomberg Business, June 26, 2015, http://www.bloomberg.com/quote/GEO:US.

10. Greg Bishop, "After Protests, Prison Firm Pulls Donation," *New York Times*, April 2, 2013, http://www.nytimes.com/2013/04/03/sports/ncaafootball/stadium-wont-be-named-for-private-prison-company.html?_r=0.

11. "Overview and Mission," Management & Training Corporation, accessed June 28, 2015, https://www.mtctrains.com/overview-mission.

12. Paul Ashton, "Gaming the System; How the Political Strategies of Private Prison Companies Promote Ineffective Incarceration Policies," (Washington, DC: Justice Policy Institute, June 22, 2011), http://www.justicepolicy.org/research/2614.

13. "Political Activity and Lobbying Report, 2014" GEO Group, accessed June 30, 2015, http://geogroup.com/documents/Political_Activity_Report_2014.pdf.

14. "Political Activity and Lobbying Report 2013," Corrections Corporation of America, accessed June 30, 2015, http://phx.corporate-ir.net/External.File?item=UGFyZW5 0SUQ9MjQ4MzExfENoaWxkSUQ9LTF8VHlwZT0z&t=1.

15. Ashton, 21–25.

16. "Political Activity and Lobbying Report, 2014" GEO Group, accessed June 30, 2015, http://geogroup.com/documents/Political_Activity_Report_2014.pdf; "Political Activity and Lobbying Report 2013," Corrections Corporation of America, accessed June 30, 2015, http://phx.corporate-ir.net/External.File?item=UGFyZW50SUQ9MjQ4MzExfENoaWxkSUQ9LTF8 VHlwZT0z&t=1.

17. Deborah Baker, "Ex-Prison Official Back at Firm," *Albuquerque Journal*, November 20, 2011, http://www.abqjournal.com/70584/north/exprison-official-back-at-firm.html.

18. Andrew L. Spivak and Susan F. Sharp, *Crime & Delinquency* 54, no. 3 (July 2008): Abstract.

19. Ibid.

20. Grant Duwe and Valerie Clark, "The Effects of Private Prison Confinement on Offender Recidivism," *Criminal Justice Review* 38, no. 3 (2013): Summary.

21. Brett C. Burkhardt, "Where Have All the (White and Hispanic) Inmates Gone? Comparing the Racial Composition of Private and Public Adult Correctional Facilities," *Race and Justice* 5, no. 1 (2015): 33–57, http://ir.library.oregonstate.edu/xmlui/bitstream/handle/1957/53197/BurkhardtBrettSociologyWhereHaveAll.pdf?sequence=1.

22. "Border Patrol Agent Staffing by Fiscal Year (as of September 30, 2104)," (Washington, DC: U.S. Border Patrol), http://www.cbp.gov/sites/default/files/documents/BP%20 Staffing%20FY1992-FY2014_0.pdf.

23. "Removal Statistics," (Washington, DC: U.S. Immigration and Customs Enforcement), accessed June 28, 2015, http://www.ice.gov/removal-statistics/.

24. Laura Sullivan, "Prison Economics Help Drive Ariz. Immigration Law" NPR, October 28, 2010, http://www.npr.org/2010/10/28/130833741/prison-economics-help-drive-ariz-immigration-law.

25. Beau Hodai, "Corporate Con Game," In These Times, June 21, 2010, http://inthesetimes.com/article/6084/corporate_con_game.

26. "Department of Justice Releases Investigative Findings on the Walnut Grove Youth Correctional Facility in Mississippi," (Washington, DC: U.S. Justice Department, March

21, 2012), http://www.justice.gov/opa/pr/department-justice-releases-investigative-findings-walnut-grove-youth-correctional-facility.

27. Order Approving Settlement, Depriest v. Epps and Burnham, American Civil Liberties Union, March 26, 2012, http://www.aclu.org/files/assets/order.pdf.

28. "The GEO Group Announces Decision to Discontinue East Mississippi Correctional Facility Contract," Bloomberg, April 19, 2012, http://www.bloomberg.com/article/2012-04-19/ai9L1FMs.MWc.html.

29. Sullivan.

30. Abbe Smith, "Undue Process, 'Kids for Cash' and 'The Injustice System,'" New York Times, March 29, 2013, http://www.nytimes.com/2013/03/31/books/review/kids-for-cash-and-the-injustice-system.html?pagewanted=all&_r=0.

31. "FY 2010 Operating Per Capita Cost Report; Cost Identification and Comparison of State and Private Contract Beds," (Phoenix: Arizona Department of Corrections, April 13, 2011), http://www.azcorrections.gov/adc/reports/ADC_FY2010_PerCapitaRep.pdf.

32. Found at Chris Kirkham, "Private Prison Corporation Offers Cash in Exchange for State Prisons," Huffington Post, February 14, 2012, http://big.assets.huffingtonpost.com/ccaletter.pdf.

33. Brad Lundahl, Chelsea Kunz, Cyndi Brownell, Norma Harris, and Russ Van Vleet, "Prison Privatization: A Meta-Analysis of Cost Effectiveness and Quality of Confinement Indicators," (Salt Lake City: Utah Criminal Justice Center, 2007): 2, http://ucjc.utah.edu/wp-content/uploads/861.pdf.

34. Cindy Chang, "Louisiana Is the World's Prison Capital," Times-Picayune, May 29, 2012, http://www.nola.com/crime/index.ssf/2012/05/louisiana_is_the_worlds_prison.html.

35. Associated Press, "Con Man in Hardin Jail Deal Claims He's Broke," Missoulian, October 30, 2009, http://missoulian.com/news/state-and-regional/con-man-in-hardin-jail-deal-claims-he-s-broke/article_ca4e19d9-4294-53f7-a840-b5c769260290.html.

36. "Two Rivers Detention Facility," Two Rivers Authority, accessed May 29, 2013, http://tworiversauthority.homestead.com/Detention-Center.html.

37. "Long Empty, Hardin Jail to House Native American Inmates," Missoulian, October 9, 2014, http://missoulian.com/news/state-and-regional/long-empty-hardin-jail-to-house-native-american-inmates/article_f48374e4-4fad-11e4-964e-6fa7dbfcf380.html.

38. See, for example, Susan Kinzie, "New Virginia Prison Sits Empty, at a Cost of More Than $700,000 a Year," The Washington Post, May 30, 2011, http://articles.washingtonpost.com/2011-05-30/local/35265131_1_prison-budget-state-budget-number-of-state-inmates.

39. Chris Megerian, "Essex County Immigrant Detention Center a House of Controversy," New Jersey Real-Time News, September 22, 2011, http://www.nj.com/news/index.ssf/2011/09/essex_county_immigrant_detenti.html.

40. Judy Harrison, "Private Prison Will Create Jobs, Milo-Erea Legislators Argue," Bangor Daily News, April 29, 2011, http://bangordailynews.com/2011/04/29/politics/private-prison-construction-will-create-jobs-milo-area-legislators-argue.

41. Paul Feely, "Berlin Prison Bill Nears Obama's Desk," New Hampshire Union Leader, November 17, 2011, http://www.unionleader.com/article/20111117/NEWS06/711179967.

42. Sara Young-Knox, "Prison Puts Berlin Back in Business," New Hampshire Union Leader, August 22, 2012, http://www.unionleader.com/article/20120822/NEWS02/708229950.

43. "Berlin Prison," City of Berlin, New Hampshire, accessed May 29, 2013, http://berlinnh.gov/Pages/BerlinNH_Prison.

44. Anthony P. Carnevale, Nicole Smith, and Jeff Strohl, "Help Wanted, Projections of Jobs and Education Requirements through 2018," (Washington, DC: Center on Education and the Workforce, Georgetown Public Policy Institute, June 15, 2010), http://cew.georgetown.edu/jobs2018/.

45. "Occupational Employment and Wages, May 2014: Correctional Officers and Jailers," (Washington, DC: U.S. Bureau of Labor Statistics), http://www.bls.gov/oes/current/oes333012.htm.

46. Ryan S. King, Marc Mauer, and Tracy Huling, "Big Prisons, Small Towns: Prison Economics in Rural America," (Washington, DC: The Sentencing Project, February 2003), http://www.sentencingproject.org/detail/publication.cfm?publication_id=80, 1.

47. "Occupational Outlook Handbook, Correctional Officers," (Washington, DC: U.S. Bureau of Labor Statistics, January 8, 2014), http://www.bls.gov/ooh/protective-service/correctional-officers.htm.

48. "Careers with the Bureau of Prisons," (Washington, DC: Federal Bureau of Prisons), accessed May 29, 2013, http://www.bop.gov/jobs/index.jsp.

49. Tony Gugliota, "RI Correctional Officers Union Seeks Less 'Good Time,'" Turnto10.com, December 13, 2012, http://www.turnto10.com/story/21120862/ri-correctional-officers-union-seeks-less-good-time.

50. "End the Violence, RI," Rhode Island Brotherhood of Correctional Officers, accessed June 28, 2015, http://endtheviolenceri.com/.

51. "Archive for Category 'Parolee News,'" California Correctional Peace Officers Association, accessed June 28, 2015, http://www.ccpoa.org/category/news/parolee/.

52. Fox Butterfield, "Eliminating Parole Boards Isn't a Cure-All, Experts Say," New York Times, January 10, 1999, http://www.nytimes.com/1999/01/10/us/eliminating-parole-boards-isn-t-a-cure-all-experts-say.html.

53. The firm of Lackie, Dammeier, McGill & Ethir removed this language from its website after receiving media criticism. The site now states, "This portion of the material has been removed from the website. What was intended to be informational, historical and educational material has been misconstrued by some as advice on negotiations 'tactics.' Accordingly, to avoid the misperception, the information has been removed." "Negotiations after Impasse," Lackie, Dammeier, McGill & Ethir, accessed May 29, 2013, http://www.policeattorney.com/node/164.

54. Tim Kowal, "The Role of the Prison Guards Union in California's Troubled Prison System," The League of Ordinary Gentlemen, June 5, 2011, http://ordinary-gentlemen.com/blog/2011/06/the-role-of-the-prison-guards-union-in-californias-troubled-prison-system.

55. Todd Shields, "Crime Pays—for Phone Companies," Bloomberg Businessweek, October 25, 2012, http://www.businessweek.com/articles/2012-10-25/crime-pays-for-phone-companies.

56. "About Securus," Securus, accessed June 30, 2015, http://www.securustechnologies.com/about-us.

57. "Company Profile," Global Tel*Link, accessed June 30, 2015, http://www.gtl.net/about-us/company-profile/.

58. Shields.

59. Justin Moyer, "After Almost a Decade, FCC Has Yet to Rule on High Cost of Prison Phone Calls," Washington Post, December 2, 2012, http://articles.washingtonpost.com/2012-12-02/local/35585388_1_prison-phone-phone-providers-phone-companies.

60. "FCC Continues Push to Rein in High Cost of Inmate Calling," (Washington, DC: Federal Communications Commission, October 17, 2014), http://www.fcc.gov/document/fcc-continues-push-rein-high-cost-inmate-calling.

61. Ben Walsh, "Prisoners Pay Millions to Call Loved Ones Every Year. Now This Company Wants Even More," *Huffington Post,* June 10, 2015, http://www.huffingtonpost.com/2015/06/10/prison-phone-profits_n_7552464.html.

62. Renovo Software, "Revenue Generation," accessed June 28, 2015, http://www.renovosoftware.com/corrections-solutions/revenue-generation/.

63. Ibid.

64. Ibid.

65. "Annotated Bibliography: Offender Reentry," (Washington, DC: National Institute of Corrections, July 2012, revised January 2013), http://static.nicic.gov/Library/026286.pdf; Jeremy Travis, *But They All Come Back: Facing the Challenges of Prisoner Reentry,* (Washington, DC: Urban Institute Press, 2005); Creasie Finney Hairston, "Prisoners and Their Families: Parenting Issues during Incarceration," in *Prisoners Once Removed: The Impact of Incarceration and Reentry on Children, Families, and Communities,* ed. Jeremy Travis and Michelle Waul (Washington, DC: Urban Institute Press, 2004): 259–282; Joan Petersilia, *When Prisoners Come Home: Parole and Prisoner Reentry,* (New York: Oxford University Press, 2003).

66. "About Western Union Inmate Services," Western Union, accessed June 28, 2015, https://www.inmateservices.westernunion.com/WUCOMWEB/staticMid.do?pagename=inmateHome&method=load&countryCode=US&languageCode=en&nextSecurePage=Y.

67. Ibid.

68. "Inmate Services," MoneyGram, accessed May 29, 2013, http://www.moneygram.com/MGICorp/campaigns/inmateaccountfunding/index.htm.

69. "Access to Entertainment," Keefe Group, accessed June 28, 2015, http://www.keefegroup.com/services/mp3-program-125.

70. "Your Home for Corrections Services," JPay accessed June 28, 2015, http://www.jpay.com/.

71. "Keefe Rap Sheet," Private Corrections Working Group, October 11, 2006, http://www.privateci.org/rap_Keefe.html.

72. James Renner, "News: Pros and Cons: Ohio Privatizes Prison Goodies," City Beat Cincinnati, May 30, 2007, http://www.citybeat.com/cincinnati/article-2698-news_pros_and_cons.html.

73. "Committee Summary: Contributions to People against the Proposition 5 Deception," Follow the Money, accessed June 28, 2015, http://www.followthemoney.org/database/StateGlance/committee.phtml?c=3357; "Committee Summary: Contributions to Public Safety First—No on Proposition 19," Follow the Money, accessed June 28, 2015, http://www.followthemoney.org/database/StateGlance/committee.phtml?c=4257.

74. Lee Fang, "Exclusive: Why Can't You Smoke Pot? Because Lobbyists Are Getting Rich off of the War on Drugs," *Republic Report,* March 7, 2012, http://www.republicreport.org/2012/exclusive-why-cant-you-smoke-pot-because-lobbyists-are-getting-rich-off-of-the-war-on-drugs/.

75. "About ALEC," American Legislative Exchange Council, accessed June 28 2015, http://www.alec.org/about-alec/history/.

76. "ALEC Exposed; Minimum Mandatory Sentencing Act," Center for Media and Democracy, accessed June 28, 2015, http://alecexposed.org/w/images/e/eb/7D6-Minimum-Mandatory_Sentencing_Act_Exposed.pdf.

77. Ibid.

78. Jessica Wohl, "Wal-Mart Ending Membership in Conservative Group," *Reuters*, May 31, 2012, http://www.reuters.com/article/2012/05/31/us-walmart-alec-idUSBRE84U05N201 20531?irpc=932.

79. "Corporations that Have Cut Ties to ALEC," Source Watch, April 2015, http://www.sourcewatch.org/index.php/Corporations_that_Have_Cut_Ties_to_ALEC.

80. "ALEC Sharpens Focus on Jobs, Free Markets and Growth—Announces the End of the Task Force that Dealt with Non-Economic Issues," American Legislative Exchange Council, April 17, 2012, http://www.alec.org/alec-sharpens-focus-on-jobs-free-markets-and-growth-announces-the-end-of-the-task-force-that-dealt-with-non-economic-issues/.

81. "ALEC Caves to Pressure, Shuts Key Task Force," Common Cause, April 17, 2012, http://www.commoncause.org/press/press-releases/alec-caves-to-pressure-shuts-key-task-force.html.

Chapter 7

Let's Fix the Problem

Thus far, we have identified some of the problems with the American correctional system. We conclude with our suggestions on how to improve it. By improve, we mean moving toward attitudes, processes, and laws that send fewer people to prison. This requires remediating the current overcriminalization of certain activities and by decriminalizing certain activities. It also entails adopting new measures for how Congress and state legislatures enact new criminal legislation in the future.

For those convicted of crimes, we suggest alternatives to incarceration that include a therapeutic approach rather than a punitive one while still demanding personal accountability, and look at the role of community corrections in diverting offenders from prison. When determining whether an offender should be imprisoned and for how long, we support sentencing reforms that move away from legislatively imposed mandatory minimum sentences and allow judges more flexibility and discretion in sentencing. We also advocate for prison programming that helps prisoners prepare to reintegrate successfully in free society, and for post-incarceration programming that helps sustain successful reintegration.

Overcriminalization

"There is no one in the United States over the age of 18 who cannot be indicted for some federal crime. That is not an exaggeration." John Baker, retired Louisiana State University law professor, *Wall Street Journal*, July 23, 2011[1]

We need criminal laws. Criminals cause direct physical, psychological, and financial harm to their victims and indirect harm to all of society. However, we have too many criminal laws, and for many of those laws, the possible punishment can be greatly disproportionate to the actual social harm. A now-infamous game supposedly played in the U.S. Attorney's Office for the Southern District of New York had junior prosecutors identify a celebrity such as Mother Theresa or John Lennon, then try to identify a crime that the person could be charged with and potentially imprisoned. The scary part is that they could always find one.[2]

Because prosecutors have thousands of criminal laws at hand, it is easy to overcharge. As we discussed in Chapter 5, this can lead to prosecutorial abuses in plea bargaining, as defendants can be facing "stacked" series of charges that could result in many years of incarceration. In some of these cases, the defendant may plead guilty to crimes s/he did not commit in order to avoid the uncertainty of going to trial. As we also discussed in Chapter 5, the grand jury system, originally intended as a safeguard from overzealous prosecutors, has often proven today to be merely another prosecutorial tool. We suggest that the federal government and those states that provide grand juries examine ways to assure that the grand jury is an independent procedural safeguard.

We Call Our Legislators "Lawmakers" for a Reason; But Do We Need All These Laws?

As discussed in Chapter 5, there is constant public pressure on legislators to make new laws in an attempt to remedy perceived social problems. When evaluating whether we need new criminal laws to address an identified problem, an ideologically disparate alliance of the American Legislative Exchange Council, the Heritage Foundation, the Texas Public Policy Foundation, the National Association of Criminal Defense Lawyers, the Washington Legal Foundation, and Families Against Mandatory Minimums have drafted a set of guidelines. These guidelines seek answers to a series of questions, which we expand upon.[3]

1. Should the behavior be treated as a crime? Or are there other ways to regulate the problem through civil litigation, administrative fines, etc.? Does the threat the crime poses to society justify the costs to taxpayers of enforcing the law? These costs include investigation, prosecution, and possible incarceration. There are also opportunity costs, as resources are used to punish these crimes rather than other crimes that pose more of a threat to society. For example, it is a crime in many states to turn back an odometer on a motor vehicle. Stealing trade secrets is also commonly a crime. Civil litigation or administrative fines may serve as effective deterrents and retribution for these offenses.

In Chapter 4, we discussed the British practice of "cautioning" for some offenses. Formal cautioning can include confiscation of drugs, and a formal warning of prosecution for a repeated offense; informal cautioning can include simply encouraging the drug user to seek treatment. Another British policing alternative is the penalty notice, which assesses a civil fine rather than issuing a criminal citation for situations such as shoplifting, simple possession of marijuana, or being drunk and disorderly. Not every wrong requires handcuffs and a criminal record.

2. If it is to be treated as a crime, what should the *mens rea* (state of mind) requirement be? There should be a return to the old common law philosophy that the more severe the punishment is for an offense, the more difficult it should be for the prosecution to prove *mens rea*. If it is a crime that poses a grave threat to society for which a defendant can receive a harsh sentence, then the prosecutor should have to prove that the defendant intended to commit the unlawful act (general intent under the common law, or "knowingly" under the Model Penal Code). For the worst of crimes, the prosecutor should prove that the defendant intended the act to result in a particular harm (specific intent under the common law, or "purposefully" under the Model Penal Code). If it is a lesser crime, then the prosecutor should be required to prove that the defendant knew (was reckless) or reasonably should have known (was negligent) of potential harm, although the harm that occurred was unintended.

3. Is the crime serious enough that those convicted of the crime should be treated as felons, which can hurt their livelihoods and families? An overcriminalization study by the nonpartisan group Florida Tax Watch identifies some acts that are treated as felonies in Florida that include the "teen or college student who carries false identification in order to get admitted to adult activities" and the "internet shopper that fails to file and pay use tax."[4] As the study goes on to say, "[T]hese behaviors are not meritorious, that is not the question. The issue is whether these offenses are so harmful to society that a state prison term is necessary, as opposed to jail or other sanctions available for misdemeanants."[5]

Certainly, some criminal activity that is currently treated as felonious should be downgraded to misdemeanor status. This would be done in part by raising the threshold for certain felonies. For example, stealing something worth more than $250 is a felony in Massachusetts.[6] In Florida, the threshold is $300; in Wyoming, it's $1,000.[7] We suspect that money isn't worth any more in Florida or Massachusetts than it is in Wyoming, and suggest that Florida and Massachusetts look to Wyoming for guidance. Similarly, threshold amounts for drugs should be revisited, as we discuss later in this chapter.

4. What would the appropriate punishment be? What aggravating factors must the prosecutor prove? What mitigating factors can the defense introduce at trial? Is incarceration necessary to provide specific deterrence to the offender and general deterrence to other members of society?

The Colorado Model

In response to questions such as these, in 2011 the Colorado Legislature established guidelines for the introduction of any legislation that creates a new crime or that modifies an existing crime. With House Bill 11-1239, Colorado took a giant step away from overcriminalization. The new guidelines require that future criminal legislation include:

- A description of the elements of the proposed new crime, or a description of the new, amended, or additional elements of an existing crime;
- An analysis of whether the new crime, or changes to an existing crime, may be charged under current Colorado law;
- A comparison of the proposed crime classification to similar types of offenses; and
- An analysis of the current and anticipated future prevalence of the behavior that the proposed new crime, or changes to an existing crime, intends to address.[8]

The law passed with broad bipartisan support, sailing through the Republican-controlled House by a vote of 64-1, passing unanimously in the Democratic-controlled Senate, and signed into law by Democratic Governor John Hickenlooper.[9] In 2013, the Colorado legislature added a fifth requirement for prospective criminal legislation, "A description of gender and minority data as it relates to the general Colorado population and available data on gender and minority offender and crime victim populations potentially affected by the proposed measure."[10] As we discuss below, the effect of a criminal record is not racially color-blind.

At the federal level, the House Judiciary Committee authorized the bipartisan Over-Criminalization Task Force in 2014. House Judiciary Committee Bob Goodlatte said in a statement:

> Over the past few decades, the federal criminal code has expanded dramatically, creating an ever-increasing labyrinth of federal statutes and regulations, many of which impose criminal penalties without requiring that criminal intent be shown to establish guilt. We need to make sure our laws and regulations protect freedom, work as efficiently and fairly as possible, and do not duplicate state efforts. This Task Force is taking a detailed look at our criminal code, seeking input from recognized experts in the field, and intends to examine many issues this year.[11]

The task force held ten hearings in 2014. The result of those hearings is congressional awareness of the problem; how Congress will respond remains to be seen.

We suggest that the states and the federal government address the questions put forward by the American Legislative Exchange Council, the Heritage Foundation, the Texas Public Policy Foundation, the National Association of Criminal Defense Lawyers, the Washington Legal Foundation, and Families Against Mandatory Minimums about the issue of overcriminalization. Guidelines such as those set out by Colorado are a great place to start.

Decriminalization

You have probably heard of any number of dumb laws, some of which are fictional or have long since been repealed, but many are real and still exist. Times change, while our criminal codes continue to expand. Still on the books are countless arcane crimes from long ago. "Whoever wilfully blasphemes the holy name of God" can be imprisoned for up to a year in Massachusetts.[12] Alabama bans "shooting, hunting, gaming, card playing or racing" on Sunday.[13] To "teach another the doctrines, principles, or tenets, or any of them, of polygamy" can get you locked up for up to six months in Mississippi.[14] Each state and the federal government has its share of such laws. They are rarely enforced, but when they are, it is typically due to an abuse of prosecutorial power— the prosecution is pursuing this case because it can, not because it should.

Paxson teaches a criminal law course and finds that his students are amazed to learn that the following morals crimes are still on the books and technically enforceable in Massachusetts.

- Consensual sex between two people who are both under the age of sixteen.[15] (Both participants are guilty of statutory rape.)
- Living together after divorce.[16] (One can only wonder why this would ever occur.)
- Consensual oral or anal sex between two adults. (The language of the Massachusetts statute and its potential punishment are extraordinary: "Whoever commits the abominable and detestable crime against nature, either with mankind or with a beast, shall be punished by imprisonment in the state prison for not more than twenty years."[17])

We are fortunate enough not to have bedroom police in the U.S., and thus, the situations above rarely result in prosecutions. However, having "deadwood" legislation on the books poses two problems. First, it clutters an already overwhelming body of criminal law. Second, the continued presence of archaic criminal statutes in contemporary society causes some members of society to have skepticism and disregard for criminal laws in general. If a law is on the books as a crime, the behavior identified in that law should represent a contemporary social harm.

Unfortunately, politics gets in the way, once again. Suppose that an energetic legislator takes on the task of stripping such laws out of the criminal code. How will that legislator's political opponents cast that activity in the next election cycle? Is that legislator soft on crime? If there was an effort to remove antiquated morals laws from the criminal code, will political opponents attempt to portray that legislator as an enabler of sexual deviants?

Perhaps a fixed percentage of the criminal code should automatically come up for review every legislative term under a sunset system, whereby laws lapse unless they are specifically renewed. The review process would be undertaken by a legislative subcommittee assigned to the task, with the subcommittee voting whether to keep each reviewed law on the books in its current state, let it lapse, or identify it as needing modification. Modification would include providing a clearer, broader, or narrower definition of the criminal act, changing (or in some cases, adding) the state of mind requirement for that crime, and assessing a different range of punishments for the prohibited behavior. Any law identified for deletion or modification would then be taken up by the entire legislative body.

The bulk of the laws would likely remain unchanged. We are not arguing that all or most of our criminal laws are unneeded or unclear, but we are arguing that too many are. Legislative review of existing laws would indeed be an arduous task given the number of criminal laws scattered throughout state and federal statutes today. Nevertheless, the result would be a more efficient penal code, which would allow prosecutors to focus on those crimes that are the most harmful to society.

There is something of a precedent here. In 1962, the American Legal Institute introduced the Model Penal Code (MPC). Noted legal scholars labored for years in the drafting of the MPC, at times accompanied by heated debate. The American Legal Institute states, "The purpose of the Model Penal Code was to stimulate and assist legislatures in making a major effort to appraise the content of the penal law by a contemporary reasoned judgment."[18] The MPC sought to standardize and modernize criminal laws. For example, the old common law definition of larceny required that the item stolen must be tangible. Under the MPC, the crime of theft includes stealing tangibles such as a diamond ring and intangibles such as cable television service.

The MPC was proffered to Congress and the state legislatures. State and local bar associations were among the groups that lobbied legislatures to adopt all or part of the MPC. Some states have adopted significant parts of it, while some have largely declined to do so. In a few states, legislators resisted the

MPC in part because it categorized some of the old morals laws as only mis-demeanors, or decriminalized them altogether.[19]

The MPC itself continues to be revised. If our suggestion that legislatures regularly revisit and revise their respective penal codes proves to be too bur-densome, then it may be more practical to considering replacing existing statutes with those that have been subjected to previous consideration and debate in the Model Penal Code.

Drug Laws

Ironically, the Model Penal Code lacks a section on controlled substances. A lot has changed since 1962. Then again, the government's approach to drugs has twisted and turned in the last century. Very small amounts of cocaine were present in Coca-Cola until 1903, and it would be another eleven years until the federal government first regulated cocaine and opium with the passage of the Harrison Narcotics Tax Act of 1914.[20]

By 1914, all but two of the forty-eight states at the time had regulations on cocaine.[21] Massachusetts was the first state to ban marijuana in 1911.[22] Texas did so in 1923, when marijuana was considered more of an oddity than a men-ace to society. The *Austin Statesman* explained to readers at the time, "Mari-huana is a Mexican herb and is said to be sold on the Texas-Mexican border."[23] By 1931, marijuana's stature in Texas had ascended from an herb to, in the words of the *San Antonio Light,* that of a "dangerous and insanity-producing narcotic."[24] Apparently, this remained the Texas criminal justice community's perception of pot in 1972, when Dallas activist Stoney Burns (yes, really) was convicted for possession of about one-tenth of an ounce of marijuana and sen-tenced to ten years and one day in prison. The extra day made Burns ineligi-ble for probation.[25]

There is significant overlap in American drug laws between the states and the federal law enforcement. As the United States Sentencing Commission tells us:

> Within the Departments of Justice, Treasury, Transportation, Defense, and State and the U.S. Postal Service, there are numerous agencies with operational and law enforcement responsibilities for drug con-trol. These include, for example, the Drug Enforcement Administra-tion, the Federal Bureau of Investigation, the United States Attorneys, the Immigration and Naturalization Service, the United States Mar-shals Service, the United States Customs Service, the Bureau of Alco-hol, Tobacco and Firearms, the United States Coast Guard, and the

Federal Aviation Administration. Defining the federal role in drug enforcement among and between these agencies and the myriad of state
and local law enforcement agencies is difficult at best.[26]

With voters in some states having recently approved laws that allow for medical marijuana, for decriminalization of simple possession of marijuana, and
for outright legalization of recreational marijuana, there is now significant
conflict between federal law and the law of some states on the subject of pot.
We emphasize here that most of the evolving marijuana laws in the states are
the result of the petition and referendum process by citizens rather than legislative action. As we discussed in Chapter 6, there is powerful opposition to
legalized marijuana, and this organized opposition lobbies legislatures heavily to keep existing marijuana prohibitions in place.

A recent example comes from the nation's capital. In November 2014, almost two-thirds of voters approved Initiative 71, allowing recreational marijuana in the District of Columbia. Washington mayor Muriel Bowser announced
that the new law would take effect on February 26, 2015. U.S. Representative
Jason Chaffetz, chair of the House Oversight and Government Reform Committee, and House Oversight Government Operations Subcommittee chair
Mark Meadows sent Mayor Bowser a sharply worded letter telling her that,
"[Y]our assertion that Initiative 71 takes effect on Thursday is contrary to law.
We strongly suggest you reconsider your position."[27] Speaking of the decision
by Washington's city leaders, Chaffetz told the *Washington Post*, "[U]nder any
illusion that this would be legal, they are wrong. And there are very severe consequences for violating this provision. You can go to prison for this. We're not
playing a little game here."[28]

We suggest that the nation's legislators pay more heed to voters than to lobbyists and legalize marijuana. This would provide our nation's law enforcement agencies, courts, and corrections agencies more time and resources to
deal with more significant social harms. We also suggest that the states and
federal government evaluate whether a prison sentence is preferable to community substance abuse treatment for drug abusers and small-time drug dealers, many of whom themselves are drug abusers.

In addition, drug "mules"—the couriers who carry large amounts of drugs
for their drug-trafficking bosses—can currently receive the same sentence as
those bosses in many jurisdictions. We suggest that government officials devote
more attention to the organizational charts of drug-trafficking organizations
when they prosecute lower-echelon members of those organizations. We are
pleased to see bipartisan support in Washington for the Smarter Sentencing
Act, which restores discretion to federal judges that mandatory minimum sen-

tences previously stripped them of, and distinguishes between the mules or couriers caught with large amounts of drugs in their possession and their high-level bosses who enjoy most of the financial gain.[29]

Mandatory Minimums

"Too many people go to too many prisons for far too long for no good law enforcement reason. We need to ensure that incarceration is used to punish, deter, and rehabilitate—not merely to warehouse and forget."[30] Former U.S Attorney General Eric Holder, August 12, 2013

Mandatory minimums are great politics but horrible policy. Speaking before a congressional subcommittee in March 2015, U.S. Supreme Court Justice Stephen Breyer said that mandatory minimums are "a terrible idea."[31] We agree. We are encouraged by the new "safety valve" legislation that some states have recently enacted and that is currently being considered by Congress with bipartisan support, which we discussed in Chapter 5. This legislation allows judges to make departures from mandatory minimums under certain specific circumstances. The next step is to remove mandatory minimum sentences altogether.

Life Sentences

The federal courts imposed a life sentence in 153 cases in fiscal year 2013 (October 1, 2012 through September 30, 2013).[32] Guess what the most common offense was to receive a life sentence. Was it murder? Rape? Kidnapping? Distribution of child pornography? Nope; it was drug trafficking. Number two on the list was firearms offenses. We don't mean to make light of this. Drugs ruin the lives, and often take the lives, of far too many people. The drug traffickers in these cases had their contraband measured in pounds, not grams. Most of the firearms cases involved felons in possession of firearms or the use of firearms in other dangerous crimes. Should these folks be in prison? No question. Should they be serving life sentences? That remains a question.

Life without parole sentences (LWOP) among the states have arisen more recently than you may have thought. Only seven states had them before the 1970s. Twenty-six states added LWOP sentences in the 1970s and 1980s, and another seventeen states have added them since.[33] The number of prisoners serving LWOP sentences in the U.S. increased from 12,453 in 1992 to 49,081 in 2012.[34] In a study released in 2013, the American Civil Liberties Union found:

[A]s of 2012, there were 3,278 prisoners serving LWOP for nonviolent drug and property crimes in the federal system and in nine states that provided such statistics (there may well be more such prisoners in other states). About 79 percent of these 3,278 prisoners are serving LWOP for nonviolent drug crimes.... The overwhelming majority (83.4 percent) of the LWOP sentences for nonviolent crimes surveyed by the ACLU were mandatory.[35]

In 2013, the European Court of Human Rights ruled that life sentences without the possibility of parole are inhumane.[36] Italy, Germany, and France had already forbidden life sentences without parole.[37] In Canada, a person with a life sentence is eligible for parole review after serving twenty-five years, although Conservative Prime Minister Stephen Harper announced in 2015 that he favors legislation that would create a literal life sentence.[38]

Most Americans would agree that some criminals deserve life sentences. The problem with "lifers" is that they have little to lose while incarcerated, while the risks they pose to correctional workers and other prisoners are substantial. A partial solution is to make those serving life sentences eligible for parole after a certain number of years. For example, Texas grants parole reviews to those serving life sentences after they have served forty years, good time notwithstanding. Thus, most lifers are no younger than sixty years old when they first become eligible for parole review. At least they have hope while serving those forty years; for many prisoners, the desire not to die in prison becomes paramount.

A quick review of parole eligibility guidelines shows the effect of "get tough" politics, with offenders sentenced more recently being subject to more years of imprisonment in order to become eligible for parole than were offenders convicted earlier. For example, before 1995, a person serving a life sentence for a serious violent felony (murder, rape, etc.) in Georgia was eligible for parole review after serving seven years. In 1995, the period was extended to fourteen years; in 2006, it was extended to thirty years.[39]

Some lifers will never earn parole, even if they live long enough to become eligible for parole review. For example, Charles Manson has had his case reviewed by the California Parole Board twelve times during his more than forty years in prison for his role in the Tate-LaBianca murders. Manson is now over eighty years old and did not bother to attend his last parole board hearing.

As we saw in Chapter 4, some nations such as Norway evaluate serious offenders in a process that is the opposite of how we address those offenders in the U.S. In the U.S., although we use the standard of innocent until proven guilty at trial, the burden shifts to the offender once the offender has been found guilty and sentenced. The sentence focuses on the maximum number of years to be served and places the burden at the parole review hearing on the prisoner seeking early release. In Norway, even mass murderers such as Anders Breivik are given a term of no more than twenty-one years. At the expiration of that period, the government evaluates whether the offender remains a threat to society. (Most bets are on Breivik remaining in prison the rest of his life.)

Our suggestion is that even those serving life sentences should be eligible for parole review after a period of years. The hope of someday being released provides an incentive to those prisoners for good behavior, making prisons safer. Because most of those serving life sentences will be older, they are more expensive to house and care for in prison, and present little threat to society if released. As we quoted a federal judge in Chapter 5, sentences for non-violent crimes that extend past the age of 60 are "pointless."[40] Geriatric prisoners cost taxpayers millions of dollars and many of those prisoners can be released safely.

For those who become eligible, the review process should be rigorous, evaluating not only the conduct of the prisoner while incarcerated, but the likelihood of successful reintegration back into the community. Corrections officials must address the reality that offenders who have served many years in prison will have difficulties in readjusting to the changes that have happened in free society while they were incarcerated.

Parolees screwed up the last time they were in free society, and they leave prison with criminal records and diminished real world skills. The media and members of the public are often quick to pounce on those cases where parolees reoffend. Parole success stories rarely receive publicity. Recidivism will never go away, but we argue that by providing parolees with proper support and guidance for reintegration, recidivism can decrease. We suggest providing parolees with not merely supervision but also assistance in finding and maintaining suitable housing and employment, continuing substance abuse treatment, and personal and family counseling.

Diversion from Prison

U.S. Supreme Court Justice Anthony Kennedy is viewed as the centrist of the court, and is often the swing voter among its nine members. Appearing before the House Appropriations Subcommittee on Financial Services and General Government in March 2015, Kennedy spoke about the current state of the American correctional system, saying, "[T]his idea of total incarceration just isn't working." Kennedy advocated for putting more offenders on probation and other supervised programs. "This is cost-effective," he said, even "without reference to the human factor" involved in incarceration. "We have a very low recidivism rate for those who are on release."[41]

We suggest that alternatives to prison should be used instead of incarceration whenever practical; we recognize that this requires a significant change in prevailing correctional policy in the U.S. today. We endorse the Danish model discussed in Chapter 4 that strives for the least disruptive approach in rehabilitating offenders; the American model tends to emphasize maximum disruption, removing offenders from their family and friends, and placing them in an environment completely alien to that of free society.

Of course, there are also many situations in which offenders do need to be separated from their current situations. This includes gang membership and other associations with criminal offenders. In these cases, effective monitoring of offenders in the community will allow them to stay out of prison while also keeping them away from the people and the situations that got them in trouble in the first place.

Community Corrections

First, a quick discussion of probation and parole. Parole is supervised early release from a correctional institution. Its goal is to reduce the costs of incarceration and to help parolees reintegrate into free society. In many jurisdictions, parole is part of the department of correction. Probation is an alternative to incarceration, and many of the terms of probation are within the purview of the sentencing judge.

Prison is far more expensive than probation, and incarceration is no more effective a deterrent against recidivism than is probation. The Florida Tax Watch study discussed above points to adult civil citation programs in which the offender pleads guilty, pays a fine, and participates in community service.[42] We have also discussed a similar British practice called the penalty notice, which assesses a civil fine rather than issuing a criminal citation for situations such as shoplifting, simple possession of marijuana, or being drunk and disorderly.[43]

Technology can also help. Alternatives to incarceration include the use of GPS tracking devices to supervise and enforce house arrest and other community control measures. Three Florida State University criminologists studied data on 75,661 offenders placed on home confinement in Florida between 1998 and 2002. They found that "both radio-frequency and global positioning system monitoring significantly reduce the likelihood of technical violations, reoffending, and absconding for this population of offenders."[44] For offenders with alcohol abuse issues, there are several remote alcohol-sensing devices available today. One has the offender blow into a breathalyzer while a camera with face recognition technology makes certain that the offender is performing the test, not a five-year-old niece. There is also a transdermal monitor that is worn like a GPS tracking cuff, analyzing sweat vapors for alcohol content. Additionally, there are drug patches worn by offenders that can detect the use of marijuana, opiates, cocaine, PCP, and amphetamines. On probation or parole visits, the patches are removed and tested, providing the probation or parole officer with a window of ten days or more on the offender's abuse or abstention.[45]

We suggest that government agencies examine how technology can help offenders remain in their communities while being monitored by community corrections officials.

Intensive Supervised Probation

Intensive supervised probation (ISP) varies in its approach among different jurisdictions, but typically includes the following components:

1. Multiple weekly contacts with the probation officer—an ISP officer should have no more than twenty-five probationers as a caseload.

2. Random and unannounced drug testing.

3. Stringent enforcement of probation conditions. Probationers on ISP know that they can be sent to prison for technical violations of probation (violation of curfew, consuming alcohol, etc.) rather having to commit an arrestable offense. (Because "failing" ISP can occur because of a technical violation, and because those on ISP are so carefully scrutinized, the recidivism rate for ISP can be deceptively high.)

4. Requirement to participate in regular treatment, hold a job, and perhaps perform community service. By treatment, we mean substance abuse treatment, anger management, and other forms of cognitive behavioral therapy.[46]

ISP may be a diversion from prison, or it may be in response to a probationer's infractions during more traditional, less intensive probation. Because each ISP officer carries a smaller caseload than does a routine probation officer, ISP is much more expensive than routine probation. Yet it is generally less expensive than incarceration. We qualify this, because there are situations where ISP may last much longer than the period of incarceration an offender would otherwise serve. We suggest that policymakers conduct a careful cost/benefit analysis of intensive supervised probation relative to incarceration.

Drug Courts

Drug abuse takes a toll on those who abuse drugs, the people who love them, and their communities. However, the prevailing strategies and tactics used in the years since Richard Nixon declared the nation's War on Drugs in 1971 simply have not proven to be effective in reducing drug abuse and are a major factor in the U.S.'s shift to mass incarceration. As the conservative policy group Right on Crime states, "Recidivism rates are high in American prisons, and there is little evidence that drug abusers who enter prison leave having conquered their addiction."[47]

In 1999, Paxson worked as a public defender in Cambridge, Massachusetts, while on sabbatical leave from his teaching job. He remembers taking the commuter train home in the evenings, thinking about how many of his clients wouldn't be in court if it wasn't for drug or alcohol abuse. The answer was, most of them, and most of them knew that. Paxson and Watson actually agree with Right on Crime on several key principles, including our shared advocacy of drug courts.

The first drug court began in Miami in 1989. As of June 30, 2013, the Justice Department estimated that there are over 3,400 drug courts, including 433 juvenile drug courts. The typical drug court offers screening and assessment of risks, needs, and responsivity; judicial interaction; drug testing and supervision; graduated sanctions and incentives; and treatment and rehabilitation services.[48]

Do drug courts work? Researchers for the U.S. Justice Department's National Institute of Justice have found that, based on a series of studies, "drug courts may lower recidivism rates (re-arrests) and significantly lower costs."[49] Due in part to cost savings by diverting drug offenders from incarceration, the National Institute of Justice says, "Reduced recidivism and other long-term program outcomes resulted in public savings of $6,744 on average per participant."[50] The National Association of Drug Court Professionals (NADCP) is predictably more strident, stating, "We know beyond a reasonable doubt that Drug Courts significantly reduce drug use and crime and do so with substantial cost savings."[51] The NADCP is more tentative about the success of juvenile drug courts, conceding, "Early studies on [juvenile drug treatment courts] yielded mixed results," but adding that, "recent findings are giving cause for greater optimism as the programs have become more adept at their operations."[52]

Our suggestion is that the states and federal government continue to embrace drug courts as a more cost-effective way to deal with drug abuse than prison.

Mental Health Courts

Paxson's late father, a trial judge, told him that he was "tired of putting people who are sick and crazy in prison." A 2006 Justice Department study found that:

> [M]ore than half of all prison and jail inmates had a mental health problem, including 705,600 inmates in State prisons, 78,800 in Federal pris-

ons, and 479,900 in local jails. These estimates represented 56% of State prisoners, 45% of Federal prisoners, and 64% of jail inmates.[53]

In response to this widespread problem, in 2004 Congress created the Justice and Mental Health Collaboration Program. The program has distributed money to forty-nine states and the District of Columbia, allowing local officials to craft their own programs that help assess the needs of the mentally ill and develop programs that divert the mentally ill from incarceration. However, the program's budget for fiscal year 2015 was a mere $8.5 million, a thirty percent decrease from FY 2010's appropriation, which was only $12 million.[54]

We suggest that more resources be dedicated to mental health courts. Mass incarceration can decrease if there are more therapeutic and less punitive measures for treating mentally ill offenders.

Veterans Treatment Courts

What people had commonly called "shell shock" or "combat fatigue" was identified as Post Traumatic Stress Disorder (PTSD) in the American Psychiatric Association's *Diagnostic and Statistical Manual of Mental Disorders III* in 1980.[55] This advance arose from the high number of returning veterans from the Vietnam War who had suffered psychological trauma during the war that led them to readjustment problems and often criminal behavior when back home. The Bureau of Justice Statistics began tracking the number of veterans in American prisons in the 1980s. The National Vietnam Veterans Readjustment Survey, conducted between 1986 and 1988, found that fifteen percent of male Vietnam combat veterans suffered from PTSD, and of that group, nearly half had been arrested at least once.[56] The more recent Gulf wars and our more than decade-long military presence in Afghanistan have heightened Americans' awareness of the need to protect those who have protected us.

The first veteran treatment court was created in Anchorage in 1994 by Judges Jack W. Smith, a retired U.S. Air Force Academy colonel, and Sigurd E. Murphy, a retired brigadier general in the Army.[57] A few years later, Judge Robert T. Russell, Jr. founded the first veteran treatment court in Buffalo. Russell also established Buffalo's mental health court in 2002, and previously created Buffalo's drug court in 1995, over which he continues to preside. (Watson and Paxson want to meet this gentleman.) In January 2010, the U.S Department of Veterans Affairs and the Justice Department announced the Veterans Treatment Court Planning Initiative, a veteran treatment court training program, with initial grants to ten jurisdictions. Veteran treatment courts are partially modeled after drug courts, which have existed long enough (over twenty years) for researchers to recognize that their programs work.[58] While the first veteran treatment courts were created by empathetic judges, at least seven states have created them through legislation.[59]

The organization Justice for Vets identifies 220 veteran treatment courts in approximately half of the fifty states as of June 30, 2014, which means that about half of the states have yet to create them.[60] The veteran treatment court model requires regular court appearances (a bi-weekly minimum in the early phases of the program), mandatory attendance at treatment sessions, and frequent and random testing for substance use.[61] These courts rely on the spirit of camaraderie instilled in military training, connecting veterans in trouble with trained volunteer mentors who are themselves veterans.[62]

Because veteran treatment courts are relatively new, there is little data about their effectiveness thus far. However, veteran treatment courts borrow many of the practices used in drug courts, which have existed for several decades and have produced encouraging results, including reduced recidivism. Early data from Alaska indicates that the recidivism rate for the veteran treatment court is forty-five percent, a little less than Alaska's overall recidivism rate of 50.4%.[63] Our suggestion is to continue to fund veteran treatment courts, evaluate them, and determine best practices. While the effectiveness of veteran treatment courts has yet to be proven conclusively, the U.S. should continue this experiment in our effort to help those men and women whose military experiences have taken a toll.

Prisons

Have you ever been to prison? Watson has. He didn't like it. Paxson has been to prison, but always with the luxury of knowing that he was going to be able to leave after a few hours. We have found that the public, whose perceptions of prisons are based largely on what they hear and see in popular culture, tend to hold one of two very different ideas of what prisons are like. Many think that prisons are country clubs, while some others think that prisons are hellholes. The truth is that the average American prison is neither.

Because the American phenomenon of mass incarceration is a recent one, many prisons today are fairly new. There were 592 state prisons in 1974; by 2000 there were 1,023, with more under construction or planned.[64] Texas alone built 120 new prisons between 1979 and 2000.[65] Most prisons in the U.S. today comply with what would be considered relatively humane standards in terms of contemporary measures of decency.

Unfortunately, as we discussed in Chapter 6, one problem with the current trend in building prisons is placing them in rural areas where land is cheap and local residents are eager for jobs. By contrast, corrections officials in Germany attempt to keep prisons close to the cities where the prisoners' families are. This benefits prisoners and their families during a stressful period in the lives of both. Norwegian officials attempt to integrate local community resources, including educational and health services, rather than isolate prisoners. We suggest that American corrections officials investigate how keeping prisoners connected to the world outside can help reintegrate prisoners upon release.

The prison population is aging, and older prisoners tend to be less impulsive and more institutionalized than younger prisoners are. Many prisoners are dangerous, but they are also in environments over which corrections officials maintain custody and control. During his period of being involuntarily embedded in local and federal correctional facilities, Watson was never physically abused. Yet he was still miserable the entire time.

We have also found that many people mistake the term "prison dormitory" for a facility similar to a college dormitory, with a few people sharing a sleeping area and a bathroom. In reality, dorms are large rooms where perhaps hundreds of prisoners sleep in rows of bunk beds, with no privacy and very little security for their property or themselves. Dorms are a common response to prison overcrowding, often using what were once gymnasiums. Overcrowded conditions are dangerous for both prisoners and corrections workers. Spaces built to provide programming often must give way to more bunks, impairing the delivery of rehabilitative services to prisoners. We suggest that prison overcrowding be addressed as both a safety issue and an impediment to successful rehabilitation and reintegration.

Recall from Chapter 2 that the federal judge who sentenced Watson referred to federal prison camps as country clubs. Has he ever visited such a facility? Watson believes that one of the best ways to improve our criminal justice system would be for everyone involved in the system, including judges, prosecutors, the U.S. Sentencing Commission, and all U.S. Bureau of Prisons personnel and state correctional personnel, spend at least fourteen days in the equivalent of a federal prison camp, including three consecutive days in solitary confinement. (Paxson thinks two days and one night might be enough.) The visitors should also eat the same food and be subject to the same rules as other prisoners, and wear the same clothes. Recall from Chapter 2 that Watson's camp was prepared prior to its inspection by the American Correctional Association. There should be a procedure in place that allows for unannounced visits, in order for prison conditions to be as they normally are, while still providing stringent security for the visitors. The knowledge and personal insights gained from this would be invaluable in helping shape a more effective criminal justice system.

Solitary Confinement

At least prisoners living in dorms have social interactions. At so-called "super max" facilities, prisoners have little interaction with other humans. They typically sleep, shower, and eat in their single-bed cells, and are segregated during recreation time as well. As we discussed in Chapter 3, government officials refer to these conditions as administrative rather than punitive, using semantics to avoid claims that solitary imprisonment violates the Eighth Amendment's prohibition against cruel and unusual punishment.

At the time of writing, court proceedings were swirling around the status of Albert Woodfox, a sixty-eight-year-old prisoner in Louisiana who is said to have been in solitary confinement in a six-by-nine foot cell for forty-three years, believed to be a record. Woodfox was convicted of killing a corrections officer during a 1972 prison riot, although no physical evidence linked him to the crime and the officer's widow has stated publicly that she believes Woodfox is innocent.[66] Louisiana correctional officials have expressly denied that Woodfox was being held in solitary confinement, saying instead that his confinement was categorized as "closed cell restricted."[67] The state's attorney general has vowed to keep Woodfox imprisoned.

A 2011 United Nations report estimated that 20,000 to 25,000 U.S. prisoners are being held in solitary confinement. [68] The UN went on to say that solitary confinement should be eliminated in all but exceptional cases and for as short a period as possible. The report also called for an absolute prohibition of solitary confinement for juveniles and people with mental disabilities. (Use the search terms "mentally ill" and "solitary confinement" on YouTube—viewer discretion is advised.) There is also widespread concern about solitary confinement driving even the most mentally stable of human beings to madness.

Our suggestion is that U.S. correctional officials adopt the U.N.'s guidelines. There are certainly offenders who need to be segregated from the general population in order to protect other prisoners and corrections officers. However, it seems to us that the number of prisoners who meet this definition falls far below the 20,000 to 25,000 currently held in solitary confinement in the U.S.

Programming

The "nothing works" philosophy that spread through the nation's corrections agencies in the last quarter of the last century remains in place in too many American prisons. Warehousing prisoners until they have completed their sentences is relatively inexpensive in the short term. There are lower supervision costs when prisoners remain locked in their cells most of the day, and personnel costs represent the largest portion of correctional facilities' budgets. Programming costs money and many Americans perceive prison programming as coddling prisoners. In the long term, however, warehousing does little to lower recidivism, and warehousing is thus a false economy.

Despite some members of society lumping all offenders into one category as "evil," criminals end up in prison for a number of reasons, some simple, but many complex. The corrections community has long experimented with a wide variety of rehabilitative programming. Some works, some does not work. Some types of programing go in and out of fashion, depending in part on the political climate of the time. The key term used today is "evidence-based practices," borrowed from the medical field, referring to correctional programming with proven results that are reproducible.

Choice Architecture

We introduced choice architecture in Chapter 3. In their 2008 book *Nudge: Improving Decisions About Health, Wealth, and Happiness*, behavioral economists Richard H. Thaler and Cass R. Sunstein discuss how choice architecture provides nudges to help people make better decisions. A nudge is "any aspect of the choice architecture that alters people's behavior in a predictable way without forbidding any options or significantly changing their economic incentives."[69] Paxson last took students from his Principles of Correction course to a Massachusetts correctional facility in 2014. That facility is comprised of an older, more traditional structure built during the Great Depression. Adjacent is a set of four modern "podular" buildings, with inmates housed according to the types of programs provided in each building. These include some of the programs we discuss below.

However, inmates housed in the older building do not participate in any programming, and spend more than twenty hours a day in their cells. The problem here is that the nudge is *counterproductive*; those inmates who do not want to share a cell with other inmates volunteer to live in the older building in single-person cells, thereby avoiding participating in programs that can help them reintegrate into society. Unfortunately, the reason most people are in prison is due to faulty decision-making, and some prisoners are their own worst enemies.

We suggest that corrections officials identify incentives that can be offered to encourage prisoners to participate in programs. Nudging rather than forcing prisoners to participate can help foster a sense of self-affirmation through making positive choices. In addition, when inmates choose to be in a program they are likely to have a higher level of engagement.[70]

Substance Abuse Treatment

Over fifty percent of prisoners reported using illegal drugs in the month prior to the offense for which they were incarcerated; almost a third reported they were using an illegal drug at the time of the offense.[71] We advocated earlier for the use of drug courts as a diversion from incarceration. For those substance abusers who do find themselves incarcerated, our suggestions here fall within the phrase, "whatever works." Many behavioral programs are religion-based. These include Alcoholics Anonymous and Narcotics Anonymous. The Religious Land Use and Institutionalized Persons Act of 2000 protects prisoners' practice of religion in correctional institutions.[72] If religion helps a prisoner prepare to reenter society successfully, we endorse it. Of course, not all prisoners subscribe to religion. Paxson once asked a friend who is a recovering alcoholic what an atheist who wanted help with substance abuse should do. The answer was simple, "Get in a group. It's got to be something bigger than you." For those who do not believe in a higher power, group sessions can still help, and group counseling is a key component of modern correctional theory and practice.

Cognitive Behavioral Therapy

Watson's experience in the Residential Drug Abuse Treatment Program (RDAP) exposed him to a form of cognitive behavioral therapy (CBT) that he believes can help countless offenders while incarcerated and after release. As a study for the National Institute of Justice simply states, "Cognitive behavioral therapy reduces recidivism in both juveniles and adults."[73] The study goes on to say that "in most cognitive behavioral therapy programs, offenders improve their social skills, means-ends problem solving, critical reasoning, moral reasoning, cognitive style, self-control, impulse management and self-efficacy."[74]

While psychotherapy is egocentric, focused on the individual, CBT emphasizes a sociocentric approach, with the offender focusing on how to interact successfully with others. There are multiple types of CBT, some of which have trademarked names. The common elements in each are developing thought processes that lead to positive behavior and strengthening behavior through the positive consequences of good behavior.

CBT is a combination of cognitive therapy that focuses on the importance of thinking and how it affects our feelings and behaviors, and behavioral therapy that uses behavior to affect thinking and feelings. One technique of CBT is to examine our thoughts and beliefs and determine if they accurately mirror reality. Coupled with this is work on understanding how those thoughts and feelings influence our behaviors, especially when those thoughts are inaccurate and destructive, resulting in negative and harmful behaviors. Coupled with helping the patient achieve this self-awareness, the therapist will require the patient to engage in certain behaviors to help the patient change his thoughts and feelings about himself and the world around him.

Watson witnessed several "ah ha" moments in the RDAP class and in the personal development class he taught when he saw other inmates begin to understand that their feelings about the world were a function of how they chose to respond to events and not the events themselves. Watson felt it was especially gratifying when inmates in the personal development class took it a step further and began to understand the power of childhood events in shaping how a person responds to the world, and how important it was for them to pay attention to how they were shaping their children's feelings of self-worth and their worldview.

Education

More than a third of prisoners in the U.S. have only some high school education or less, compared to less than twenty percent of the U.S.'s general adult population. Adding those prisoners with GEDs, nearly two-thirds of American prisoners do not have a high school diploma, compared to twenty-four percent of the general adult population.[75] The lack of sufficient education and a criminal record are two significant obstacles to successful reintegration. In addition, with increasingly accelerated technological changes in the workplace, years spent serving a prison sentence can put ex-offenders at a distinct disadvantage relative to other job seekers. As we mentioned earlier in the book, Watson witnessed halfway house residents in San Antonio who did not know how to use a computer to search for a job.

In a 2014 meta-analysis (a study of studies) researchers for the RAND Corporation found that "inmates who participated in correctional education programs had a 43 percent lower odds of recidivating than those who did not, thus indicating that correctional education is an effective strategy for reducing recidivism."[76] The RAND study further found that "the direct costs of reincarceration were far greater than the direct costs of providing correctional education."[77] Correctional education has several components.

Literacy

The average reading level of prison inmates is very low: below the fifth grade in one study and below the eighth grade in another. About 67% of prison inmates cannot write a brief letter explaining a billing error, read a map, or understand a bus schedule.[78] This lack of basic literacy is attributable to cognitive disabilities among some prisoners, and dysfunctional childhoods among many prisoners. With few distractions in prison, illiterate prisoners have time to develop their reading and writing skills. For some prisoners, courses in English as a second language are necessary.

Adult Basic Education

Adult basic education covers some of the most basic skills of successful adulthood. Can prisoners preparing to reenter the community read job listings on the internet? Can they fill out an employment application? Can they read the warning label on the side of an over-the-counter drug? Can they create a monthly budget and live within it? What parenting skills do they have? What parenting skills do they need? These basic skills are vital for successful reintegration back into the community.

Secondary Education

It is hard to imagine how anyone in the U.S. today can make a decent living without a high school diploma or a GED. Much has been written about the "school to prison pipeline." Many prisoners who did not finish high school did not drop out; they were expelled. We discuss this in our look at juveniles below.

For prisoners seeking an education, prison overcrowding has meant that demand for educational programming is increasing while available resources have declined. A 2012 study by the U.S General Accountability Office (GAO) found that about fourteen percent of federal prisoners were enrolled in GED courses. However, another twelve percent of prisoners at those facilities were on waiting lists for those classes.[79] The GAO study attributed much of the problem to overcrowded facilities.

Vocational Training and Job Readiness Training

Many offenders have never had a "real job" and come from families in which that was also the case. For these folks, something as simple as janitorial work or making license plates requires reporting to a supervisor and working a shift, which are life skills that translate to the real world. Paxson has found that many of his law-abiding students do not know how to draft an effective résumé, nor prepare for and present at a job interview. Obviously, it is much harder for ex-offenders, who have to explain gaps in their employment record due to incarceration.

While there is much to criticize about how criminals think, one characteristic of many offenders than can be redirected in a positive manner is their willingness to assume risks. A particularly notable vocational program is the Leonard Greenstone Marine Technology Training Center at the California Institution for Men in Chino, California. This program teaches prisoners how to be underwater welders. Underwater welding requires technical skills and risk-taking; accordingly, it pays well, with experienced welders earning six-figure annual incomes.[80] Not all who enter this rigorous problem complete it, but those who do leave Chino with a guaranteed job. We suggest that corrections officials identify skill sets needed in the labor market and provide appropriate vocational programming.

Entrepreneurial Training

Because many ex-offenders will have trouble getting jobs due to their criminal record, creating one's own job may be the best option for some. Many ex-offenders were effectively self-employed business people in their criminal lives; the problem was that their businesses were illegal. Repurposing existing entrepreneurial skills and refining them for legal occupations is the focus of such programs as California's The Last Mile. Part of the program focuses on developing interpersonal skills, social media usage, and generating a business plan, and culminates with a five-minute sales pitch before an audience.[81] We suggest that corrections officials offer similar forms of entrepreneurship programming.

College

In Chapter 3 we discussed Congress abolishing Pell Grants for prisoners in 1994. Partly because of this, the GAO found that only one percent of prisoners at the facilities it studied were enrolled in college courses, and the GAO pointed that college courses are "funded by inmates' personal funds rather than through BOP's salaries and expenses budget account."[82] Fortunately, private foundations and private colleges have helped some prisoners obtain a post-secondary education.

After Congress banned college funding for prisoners and the state of New York followed suit, a collaboration of colleges, prisoners, and community organizations founded Hudson Link. Hudson Link offers courses through a consortium of five colleges that operate at five correctional facilities in New York.

Over 300 prisoners have earned degrees through the program; the recidivism rate among its graduates over sixteen years is a meager two percent.[83]

The VERA Institute for Justice's privately funded Pathways from Prison to Postsecondary Education Program offers a two plus two design; as prisoner prepare to reenter the community, they spend the last two years of their sentences in prison taking coursework and continue attending college for two years upon release. The VERA Institute points to reducing recidivism and the goal that "increasing the education attainment of parents could impact the education achievement of their children."[84]

We are encouraged by the announcement in May 2015 that the Obama Administration is planning to provide Pell Grants to some prisoners, characterizing the move as a small-scale experiment that could lead to overturning the 1994 congressional ban on Pell Grants for prisoners. That same month, U.S. Representative Donna Edwards of Maryland introduced the Restoring Educating and Learning (REAL) Act to restore Pell Grants for prisoners. Representative Edwards explained:

> The REAL Act is about restoring education opportunities for our nation's prisoners so they will have the opportunity to reintegrate as productive members of the community post-incarceration. We know that helping economically challenged individuals work toward postsecondary study and training provides a better future for all Americans. We should provide such opportunities to all to ensure that the cyclical process of repeat incarceration does not continue.[85]

Co-sponsor Danny Davis said,

> A lack of federal funding is the primary barrier to correctional education. This is another reason why we need to expand Pell Grants and restore eligibility for the incarcerated. Expanding and restoring Pell is a common-sense federal investment that dramatically increases successful reentry and builds stronger communities and families.[86]

Much of the online reaction to the REAL Act is negative, assailing the idea that the government will help convicted criminals pay for college while not doing enough to help law-abiding citizens who are struggling to pay college tuition. We suggest that policymakers focus on the data cited in the RAND report that draws a causal link between prison education and lower recidivism, as well as the very successful results from the Hudson Link. In most states, it remains more expensive to house a prisoner for one year than it does to attend public college for one year.

Prisons and Profits: A Horrible Idea

For-profit prison firms claim that they can save taxpayers money relative to government-operated prisons; we ask that the public and our government leaders scrutinize for-profit prison companies and the claims that they make. First, they cherry pick their data. For example, the resource center on CCA's website (http://www.cca.com/cca-resource-center) directs its visitors to a section titled "*Independent* Research on Public-Private Partnerships" (emphasis added). As of the time of writing, the first study listed is one by Temple University economics professors Simon Hakim and Erwin A. Blackstone, "Contracted Prisons Cut Costs without Sacrificing Quality: A Report from Economics Professors from Temple University's Center for Competitive Government." However, in the description of that study, the CCA website (now) states, "This study received funding by members of the private corrections industry." Namely, CCA, the GEO Group, and Management and Training Corp., the big three of the for-profit prison industry. If the for-profit prison industry funds a research project, that research project is hardly independent.

Moreover, the study itself did not originally disclose that the Temple professors had received money from the for-profit prison operators. After an ethics complaint was lodged with Temple, the university conducted an inquiry; the complainant was Alex Friedmann, who served six years at a CCA-owned facility and is now an editor at the Prison Legal News website. Michele Masucci, Interim Vice Provost for Research at Temple, stated in a July 2014 letter to Friedmann:

> I conclude my examination of the allegation you raised that Drs. Simon Hakim and Erwin Blackstone neglected to mention funding sources in a working paper containing research results and in at least three newspaper editorials.
>
> As you know, the working paper was withdrawn and is no longer widely available. Additionally, University records do not reveal that it received grant funds for specific work under consideration. Consistent with this information many months ago we directed that correction be made to any publication that inaccurately attributed Temple's connection to this work.
>
> The University will address its conclusions, including any action specific [sic] pertaining to the respondents, individually with Drs. Hakim and Blackstone.[87]

Nevertheless, Hakim and Blackstone's work may still have assisted the privatization of American corrections. In an article entitled, "How a Bogus, Industry-

Funded Study Helped Spur a Privatization Disaster in Michigan" published on Bill Moyers's website only two weeks after Masucci's letter to Friedmann, the author cites numerous problems that the Michigan Department of Corrections was experiencing after the state had recently laid off approximately 370 kitchen workers and contracted with for-profit Aramark to feed its prisoners.[88] The article points out that during the period when the Michigan Legislature was debating whether to outsource, Hakim and Blackstone published an op-ed article in the *Detroit Free Press* entitled, "Data Shows Running Prisons for Profit Is a Win-Win."[89] The article relies on the data from their study, but does not state that for-profit prison companies funded that study. Hakim and Blackstone also told readers that, "The use of contractor-operated prisons is not new for Michigan; a private facility in Baldwin housed inmates until 2005."[90] What they neglected to mention is that, having only opened in 1998, the Baldwin juvenile facility was "shut down amid reports it was too costly to run and neglected the health and educational needs of its young inmates."[91]

In an open letter to CCA, University of California at Berkeley doctoral candidate Christopher Petrella points out that "the Temple University report fails to acknowledge that an exceedingly small percentage of prisoners with high-cost health conditions—precisely those your company will never house—account for a disproportionately large slice of specialty health care expenditures."[92] This brings us to the second problem with for-profit prisons; they often get to cherry pick the prisoners that they will house, specifying in their contracts with governmental jurisdictions that they will only accept young and healthy prisoners, who are the cheapest to house. Petrella's research of for-profit prisons cites language from contracts in four states in which the for-profit contractor is allowed to ship sick prisoners back to the custody of the state.[93]

Petrella also found that younger prisoners are also more likely to be prisoners of color than white; "This fact results in a prisoner profile that is far younger and far 'darker' in minimum and/or medium security private facilities than in select counterpart public facilities."[94] Criminals have few powerful friends. It should come as no surprise that for-profit companies have had great success in gaining contracts to house those with the least socio-economic power, including minority group members, illegal immigrants, and juvenile offenders. These groups represent the low-hanging fruit of the corrections system.

The bottom line for the firms that operate for-profit prisons is of course financial. As members of society, we argue that the ultimate metric must be recidivism. Are those held in for-profit prisons less likely to commit future crimes upon release than prisoners held in government-operated facilities are? No; as we pointed out in Chapter 6, the operators of for-profit prisons cannot afford to be too successful in rehabilitating prisoners, as their business models rely on repeat offenders, and studies have shown that the recidivism rates at private fa-cilities tend to be higher than those at public prisons.

Although we find ourselves agreeing with the conservative organization Right on Crime on many topics, this is one where we diverge. We need to get rid of privately owned prisons. Watson believes that privately owned prisons violate the Thirteenth Amendment, reasoning that taking another human being's freedom away from them for the financial profit of another is engag-ing in slavery. If the courts hold otherwise, Watson argues that we need a new constitutional amendment that specifically prohibits private prisons. Paxson, a little more dispassionate about the topic, simply doesn't trust the business model of for-profit prisons, for the reasons laid out in Chapter 6. Governmental en-tities should cease from contracting with private, for-profit firms to house the government's prisoners. Existing government contracts with private prison firms should be allowed to lapse without renewal.

This will require many government leaders to reassess their current reliance on for-profit prison companies. The 2014 annual report of Corrections Cor-poration of America (CCA) boasts that the firm "achieved a 100% renewal rate for the 22 contracts up for renewal with our government partners in 2014."[95] The report also states that CCA planned to add almost 6,500 new beds in 2015.[96]

Juveniles: Almost All of Them Will Get Out

A financially comfortable family with a trouble child has a variety of re-sources available to it, including substance abuse programs and behavioral health resources. The young offenders who end up in juvenile facilities are more likely to come from poor, dysfunctional families.

As we discussed in Chapter 4's comparison of the American justice system with that of other nations, American treatment of juvenile offenders remains one of many facets of American exceptionalism, and not a good one. One of the differences in the American juvenile justice system is how frequently juve-nile offenders are transferred out of the juvenile justice system and tried in adult courts. All fifty states have laws that allow or require the transfer of ju-venile cases from juvenile jurisdiction to regular criminal courts. This can in-clude children who are as young as ten years old.[97]

We often hear the expression, "If you do the crime, you do the time," a one-size-fits-all approach to criminal justice. If you've been reading this book this far, you have seen numerous arguments that oppose this kind of thinking. It doesn't make sense that a juvenile is not allowed to vote, drink beer, sign a business contract, or run for political office, but can be treated as an adult by the criminal justice system. The popular argument that punishing juveniles as adults will serve as an effective deterrent to juveniles makes little sense when considering how ineffectively punishing *adults* as adults deters them from committing crimes.

Several recent developments at the federal and state level concerning juvenile offenders are encouraging. Six states that previously treated seventeen-year-olds as adults have raised the age to eighteen. However, at the time of this writing, nine states still treat seventeen-year-olds automatically as adult offenders; New York and North Carolina automatically treat sixteen-year-olds as adults.[98] For those who say, "You do the crime, you do the time," consider this: juvenile offenders who are transferred to the criminal justice system rather than the juvenile system have consistently been found to have higher recidivism rates than do juveniles processed through the juvenile system. A federally funded study for the Florida Department of Juvenile Justice found that "nearly 50 percent of the transfers re-offended after age 18 but only 35 percent of the juvenile cases did."[99] Part of the explanation for this difference is simple: many adult prisons focus on warehousing, not rehabilitation, and do not offer the types of programs necessary to help youthful offenders get on the right track.

In 2012, the U.S. Supreme Court ruled in *Miller v. Alabama* that an offender who was a juvenile at the time of the offense cannot be given a sentence of life without parole.[100] (As Chief Justice John Roberts pointed out in his dissent, the majority of states in 2012 allowed life without parole sentences for juvenile offenders.) At the time of this writing, the U.S. Supreme Court had not yet heard oral arguments in *Montgomery v. Louisiana*, which will determine whether *Miller* should be applied retroactively throughout the U.S. Some states are not waiting for the *Montgomery* decision and have already applied *Miller v. Alabama* retroactively, allowing juveniles offenders who were convicted to life without parole before the *Miller* decision to become eligible for parole review. As of the time of this writing, nine states have done so, although Michigan specifically refused to do so, as did Louisiana, which is why the *Montgomery* case is now before the court.[101]

Paxson recalls a conversation he had with David Rosmarin, a forensic psychiatrist in Massachusetts who has evaluated over 150 murderers.[102] Rosmarin told him that a twenty-five-year-old who kills is likely a stone-cold killer, while a fifteen-year-old who kills can likely still be fixed. We suggest that juvenile offenders' immaturity and impetuosity, as well as the fact that the brains of juvenile offenders are still developing, must be considered by all actors in the criminal justice process, beginning with the legislatures that determine punishment ranges.

As the saying goes, it takes a village to raise a child. We suggest that Americans begin to reassess troubled youths as a community problem rather than an individual one. This philosophy brought about the first neighborhood conference committees in Texas as a means of diverting some young offenders from detention facilities. These committees consist of volunteers who meet with the child and parents to draw up a contract, which all parties sign. The contract identifies the activities that the young person in question must successfully participate in order to have the case closed. This includes regularly attending school and can include undergoing therapy and participation in community projects.

Policymakers have also been giving more scrutiny to school disciplinary procedures; as we mentioned above, many juvenile and adult offenders who lack high school diplomas did not drop out of school, they were expelled. We discussed how negative experiences early in childhood could lead to future criminality in our brief look at life course theories in Chapter 3. Unfortunately, in the aftermath of the tragedy at Colorado's Columbine High School in 1999, many school districts adopted zero-tolerance policies for troubled students.

Among those students who are expelled, race, unfortunately, seems to be a factor, with suspensions and expulsions affecting a disproportionate number of black students relative to other groups. A study by the American Psychological Association (APA) found that "[e]merging professional opinion, qualitative research findings, and a substantive empirical literature from social psychology suggest that the disproportionate discipline of students of color may be due to lack of teacher preparation in classroom management ... lack of training in culturally competent practices ... or racial stereotypes."[103] Not surprisingly, the APA's study advocates for policies that allow for variances from zero-tolerance policies in schools.[104]

The U.S. Department of Health and Human Services and the Department of Education have issued guidance on preventing and severely limiting expulsion and suspension practices in early childhood settings.[105] In September 2011, U.S. Secretary of Education Arne Duncan and Attorney General Eric Holder announced the Supportive School Discipline Initiative, aimed at maintaining school discipline while attempting to keep troubled children in school. This initiative encourages collaboration among educators in identifying and expanding best practices for school discipline.[106]

In addition to engaging in a joint effort to divert children from the juvenile justice system, Duncan and Holder asked the states to improve the educational opportunities available to those young people who are held within the juvenile justice system. A December 2014 letter to state education officials and state attorneys general advocated for high-quality correctional education, "which is one important way of providing some of our most vulnerable youth with a real chance at a second chance—the opportunity to demonstrate growth and maturity and, ultimately, to fulfill their potential as human beings."[107]

At the time of writing, a new charter school was preparing to open in In-dianapolis. The school will enroll students who have been expelled from other schools or are on juvenile probation at the Marion Academy in a former school's facility. Juveniles held in the Marion County Juvenile Justice Center will at-tend the Hillside Academy within the detention facility.[108] Former juvenile court judge Clark Rogers said, "We decided not only would they be able to get their high school degree, not just a GED but a high school degree, and recover credits and also learn a certifiable skill, a vocation … or go on to Ivy Tech or a college for that matter."[109]

Life after Prison

Reintegration

"I don't know how to talk to a woman anymore."
Prisoner in conversation with Paxson at the North Central
Correctional Institution, Gardner, Massachusetts

As we first discussed in Chapter 3, reintegration is the process of former prisoners becoming members of free society again. They do so with the bur-den of having criminal records and having been apart from their families and friends for some time. In Chapter 3 we also discussed a model facility for help-ing ex-offenders reintegrate. Hampden County, Massachusetts's After Incarceration Support Systems Program (AISS) was the first program of its kind upon its founding in 1996.[110] AISS collaborates with correctional facilities holding pris-oners who are soon to be released. The Pre Release Center screens and assesses those prisoners. Occupational assistance begins with job readiness programs, then employment searching, followed by job retention support. There are sig-nificant efforts to assist clients in obtaining permanent housing, with short-term housing available in the interim.

AISS also works with a myriad of public and private agencies, including employment agencies, health and mental health agencies, and men's and women's support groups (conducted in English and Spanish). Some of the needs of those reintegrating are things that others in free society may take for granted. For example, many ex-offenders lack identifying documents such as a driver's license or a state identification card, which can make it difficult or impossible to find a job or rent housing. AISS works with Massachusetts Reg-istry of Motor Vehicles to help in this regard.

Beyond the concern for the ex-offenders and their families, there is a broader community concern. The current emphasis on restorative justice (discussed in Chapter 3) seeks to have offenders make recompense for financial losses that they have caused others. We are encouraged by John Owen Haley's work on "cooperative communities" as a means of reintegrating ex-offenders in society. Haley, a comparative legal scholar at Vanderbilt University Law School, looks to communitarian models from Japan, as opposed to individualistic approach common in the U.S. Haley worked on a pilot program in St. Louis with Joseph A. Scalise, Jr., a retired chief deputy juvenile officer.[111] Essentially, cooperative communities are similar to neighborhood conference committees in use for juvenile offenders, which we mentioned above. The goal is to create neighborhood volunteer boards, which would include police and social workers to guide ex-offenders in their communities. In accordance with the restorative justice model, victims are encouraged to participate, if they so desire. The goal is to have ex-offenders understand the costs of their actions on their community, and to have ex-offenders become a part of their communities rather than remain marginalized outsiders.

The old days of just giving a released prisoner twenty dollars and a bus ticket should be long past; we suggest that community leaders, human service agencies, correctional agencies, and law enforcement explore how to involve communities in reintegrating ex-offenders.

Earning a Living

We have already made the case that too much taxpayer money is spent on incarceration in the U.S. There is also the issue of raising tax revenue. People with decent jobs contribute to the nation's economy through their productivity. Those who are gainfully employed contribute through the payment of sales tax, property tax, excise tax, and income tax.

Criminal convictions in general and felony convictions in particular make it harder for ex-offenders to obtain decent jobs that will support them and their families. Ex-offenders can actually be punished for years after they have served their prison sentences, often losing the right to vote, to serve in the military, and to live in subsidized housing, as well as being severely impaired in their ability to find gainful employment. Another consideration is restorative justice. Ex-offenders holding jobs may be able to provide compensation to their victims.

We are encouraged that at the time of writing a major movement has arisen across the country to "ban the box." This campaign, using model legislation called the Fair Chance Act, seeks to remove questions about one's criminal record ("Check here if you have ever been convicted of a crime") from initial employment application forms. Thus far, seventeen states have adopted policies that remove the question from applications for jobs with government agencies. Six states have removed the criminal history question on job applications for private employers.[112] At the federal level, the U.S. Equal Employment Opportunity Commission (EEOC) has endorsed removing the criminal history question from initial job application forms, and treats an employer's blanket ban against hiring people with criminal records as illegal.[113]

The EEOC's stance is based in part on a now-famous study by Devah Pager published in the *American Journal of Sociology* in 2003. Pager's study found that the self-disclosure of a criminal record in response to a question on an application form diminished the applicant's chance of getting a callback from the employer by about fifty percent for white male applicants.[114] While thirty-four percent of white men without a criminal record were called back, only seventeen percent of white men with a criminal record were. For black men, the situation was particularly grim. Among black male applicants without a criminal record, only fourteen percent received a callback. (Note that a black applicant *without* a criminal record was less likely to receive a callback than a white applicant *with* a criminal record.) Among black applicants with a criminal record, only five percent received a callback. The status of being black and an ex-offender poses a significant barrier to suitable employment in the U.S. Some states such as Colorado, as we discussed above, are now looking at the effect that proposed new criminal laws may have on offenders based on their race.

To clarify, if a prospective employer determines that the applicant is a possible candidate for a job, that employer may then follow up with a criminal background check. The "ban the box" movement seeks to give ex-offenders the opportunity to be given early consideration based on their qualifications. The EEOC's guidance recognizes the business necessity of disqualifying an applicant with a criminal record because of the nature of the crime(s) involved and the nature of the job that the applicant is seeking.[115] Common sense tells us that we should not have a convicted child molester working in a daycare center nor a convicted embezzler handling large sums of an employer's money. However, many convictions are not directly related to the duties and responsibilities of a job. Watson is grateful that his employer was able to look beyond Watson's status as a felon so that Watson can support himself and his family. Paxson's employer does not ask job applicants about a criminal record, but does ask for three professional references and asks why applicants left their previous jobs.

Employers who employ ex-felons within a year of their release can receive federal work opportunity tax credits (WOTC). This provides a tax credit equal to twenty-five to forty percent of the employee's first-year wages, and forty to fifty percent of the employee's second-year wages. We suggest that the states create similar WOTC incentives to employers of ex-offenders.

We suggest that criminal justice policymakers focus on how to get offenders to become productive citizens in the community rather than prisoners who cost over \$31,000 on average to incarcerate each year.[116]

Conclusion

Although the U.S.'s embracement of mass incarceration is relatively new, we hold no illusion that the nation will completely reverse its course. As we have discussed, the reason that the U.S. has the highest incarceration rate in the world springs from cultural ideals about the role of the individual in society and the belief that people freely make the choices that they make. We know we cannot change these long-held ideals and beliefs. However, Americans are also increasingly wary of the power of government and the cost of government, concerns that are bipartisan. Here, we argue that the government's power to imprison people at great expense to taxpayers be given much more scrutiny. Every tax dollar dedicated to incarcerating prisons is a dollar that could be used to meet some other social need.

Notes

1. Quoted in Gary Fields and John R. Emshwiller, "Many Failed Efforts to Count Nation's Federal Criminal Laws," *Wall Street Journal*, July 23, 2011, http://www.wsj.com/articles/SB10001424052702304319804576389601079728920.

2. Tim Wu, "American Law Breaking," *Slate*, (October 14, 2007), http://www.slate.com/articles/news_and_politics/jurisprudence/features/2007/american_lawbreaking/introduction.html.

3. "Criminalizing America: How Big Government Makes a Criminal of Every America," American Legislative Exchange Council, 2013, http://alec.org/docs/Criminalizing_America.pdf.

4. Dan McCarthy, "Over-Criminalization in Florida—An Analysis of Non-Violent Third-Degree Felonies," (Tallahassee: Florida Tax Watch, April 2014), http://www.floridatrend.com/public/userfiles/news/pdfs/ThirdDegreeFINAL.pdf#zoom=80.

5. Ibid.

6. Mass. Gen. Laws ch. 266, §30.

7. Fla Stat. §812.014; Wyo. Stat. Ann. §6-3-402.

8. Colo. Rev. Stat. §2-2-322 (2011).

9. Mike Krause, "Legislature Restrains Its Compulsion to Overcriminalize Colorado," *Huffington Post*, May 5, 2011, updated July 7, 2011, http://www.huffingtonpost.com/mike-krause/colorado-restrains-overcriminalization_b_857771.html.

10. Colo. Rev. Stat. §2-2-322 (2013).

11. "House Judiciary Committee Reauthorizes Bipartisan Over-Criminalization Task Force," House Judiciary Committee, February 5, 2014, http://judiciary.house.gov/index.cfm/2014/2/house-judiciary-committee-reauthorizes-bipartisan-over-criminalization-task-force".

12. Mass. Gen. Laws ch. 272, §36.

13. Ala. Code §13A-12-1.

14. Miss. Code Ann. §97-29-43 (2014).

15. Mass. Gen. Laws ch. 265, §23.

16. Mass. Gen. Laws ch. 208, §40.

17. Mass. Gen. Laws ch. 272, §34.

18. "Model Penal Code," American Legal Institute, https://www.ali.org/index.cfm?fuse-action=publications.ppage&node_id=92.

19. See generally William N. Eskridge Jr., *Dishonorable Passions: Sodomy Laws in America 1861–2003*, (New York: Viking, 2008).

20. Public Law No. 223, 63rd Cong., approved December 17, 1914.

21. "Report on Cocaine and Federal Sentencing Policy," (Washington, DC: U.S. Sentencing Commission, May 2007), http://www.ussc.gov/report-cocaine-and-federal-sentencing-policy-2.

22. Massachusetts 1911 Chap. 0372. An Act Relative to the Issuance of Search Warrants for Hypnotic Drugs and the Arrest of Those Present.

23. Quoted in National Commission on Marihuana and Drug Abuse, "The Technical Papers of the First Report of the National Commission on Marihuana and Drug Abuse" (Washington: GPO, 1972): 482.

24. Ibid., 484.

25. Roy Appleton, "Stoney Burns, Leading Voice of the 1960s Dallas Counterculture, Dies at 68," *The Dallas Morning News*, April 29, 2011, updated April 30, 2011, http://www.dallasnews.com/news/community-news/dallas/headlines/20110429-stoney-burns-leading-voice-of-the-1960s-dallas-counterculture-dies-at-68.ece.

26. United States Sentencing Commission.

27. "Letter to D.C. Mayor Muriel Bowser Regarding Initiative 71," *Washington Post*, February 24, 2015, http://apps.washingtonpost.com/g/documents/local/letter-to-dc-mayor-muriel-bowser-regarding-initiative-71/1427/.

28. Mike DeBonis and Aaron C. Davis, "Bowser: Legal Pot Possession to Take Effect at Midnight in the District," *Washington Post*, February 25, 2015, http://www.washingtonpost.com/local/dc-politics/house-republicans-warn-dc-mayor-not-to-legalize-pot/2015/02/25/2f784a10-bcb0-11e4-bdfa-b8e8f594e6ee_story.html.

29. Smarter Sentencing Act of 2015, S. 502, H.R. 920, 114th Cong. (2015).

30. "Attorney General Eric Holder Delivers Remarks at the Annual Meeting of the American Bar Association's House of Delegates," U.S. Justice Department, August 12, 2013, http://www.justice.gov/opa/speech/attorney-general-eric-holder-delivers-remarks-annual-meeting-american-bar-associations.

31. Jess Braven, "Two Supreme Court Justices Say Criminal-Justice System Isn't Working," *Wall Street Journal*, March 24, 2015, http://www.wsj.com/articles/two-supreme-court-justices-say-criminal-justice-system-isnt-working-1427197613.

32. "Life Sentences," (Washington, DC: U.S. Sentencing Commission), February 2015, http://www.ussc.gov/sites/default/files/pdf/research-and-publications/research-projects-and-surveys/miscellaneous/20150226_Life_Sentences.pdf.

33. Ashley Nellis, "Life Goes On: The Historic Rise in Life Sentences in America," (Washington, DC: The Sentencing Project 2013): 3, http://sentencingproject.org/doc/publications/inc_Life%20Goes%20On%202013.pdf.

34. Ibid., 6; Ashley Nellis and Ryan S. King, "No Exit: The Expanding Use of Life Sen-

tences in America" (Washington, DC: The Sentencing Project, 2009): 9, http://www.sentencingproject.org/doc/publications/publications/inc_NoExitSept2009.pdf.

35. "A Living Death; Life without Parole for Nonviolent Offenses," (New York: American Civil Liberties Union, 2013): 2, https://www.aclu.org/files/assets/111213a-lwop-complete-report.pdf.

36. Stephen Castle, "Court Rules against Britain in Life Terms for 3 Convicts," *New York Times*, July 9, 2013, http://www.nytimes.com/2013/07/10/world/europe/10iht-britain10.html?smid=tw-share.

37. Ashley Nellis, *Throwing Away the Key: The Expansion of Life Without Parole Sentences in the United States*, 23 FED. SENT'G REP. 1, 30 (2010).

38. Ashley Csanady, "Harper Crime Bill to Throw Away the Key for 'Repulsive' Murderers Could Prove Unnecessary and Harmful: Critics," *National Post*, March 4, 2015, updated March 5, 2015, http://news.nationalpost.com/news/canada/canadian-politics/a-life-sentence-in-canada-will-henceforth-mean-just-that-harper-announces-new-tough-on-crime-bill.

39. "Life Sentences," Georgia State Board of Paroles and Pardons, accessed June 3, 2015 https://pap.georgia.gov/life-sentences.

40. David M. Zlotnick, *The Future of Federal Sentencing Policy: Learning Lessons from Republican Judicial Appointments in the Guidelines Era*, 79 U. COLO. L. REV. 1, 37 (2008).

41. Braven.

42. McCarthy.

43. "Police Cautions, Warnings and Penalty Notices," Gov.UK, last modified April 10, 2015, https://www.gov.uk/caution-warning-penalty.

44. Kathy G. Padgett, William D. Bales, and Thomas G. Blomberg, "Under Surveillance: An Empirical Test of the Effectiveness and Consequences of Electronic Monitoring," *Criminology & Public Policy* 5, no. 1 (2006): 61, article first published online, 26 April 2006.

45. See generally "Solutions," Electronic Sentencing Alternative, accessed June 13, 2015, http://esakc.com/.

46. See generally Joan Petersilia and Susan Turner, "Evaluating Intensive Supervision Probation/ Parole: Results of a Nationwide Experiment," (Washington, DC: U.S. Office of Justice Programs, 1993).

47. "Substance Abuse," Right on Crime, accessed June 12, 2015, http://rightoncrime.com/category/priority-issues/substance-abuse/.

48. "Drug Courts," (Washington, DC: National Institute of Justice, March 16, 2015), http://www.nij.gov/topics/courts/drug-courts/pages/welcome.aspx.

49. "Do Drug Courts Work?" (Washington, DC: National Institute of Justice, May 12, 2008), http://www.nij.gov/topics/courts/drug-courts/pages/work.aspx.

50. Ibid.

51. Douglas B. Marlowe, "Research Update on Adult Drug Courts," (Alexandria, VA: National Association of Drug Professionals, 2010), http://www.nadcp.org/sites/default/files/nadcp/Research%20Update%20on%20Adult%20Drug%20Courts%20-%20NADCP_1.pdf.

52. Ibid.

53. Doris J. James and Lauren E. Glaze, "Mental Health Problems of Prison and Jail Inmates," (Washington, DC: U.S. Department of Justice, September 2006, revised December 14, 2006), http://www.bjs.gov/content/pub/pdf/mhppji.pdf.

54. "The Mentally Ill Offender Treatment and Crime Reduction Act," (Lexington, KY:

The Council of State Governments, April 2014), http://csgjusticecenter.org/wp-content/uploads/2014/08/MIOTCRA_Fact_Sheet.pdf.

55. Tiffany Cartwright, *To Care for Him Who Shall Have Borne the Battle": The Recent Development of Veterans Treatment Courts in America*, 22 Stan. L. & Pol'y Rev. 295 (2010): 297.

56. "National GAINS Center, Responding to the Needs of Justice-Involved Combat Veterans with Service-Related Trauma and Mental Health Conditions," (Rockville, MD: Substance Abuse and Mental Health Services Administration, 2008): 6, http://gainscenter.samhsa.gov/pdfs/veterans/CVTJS_Report.pdf.

57. Jack W. Smith, *The Anchorage, Alaska Veterans Court and Recidivism: July 6, 2004–December 31, 2010*, 29 Alaska L. Rev. 93 (2012).

58. "Veterans Treatment Courts," (Washington, DC: Office of National Drug Control Policy, December 13, 2010), https://www.whitehouse.gov/sites/default/files/ondcp/Fact_Sheets/veterans_treatment_courts_fact_sheet_12-13-10.pdf.

59. "Veterans Treatment Court State Legislation" Justice for Vets, accessed June 13, 2015, http://www.justiceforvets.org/state-legislation.

60. "Veterans Treatment Courts Locations," Justice for Vets, accessed June 13, 2015, http://www.justiceforvets.org/veterans-treatment-court-locations.

61. "What Is a Veterans Treatment Court?" Justice for Vets, accessed June 13, 2015, http://www.justiceforvets.org/what-is-a-veterans-treatment-court.

62. "Building a National Mentor Corps," Justice for Vets, accessed June 13, 2015, http://www.justiceforvets.org/Mentor-Corps.

63. Smith, 107.

64. Sarah Lawrence and Jeremy Travis, *The New Landscape of Imprisonment: Mapping America's Prison Expansion,* (Washington, DC: Urban Institute, 2004), 8, http://webarchive.urban.org/UploadedPDF/410994_mapping_prisons.pdf.

65. Ibid., 9.

66. Emily Lane, "After 4 Decades in Solitary, Albert Woodfox's Release Ordered by Federal Judge," *Times-Picayune*, June 8, 2015, http://www.nola.com/news/baton-rouge/index.ssf/2015/06/albert_woodfox_angola_release.html.

67. Catherine E. Shoichet and Eliott C. McLaughlin, "Will 'Angola 3' Inmate Albert Woodfox Be Released?" CNN, June 8, 2015, http://www.cnn.com/2015/06/08/us/albert-woodfox-angola-3-release-ordered/.

68. "Solitary Confinement Should Be Banned in Most Cases, UN Expert Says," UN News Centre, October 18, 2011, http://www.un.org/apps/news/story.asp?NewsID=40097#.VXn2JPlViko.

69. Richard H. Thaler and Cass R. Sunstein, *Nudge: Improving Decisions about Health, Welfare, and Happiness*, (New York: Penguin, 2008): 6.

70. See also Mark Dlugash, "'Nudging' Prisons: New Hope for Real Prison Reform," *Kennedy School Review*, May 2, 2013, http://harvardkennedyschoolreview.com/nudging-prisons-new-hope-for-real-prison-reform/#_edn9.

71. Christopher J. Mumola and Jennifer C. Karberg, "Drug Use and Dependence, State and Federal Prisoners, 2004," (Washington, DC: U.S. Bureau of Justice Statistics, revised January 19, 2007), http://www.bjs.gov/content/pub/pdf/dudsfp04.pdf.

72. 42 U.S.C. § 2000cc (2000).

73. Patrick Clark, "Preventing Future Crime with Cognitive Behavioral Therapy," (Wash-

ington, DC: National Institute of Justice, May 29, 2010), http://www.nij.gov/journals/265/pages/therapy.aspx.

74. Ibid.

75. Anna Crayton and Suzanne Rebecca Neusteter, "The Current State of Correctional Education," Reentry Roundtable on Education, 2008, http://johnjay.jjay.cuny.edu/files/CraytonNeusteter_FinalPaper.pdf.

76. Lois M. Davis, Jennifer L. Steele, Robert Bozick, Malcolm V. Williams, Susan Turner, Jeremy N. V. Miles, Jessica Saunders, and Paul S. Steinberg, "How Effective Is Correctional Education, and Where Do We Go from Here? The Results of a Comprehensive Evaluation," (Santa Monica: RAND Corporation, 2014): xv, http://www.rand.org/content/dam/rand/pubs/research_reports/RR500/RR564/RAND_RR564.pdf.

77. Ibid., xvi.

78. "U.S. Adult Literacy Programs: Making a Difference," ProLiteracy America (2003), 17,http://literacyconnects.org/img/2011/11/US-Adult-Lit-Programs-Making-a-Difference-Research-review.pdf.

79. "Bureau of Prisons; Growing Inmate Crowding Negatively Affects Inmates, Staff, and Infrastructure," (Washington, DC: Government Accountability Office, September 2012): 68–69, http://www.gao.gov/assets/650/648123.pdf.

80. Stephen Green, "A Chino Hand," National Corrections Industry Association, accessed June 16, 2015, http://www.nationalcia.org/a-chino-hand.

81. "Reentry Programs," The Last Mile, accessed June 16, 2015, https://thelastmile.org/programs/reentry-programs/.

82. "Bureau of Prisons; Growing Inmate Crowding Negatively Affects Inmates, Staff, and Infrastructure," 69.

83. "Why Prison Education?" Hudson Link, accessed June 16, 2015, http://www.hudsonlink.org/about/why-prison-education.

84. "Pathways from Prison to Postsecondary Education Project," (New York: VERA Institute of Justice), accessed June 16, 2015, http://www.vera.org/project/pathways-prison-postsecondary-education-project.

85. "Real Act Would Restore Pell Grant Eligibility for Students in Prison," Legal Action Center, accessed June 16, 2015, http://lac.org/real-act-would-restore-pell-grant-eligibility-for-students-in-prison/.

86. Ibid.

87. Michele Masucci to Alex Friedmann, July 2, 2014, at https://www.prisonlegalnews.org/media/publications/Temple%20University%20response%20letter.pdf.

88. Joshua Holland, "How a Bogus, Industry-Funded Study Helped Spur a Privatization Disaster in Michigan," Moyers & Company, July 17, 2014, http://billmoyers.com/2014/07/17/how-a-bogus-industry-funded-study-helped-spur-a-privatization-disaster-in-michigan/.

89. Simon Hakim and Erwin Blackstone, "Data Shows Running Prisons for Profit Is a Win-Win," *Detroit Free Press*, June 7, 2013, http://www.freep.com/apps/pbcs.dll/article?AID=2013306070023.

90. Ibid.

91. Paul Egan, "Prison Food Supplier Has Michigan Officials at Wit's End," *Detroit Free Press*, July 13, 2014, http://www.freep.com/article/20140713/NEWS06/307130099/aramark-prison-food-privatization-michigan.

92. Christopher Petrella, "An Open Letter to the Corrections Corporation of Amer-

ica," (New York: American Civil Liberties Union, July, 2014): 3, https://www.aclu.org/sites/default/files/field_document/open_letter_to_cca_final.pdf.

93. Petrella, "The Color of Corporate Corrections, Part II: Contractual Exemptions and the Overrepresentation of People of Color in Private Prisons," *Radical Criminology*, no. 3 (2014): 84–85.

94. Ibid., 83–84.

95. "2014 Annual Letter to Shareholders," Corrections Corporation of America, http://www.cca.com/investors/financial-information/annual-reports.

96. Ibid.

97. Patrick Griffin, Sean Addie, Benjamin Adams, and Kathy Firestine, "Trying Juveniles as Adults: An Analysis of State Transfer Laws and Reporting," (Washington, DC: U.S. Office of Juvenile Justice and Delinquency Prevention, September 2011): 2–4, https://www.ncjrs.gov/pdffiles1/ojjdp/232434.pdf.

98. Maurice Chammah, "Texas among States Facing 'Raise the Age' Debate," *The Texas Tribune*, March 4, 2015, http://www.texastribune.org/2015/03/04/texas-among-states-facing-raise-age-debate/.

99. Lonn Lanza-Kaduce, Charles E. Frazier, Jodi Lane, and Donna M. Bishop, "Juvenile Transfer to Criminal Court Study: Final Report," (Washington, DC: U.S. Office of Juvenile Justice and Delinquency Prevention, 2002): 15, http://www.prisonpolicy.org/scans/juveniletransfers.pdf.

100. *Miller v. Alabama*, 567 U.S. ___ (2012).

101. Gary Gately, "High Court Asked to Weigh *Miller* Retroactivity," Juvenile Justice Information Exchange, March 13, 2015, http://jjie.org/high-court-asked-to-weigh-miller-retroactivity/.

102. "David Rosmarin, M.D.," McLean Hospital, accessed June 3, 2015, http://www.mcleanhospital.org/biography/david-rosmarin.

103. American Psychological Association Zero Tolerance Task Force, "Are Zero Tolerance Policies Effective in the Schools? An Evidentiary Review and Recommendations," (*American Psychologist*, December 2008): 854, https://www.apa.org/pubs/info/reports/zero-tolerance.pdf.

104. Ibid., 857–859.

105. "Policy Statement on Expulsion and Suspension Policies in Early Childhood Settings," (Washington, DC: U.S. Department of Health and Human Services and U.S. Department of Education), accessed June 16, 2015, http://www2.ed.gov/policy/gen/guid/school-discipline/policy-statement-ece-expulsions-suspensions.pdf.

106. "Supportive School Discipline Initiative," (Washington, DC: U.S. Department of Education and U.S. Department of Justice), accessed June 16, 2015, http://www2.ed.gov/policy/gen/guid/school-discipline/appendix-3-overview.pdf.

107. "Letter to Chief State School Officers and State Attorneys General," (Washington, DC: U.S. Department of Education and U.S. Department of Justice, December 8, 2014), http://www2.ed.gov/policy/gen/guid/correctional-education/csso-state-attorneys-general-letter.pdf.

108. Russ McQuaid, "New Indianapolis Charter School to Target Expelled, Incarcerated Students," Fox59.com, April 9, 2015, http://fox59.com/2015/04/09/charter-school-to-target-expelled-at-risk-youth/.

109. Ibid.

110. "Hampden County Sheriff's Department's After Incarceration Support Systems Program (AISS)," (Springfield, MA: Hampden County Sheriff's Department), accessed June 17, 2015, http://www.hcsdmass.org/WebsiteContentforAISS.pdf.

111. Rick Skwiot, "Cooperative Communities Reduce Crime," *Washington University in St. Louis Magazine*, Fall 2009, http://magazine-archives.wustl.edu/Fall09/John%20Owen%20Haley.html.

112. Michelle Natividad Rodriguez, "Ban the Box: U.S. Cities, Counties, and States Adopt Fair Hiring Policies," National Employment Law Project, May 2015, http://www.nelp.org/publication/ban-the-box-fair-chance-hiring-state-and-local-guide/.

113. "EEOC Enforcement Guidance," (Washington, DC: U.S. Equal Employment Opportunity Commission, April 25, 2012), http://www.eeoc.gov/laws/guidance/arrest_conviction.cfm#IIIC.

114. Devah Pager, "The Mark of a Criminal Record," *American Journal of Sociology* 108, no. 5 (2003): 955–958.

115. U.S. Equal Employment Opportunity Commission.

116. Christian Henrichson and Ruth Delaney, "The Price of Prisons: What Incarceration Costs Taxpayers," (New York: VERA Institute of Justice, January 2012, updated July 20, 2012): 10, http://www.vera.org/sites/default/files/resources/downloads/price-of-prisons-updated-version-021914.pdf.

Bibliography

Abramsky, Sasha. *Hard Time Blues: How Politics Built a Prison Nation.* New York: St. Martin's Press, 2002.

—. *American Furies: Crime, Punishment, and Vengeance in the Age of Mass Imprisonment.* Boston: Beacon Press, 2007.

Alexander, Michelle. *The New Jim Crow: Mass Incarceration in the Age of Colorblindness.* New York: The New Press, 2010.

Barash, David P., and Judith Eve Lipton. *Payback; Why We Retaliate, Redirect Aggression, and Take Revenge.* New York: Oxford University Press, 2011.

Bosworth, Mary. *Explaining U.S. Imprisonment.* Los Angeles: Sage, 2010.

Bourgois, Philippe. *In Search of Respect: Selling Crack in El Barrio.* Cambridge, UK: Cambridge University Press, 1995.

Clear, Todd R., and Natasha A. Frost. *The Punishment Imperative: The Rise and Failure of Mass Incarceration in America.* New York: New York University Press, 2014.

Cullen, Francis T., and Cheryl Lero Jonson. *Correctional Theory: Context and Consequences.* Los Angeles: Sage, 2012.

Drucker, Ernest. *A Plague of Prisons: The Epidemiology of Mass Incarceration in America.* New York: The New Press, 2011.

Ferguson, Robert A. *Inferno: An Anatomy of American Punishment.* Cambridge, MA: Harvard University Press, 2014.

Friedman, Lawrence C. *Crime and Punishment in American History.* New York: Basic Books, 1993.

Healy, Gene, ed. *Go Directly to Jail: The Criminalization of Almost Everything.* Washington: Cato Institute, 2004.

Hervivel, Tara, and Paul Wright, eds. *Prison Nation: The Warehousing of America's Poor.* New York: Routledge, 2003.

Johnson, Robert. *Hard Time: Understanding and Reforming the Prison,* 3rd ed. Belmont, CA: Wadsworth, 2002.

Kleiman, Mark A. *When Brute Force Fails: How to Have Less Crime and Less Punishment.* Princeton, NJ: Princeton University Press, 2009.

Maruna, Shadd. *Making Good: How Ex-Convicts Reform and Rebuild Their Lives.* Washington, DC: American Psychological Association, 2001.

Mauer, Marc. *Race to Incarcerate.* New York: The New Press, 1999.

Perkinson, Robert. *Texas Tough: The Rise of America's Prison Empire.* New York: Metropolitan Books, 2010.

Pratt, Travis C. *Addicted to Incarceration: Corrections Policy and the Politics of Misinformation in the United States.* Los Angeles: Sage, 2009.

Reiman, Jeffrey. *The Rich Get Richer and the Poor Get Prison: Ideology, Class, and Criminal Justice,* 5th ed. Boston: Allyn and Bacon, 1998.

Rogers, Joseph W. *Why Are You Not a Criminal?* Englewood Cliffs, NJ: Prentice-Hall, 1977.

Ross, Jeffrey Ian, and Stephen C. Richards. *Beyond Bars: Rejoining Society after Prison.* New York: Penguin, 2009.

Silverglate, Harvey A. *Three Felonies a Day: How the Feds Target the Innocent.* New York: Encounter Books, 2011.

Soering, Jens. *An Expensive Way to Make Bad People Worse: An Essay on Prison Reform.* New York: Lantern Books, 2004.

Stevens, Dennis J. *The Failure of the American Prison Complex: Let's Abolish It.* Dubuque, IA: Kendall Hunt, 2014.

Stevenson, Bryan. *Just Mercy: A Story of Justice and Redemption.* New York: Spiegel & Grau, 2014.

Stuntz, William J. *The Collapse of American Criminal Justice.* Cambridge, MA: Harvard University Press, 2011.

Terry, Charles M. *The Fellas: Overcoming Prison and Addiction.* Belmont, CA: Wadsworth, 2003.

Tonry, Michael. *Thinking about Crime: Sense and Sensibility in American Penal Culture.* New York: Oxford University Press, 2004.

Tonry, Michael, ed. *The Handbook of Crime and Punishment.* New York: Oxford University Press, 1998.

Trounstine, Jean. *Shakespeare Behind Bars: One Teacher's Story of the Power of Drama in a Women's Prison.* New York: St. Martin's Press, 2001.

Wagner, Michele, ed. *How Should Prisons Treat Inmates?* San Diego: Greenhaven Press, 2001.

Whitman, James Q. *Harsh Justice: Criminal Punishment and the Widening Divide between America and Europe.* New York: Oxford University Press, 2003.

Zimring, Franklin E., and Gordon Hawkins. *The Scale of Imprisonment.* Chicago: University of Chicago Press, 1991.

Index